THE ROLLING STONES

STONES

AN ORAL HISTORY

ALAN LYSAGHT

McArthur & Company
Toronto

First published in Canada in 2003 by
McArthur & Company
322 King St. West, Suite 402
Toronto, Ontario
M5V 1J2

National Library of Canada Cataloguing in Publication

Lysaght, Alan
    The Rolling Stones : an oral history / Alan Lysaght.

ISBN 1-55278-392-8

    1. Rolling Stones--Interviews. 2. Rock musicians--Great
Britain--Interviews. I. Title.

ML421.R754L98 2003   782.42166'092'2   C2003-903877-7

Cover & Text Design: Tania Craan
Cover Image: Everett Collection/Magma
Printed in Canada by: Transcontinental Printing Inc.

The publisher would like to acknowledge the financial support of the
Government of Canada through the Book Publishing Industry Development
Program, the Canada Council, and the Ontario Arts Council for our publish-
ing activities. We also acknowledge the Government of Ontario through the
Ontario Media Development Corporation Ontario Book Initiative.

FOREWORD

Twenty years back, when Alan Lysaght was putting the finishing touches on his twenty-one-hour radio documentary on the Rolling Stones, it was Mick Jagger who came up with the title: *The Complete History of the Rolling Stones*. The two were sitting in Jagger's suite in the George V Hotel in Paris in 1983. Mick thought Alan's earlier Stones' radio documentary had covered all the ground. What more could be done, what more could be said? Anything else, Jagger said, would have to be THE complete history.

It made perfect sense for Jagger to get involved this way. Lysaght, a rather mild-mannered guy with a serious passion for rock'n'roll, had already been documenting the band for so many years they'd come to think of him as their archivist. Alan, they realized, knew as much about their own history as they did.

Airing over the years in the United States, Canada, England, Australia, and throughout Europe, *The Complete History of the Rolling Stones* has come to be regarded as the defining radio history of the Stones. For Lysaght, a Toronto writer and radio producer, the history of the Stones has evolved over his more than thirty years' association with the band. *The Rolling Stones: An Oral History* is the culmination of countless exclusive interviews, up-dated, fleshed-out, and revised over the years.

For any rock'n'roll band, history is made day-to-day, gig-to-gig. It's done on the fly, fashioned fast and furiously, and easily forgotten. But Lysaght always knows what has happened, what should be asked for, and who to ask. The more he jogged the band's memories over the years, the sharper their memories became. In effect, the Stones re-created and re-edited their own history for Lysaght. *The Rolling Stones: An Oral History* is the result.

He knows it all, the scandals, the slip-ups, and successes alike. What really did happen when the band was busted with Marianne Faithfull? How exactly did "Satisfaction" come to be written? Lysaght became the guy the rest of us turn to when checking out some vague rumour about the band, or some missing bit of information.

I remember it well. Because of something I'd written about him during my days at *The Toronto Star* as a rock critic, Mick Jagger was on the phone early one Monday morning, furious that I'd got the story wrong. "Yeah?" I said after hearing him out. "Well, I'll just have to check with Alan about that." And that was that.

Lysaght's interests don't stop with the Stones. In 1998, he wrote *The Beatles: An Oral History* along with fellow

Torontonian David Pritchard. Within months, it was one of the best-selling Beatles books ever. Over the years, Alan's produced radio documentaries on Celine Dion, Alanis Morissette, Eric Clapton, Paul McCartney, and Whitney Houston, as well as one about Mick Jagger on his own. He's now working on TV documentaries for the Canadian Broadcasting Corporation.

True, he doesn't exactly strike you as any sort of rock'n'roll insider. He's more of the Clark Kent type next to the Supermen he gets up close and personal with. In fact, when it comes to book writing, you'd pick him to do one on business—which he has, by the way.

But like all of the rest of the great rock'n'roll insiders, Alan knows where the secrets can be found—and how to find them.

— Peter Goddard, *The Toronto Star*, Toronto, 2003

TABLE OF CONTENTS

CHAPTER 1
Blues Nights 1

CHAPTER 2
Oldham Days 46

CHAPTER 3
American Nights 79

CHAPTER 4
Satisfaction 100

CHAPTER 5
A Beautiful Guy 141

CHAPTER 6
Woody 182

CHAPTER 7
Fight Nights 208

CHAPTER 8
Steel Wheels 249

CHAPTER 9
Finale 297

Cast of Characters

Albert Maysles – Director, *Gimme Shelter* film

Alexis Korner – Father of British blues music scene

B.B. King – Musician

Bill Wyman – Musician, former Stones member

Bob Bonis – Stones tour manager 1964

Brian Jones – Musician, former Stones member

Brian Knight – Musician

Charlie Watts – Musician, Stones member

Chris Kimsey – Engineer/producer of several Stones albums

Chrissie Hynde – American musician (The Pretenders)

Chuck Leavell – Musician, Stones member

Cliff Lorimer – Radio announcer, hosted the "Blind Benefit" concert

Darryl Jones – Musician, Stones member

Dick Rowe – Decca Records recording manager; signed Rolling Stones

Dick Taylor – Childhood friend of Mick, Keith; early Stones member

Don Was – Musician, producer

Earl McGrath – President Rolling Stones Records, late '70s

Eric Clapton – Musician, friend

Eva Jagger – Mother of Mick

Gene Pitney – American musician

Geoff Bradford – Early Stones member

George Harrison – Musician (The Beatles)

George Martin, Sir – Producer of The Beatles' records

Ginger Baker – Musician

Giorgio Gomelski – Early manager

Glyn Johns – Engineer on first recordings; produced several albums

Hal Ashby – Director, "Let's Spend The Night Together"

Harold Pendelton – Owner of the Marquee Club

Howlin' Wolf – Legendary blues musician and singer

Ian Stewart – Original Stones member; lifelong band employee

Jimmy Miller – Producer "Beggars Banquet" to "Goat's Head Soup"

Joe Jagger – Father of Mick

John Gee – Manager of the Marquee Club

John Rowlands – Photographer on part of 1965 tour

Julien Temple – Video director

Keith Altham – British publicist for band

Keith Richards – Musician, Stones member

Lewis Jones – Father of Brian

Marianne Faithfull – Musician, Mick's girlfriend in '60s

Marshall Chess – Chess Records; Chicago studio Stones used in '60s

Michael Cohl – Tour manager extraordinaire from 1989 to present

Mick Jagger – Musician, Stones member

Mick Taylor – Musician, former Stones member

Nicky Hopkins – Musician, played many Stones sessions

Norman Jopling – Journalist, wrote first national story on Stones

Pat Joyce – Bartender at the El Mocambo club

Paul Kantner – Musician, witness to Altamont

Paul McCartney – Musician (The Beatles)

Paul McGrath – Journalist, *The Globe and Mail*

Pierre Trudeau – Prime Minister of Canada, husband of Margaret

Pete Townshend – Musician, friend

Peter Goddard – Journalist, *The Toronto Star*

Peter Holland – Childhood friend, of Mick

Peter Jones – British journalist; wrote for official Stones' magazine

Peter Rudge – Stones' tour manager in '70s

Reggie Bovaird – Manager, the El Mocambo club

Ron Wood – Musician, Stones member

Ronnie Spector – American musician (the Ronettes)

Roy Carr – British journalist, writer

Sid Bernstein – U.S. promoter, booked Stones in the U.S. 1st time

Sonny Barger – Hell's Angels member, part of 'security' at Altamont

Sugar Blue – American blues musician

Tony Calder – Business associate of Andrew Oldham

Vicki Wyckham – Producer *Ready, Steady, Go* TV series in '60s

William Wilkinson – School teacher of Mick Jagger

Willie Dixon – Legendary blues musician and songwriter

CHAPTER 1
Blues Nights

July 26, 1943. Michael Phillip Jagger is born to Eva and Basil "Joe" Jagger.

MICK JAGGER: People seem to like to think of me as coming from a really working-class background but it isn't true. My mother's family was a bit working class, I suppose, but my father was middle class—even bourgeois, I guess you could say. He was educated and lectured about physical education in some prestige schools, and was even appointed to the British Sports Council. Fitness was always a big thing with him.

JOE JAGGER: Mick was always very independent. Whereas I would very much have liked him to get involved in sports, he loved listening to pop music. He worked hard at school and was quite successful at his A-levels [tests] but he also loved to sing and would have his friends around the house. They would play their guitars and he would sing. They were quite good-sounding, actually.

December 18, 1943. Keith Richards is born to Doris and Herbert "Bert" Richards.

KEITH RICHARDS: I was born near the end of the war, at a time when Hitler was sending over these nasty little bombers [unmanned V1 rockets] known as "Doodlebugs." They'd come over from France meant for London but half of them only made it as far as the suburbs where we were. I'm too young to remember the war but I still cringe every time I hear the sirens. They were a constant for the first year or two of my life. At the height of the bombing we were evacuated to a place to the north and just missed being killed by "Hitler's messengers." Just after we left, a piece of the house literally went right through my bed.

PETER HOLLAND: Mick was a very good basketball player. We played on the same team together in grammar school and he was also a very good cross-country runner. I never thought of Mick as a rebel or the sort that would buck the trends. He was always very bright and keen, always helping out in class.

MICK JAGGER: I guess I was about seven when my mum bought me a guitar while we were on holiday in Spain. So I started singing all these Spanish songs even though I had no idea how to speak the language.

Pushed by his parents to succeed in school, Mick is accepted at Dartford Grammar, a prestigious high school. Grade school classmate Keith Richards enters technical school in Dartford.

KEITH RICHARDS: My mum's family, we had a lot of fun. Very musical. My granddad [Gus] played saxophone until he got gassed in the First World War so he switched to guitar. Oh yeah, he was a real nutter, a great guy. He's the one that got me playing. He used to be in a dance band in the thirties and played fiddle, guitar, saxes. There was always music around his house, and he was a great laugh, too. He'd get you into music very naturally. He was probably very important to me without me realizing it at the time, just being around instruments and music that much.

As I say, he was one of the most incredible rascals I ever met in my life . . . Living in a house with eight women, you got to know how to manoeuvre. Now I'm getting a taste of it too, with two daughters [laughs]. So he would have a guitar up on top of the piano in his room, and I always thought that's where it lived. I found out from one of my aunts a couple of years ago that he actually only put it there when he knew I was coming to visit. He never said, "Did you want to play it?" It was too tall for me to reach then. It was just like an icon to me. For some reason he recognized me as a guitar player from the age of five. I didn't actually pick one up until I was about twelve, thirteen, fourteen, but somehow he intrigued me. He saw it in me.

My grandmother [Emily] played piano. They had seven daughters and there was always music and play acting going on in the house. It was great. So my mum was into music and we used to have a radio. She would sing and dance whenever the big tunes of the day were playing. My dad was the typical absent father who worked all day and just barely kept ahead of the rent. We never really had very much.

I think I was always into music. My mother used to laugh and say I could sing perfectly to all the Sinatra records on the radio when I was just a young lad. And I was actually a choirboy for a while. Yeah, I actually sang Handel for the Queen at Westminster Abbey. Then my voice cracked and I was out on my ass. There was nowhere to go from there but rock'n'roll.

DICK TAYLOR: I was at school with Mick for about five years and we were friends. I remember when I would go around to his place his father would insist that Mick do all his exercises [i.e., homework] before he could go out. I thought that was pretty strict but Mick didn't seem to mind too much. Maybe he was scared of his father.

MICK JAGGER: When I was just a teenager I thought about being a journalist [laughs]. Then I thought about all the horrible things I'd have to do like covering the local government and weddings so I started to think about government. I was interested in how the government and the economy controlled each other.

February 1956. Lonnie Donnegan becomes an instant hit in England with "Rock Island Line." This starts the skiffle craze, which inspires hundreds of teenagers to form their own skiffle groups.

HAROLD PENDELTON: If you really know why things happened, it amuses you to read all the later histories. I can tell you exactly how skiffle started. It was because in the original band that Chris [Barber] was involved with, Ken Collier, the trumpet player, had a poor embouchure and his lip used to give out. Poor old Ken couldn't actually do more than three-quarters of an hour and then his lip went. So they started doing skiffle in between to let Ken's lip recover, and Chris would say, "I'll play bass." He'd been playing trombone, so he'd nip over to the bass and play slap bass and Donnegan would play banjo and Ken would play guitar and so on and mumble the skiffle songs, and they created—and nobody will believe this—they created skiffle in this country, Collier, Donnegan, Barber, Bill Collier, who is Ken's brother who was the manager of the band on washboard. So it was purely to give Ken's lip a rest. That was the entire and total reason for the creation of skiffle. Can you believe that? And it spawned hundreds of bands in this country.

ALEXIS KORNER: Skiffle music was very much like "rent party" music. It was all-night-long, twelve-bar instrumental music. Someone would sing every now and then. And you'd charge fifty cents to come in, and with luck you'd collect enough bread to pay the rent. And that is what skiffle music was about. It was essentially an instrumental music and essentially the blues. And we formed this skiffle group together in 1952, which was Chris Barber because it was the Barber–Collier band and Ken Collier, and Bill Collier on washboard, Ken's brother, and Lonny Donnegan on banjo until he went into the army, and me on guitar and mandolin and the first and worst harmonica player the movement had known.

I didn't like what happened with skiffle . . . I really hated it. I mean, I liked Uncle Dave Makin and people like that, but I didn't like the versions of "Sail Away Ladies" and "Won't You Rock Me Daddyo" and all that stuff that was going down . . . Now it's fine . . . but then, no, it wasn't fine. I didn't want to play that stuff, and skiffle was that stuff, so I pulled out of the skiffle thing altogether.

PETER HOLLAND: Mick would come over to my place and we'd listen to records. He had quite different tastes from most kids. He was always tuned into the American Forces network and knew all the latest hits from Chuck Berry and Bo Diddley. He loved all that stuff.

DICK TAYLOR: We were really interested in music and I used to do a bit of playing with Mick and a few other people. There were about four or five of us and we used to play at each other's places a lot. Keith wasn't involved at that time.

6

He and Mick knew each other slightly when they were really small, but never hung around together.

1957. Mick's father is hired as a consultant on the BBC-TV series *Seeing Sport* and hires Mick, then fourteen, to show the proper techniques for rock climbing and canoeing.

MICK JAGGER: When I first heard rock'n'roll I wasn't really that keen on it. I just didn't care about Elvis and Bill Haley. I liked the blacker sounds of Fats Domino and Chuck Berry. My dad used to call it "jungle music" but I really liked it.

WILLIAM WILKINSON: As I remember Mick, he was a good student, very pleasant and helpful. Some people try to make him out to have been a real troublemaker or a rebel of some kind, but that is not the case at all. He was a very sober, thoughtful student, part of a very good group of talented boys.

Keith enters Sidcup Art College, where he meets fellow student Dick Taylor. His mother Doris gives him a Rosetti acoustic guitar. He learns to play by ear while listening to blues records.

KEITH RICHARDS: My mum was great. She bought me my first guitar and encouraged me to take it seriously. Then she bought me a record player. I used to play songs over and over, from Elvis to Johnny Cash, and practise trying to get the sound right. She was my audience. My father used to call it a "bloody noise."

I'm not sure which was the first rock'n'roll record I remember hearing. "Heartbreak Hotel" or "Lucille"—it was around that time. It's difficult to remember which one it was because when rock'n'roll came in England it came in this torrent from nowhere. One minute there was nothing, next minute there was this . . . whewww . . . It was just a blur. "Where did that come from?" [laughs]. Suddenly this incredible avalanche of music struck everybody around my age like a thunderbolt.

When I first heard Chuck Berry, that was it. His style was so hip, it was loose and alive. How he could turn a twelve-bar progression into a tight commercial song was fascinating to me. I listened to [his songs] over and over again until I figured them out. He was like a spiritual father to me [laughs].

We all had to wear grey flannel pants [at technical school]. It was the regulation uniform. I was about thirteen, fourteen, and it was absolutely degrading to be seen in school flannels outside the gates, so we used to wear these skin-tight trousers underneath during classes and then we used to dash around the trees and take these horrible school flannels off and walk over there with tight trousers on. It was a minor sign of rebellion. "All right lads, trousers off!"

Later I was at Sidcup Art College, so I guess I was around fifteen or sixteen. It was a great environment full of freaks and rebels and I first heard John Lee Hooker, Muddy [Waters] and the Chicago guys. I think it saved my life.

After ordinary school, art school was very relaxed. You could wander in and out of classes, nobody bothered you much, and there were always three or four guys playing blues or folk music in the john. You'd go in there with a cigarette and sit on the seat and listen to them, and I started to pick it up from there.

With some friends we did a couple of school dances, soon after I'd learned the basic things on the guitar. I can hardly remember, I was so drunk. I remember sleeping somewhere in a bus stop near a park.

DICK TAYLOR: I guess it was about 1958 [March 14] that Mick and I went to see Buddy Holly at the Woolwich theatre. Mick was kind of cool about the whole thing at the beginning but as the show got on he was really blown away. He was watching really closely, looking at all Holly's moves. It was the first time we heard "Not Fade Away," which was amazing. We started to play it every day after that.

October 1961.

MICK JAGGER: Keith and I knew of each other because we lived very close by when we were young. But we went to different schools so we kind of lost touch with each other. Then we saw each other one day in the train station and I had all these

9

records I had just bought from America. I had written away to Chess Records in Chicago so they were kind of rare in England at the time, and so expensive. Keith noticed them and his eyes kind of lit up and we just started talking.

KEITH RICHARDS: Yeah it's true, we met one day on the railway platform. Mick had the records; I couldn't afford them. He was going to the London School of Economics, which after all must say something. I was going to art school. I was the penniless artist and he was the guy studying money, and I hadn't seen him in years. It just so happened that my journey eventually took me on the same train that he had to take. He had to go right into London and I was stuck in some suburban art school famous for producing David Bowie and Dick Taylor and some other characters that should be far more well known. And I saw these records he had under his arm and I would have mugged him for them except I knew him, so we just started talking and one thing led to another. "Where did you get 'em?" "You got any more?" "Oh, you like that shit too?" "What do you do?" "Oh, I sing a bit." "Oh, yeah? I play guitar a bit." "Fine, let's get together." "You know that girl Nora down the street, what's she like?" [laughs]. And really that was basically it.

So Mick came over for tea and we started listening to his records. He put on *The Best of Muddy Waters* and it all fell together for me. I could suddenly see the connections between all the music I liked. He was the master guide—he had the codebook. He was, after all, the "Hoochie Coochie" man. He wasn't just a singer, he wasn't just a guitar player or even just a writer. He was everything.

At that time I was going to art school with Dick Taylor, that's how I knew him. And he'd gone to a previous school with Mick so the tentacles started to spread early. We used to get together at Dick's mother's house one night a week . . . what a racket!

DICK TAYLOR: I met Keith at art college and we really got along because we were both into records like John Lee Hooker and Little Richard. We'd bring our acoustic guitars to school and play together between classes. Teachers would come by and tell us to stop but Keith would just carry on. He didn't care about anything but the music.

Keith was always great fun at art college. He was a real hooligan, which I liked. There was a field trip once to a classy furniture store named Heal's because we were studying design. Keith was sitting on this expensive couch and purposely dropping his cigarette ash all over it and rubbing it in to make a mess. He didn't care. He just wanted to play. We would stay up practising till all hours after taking any pep pills we could find to keep us awake.

We used to rehearse around my place quite a bit, and as Keith knew me, and Mick knew me, we thought, well, why not join forces? I found out later that Keith had thought he'd like to have a go with us but never had the nerve to ask, which I found really funny.

I was eighteen, which meant Mick was seventeen and Keith was sixteen. We were playing things we knew for a start, which wasn't all that varied. It was twelve bars—Bo Diddley, Jimmy Reed, Chuck Berry. We'd listen to their records and copy them. I know we used to do long versions of "La Bamba," which Mick used to get really wound up in. He used to rattle away making up all these stupid pseudo-Spanish words to "La Bamba" [laughs]. He was very good, he was really talented at that.

When Keith came along to play with the Blue Boys it was clearly a perfect match-up with Mick. Jagger was smart, really ambitious, and liked being the centre of attention. Keith was much more carefree than Mick. He didn't care what anybody thought. He'd tell anyone to go sod off. He just wanted to play his music. So they were opposites in a way and in another sense they were absolutely perfect together.

There was a tape made in my house on a crummy tape deck, and I had this same tape recorder for quite a while, for three or four years afterwards. I went off with the Pretty Things to New Zealand and there were some other people staying around my flat and one moron managed to rub out the tape of the Stones and put on some daft tape off the radio. [What he erased] was the Blue Boys—me, Mick, Keith, a guy called Alan Everington, a guy called Robert Beckwith. I was playing the drums. Actually I'm quite happy it got rubbed out [laughs] because it was pretty shocking, from my department anyway. I don't know about anybody else. Actually it wasn't bad, really. It certainly wasn't anything that could ever appear on a disc, but . . . it would have been interesting for sentimental value. It was a shame it got eliminated.

HAROLD PENDLETON: When Chris Barber came back from touring America he had a residency at my club, the Marquee, on a Wednesday night. He said to me: "We've always been cut off in England, copying the music of the American records. We were playing what we thought they were doing musically but they're not doing that now. They were doing that then, when they first made the records. Now that we've been to America we realize that. So instead of playing the music of twenty years ago, or thirty years ago, I'd like to play this, as contemporary Negro music of today. I really want to try and do that sort of music because that is today's music."

So he started experimenting with it, but musically he needed a guitar player, so he remembered Alexis Korner. Now Alexis was not really a guitar player, he was a fan. Alexis had always been into everything that Chris had brought back with him. Alexis was the number one fan and was deeply involved in the blues. While he wasn't the world's greatest guitar player, he understood the blues, so Chris felt—and I think quite rightly—that he needed somebody who understood and felt the music far more than somebody who played a good guitar but didn't feel it. Because traditional jazz is all about feeling—it's not technique. It helps to have technique, but it's not entirely about technique, you've got to feel it. And he was very lucky to find a harp player called Cyril Davis—"Squirrel," we called him—who'd been very much on the folk side, but who'd got involved in all this. So we brought Squirrel and Alexis into the band as additional people to do these sets.

And we started experimenting with them on the Wednesday nights for half an hour, and they were an instant hit. People thought this was real music, that it was really good. The skiffle thing was a bit played out and this was a new dimension and a new music with balls. It really had everything anybody wanted, so we started working on it. Quite interestingly, we were the only people doing it in the whole of the British Isles. Record producers started creeping down to listen to it—Dennis Preston, Norry Paramour, we would find them all in the audience, listening to what was going on.

And the Barber Band was doing it by itself for almost a year, with this sort of feeling. Then, Alexis who was nothing if not enterprising, decided he'd form a band to do this sort of music and nothing but this music, being a total blues devotee. He felt—and I totally agreed with him—that there was probably room for a group doing nothing but this sort of music. And he collected a band together called Blues Incorporated to do this. But the one thing they couldn't find was a drummer.

Then they found Charlie Watts, so Charlie was their first regular drummer. Now he had a complete band.

Then Cyril sent for Long John Baldry and brought him into the band. We had two groups a night ever since Chris and I founded the Marquee, because in the days when we wanted to play we used to hang around the Humphrey Littleton Club, hoping that Humph would give us a spot in the interval or to allow us to play. So we swore that when we launched a club of our own it would always have a guest group. There'd be the name group, who would bring the people in, and in the interval there would be a guest group to give them a chance to get started. Almost every group you can ever think of has started as a guest group, such as the Rolling Stones.

JOHN GEE: The Marquee at that time—we're talking about 1961, 1962—was a jazz club pure and simple, and Alexis was running a little club in the London suburb of Ealing, and he had his band there with Cyril Davis. But he wanted to break into the West End. I well remember we had a meeting in a little café just below the Marquee offices, and he told me about this group he wanted to get into the club, and I said, "Well what type of thing is it? Is it jazz?" He said, "The basis is blues, but it's an instrumental type of blues and it's steeped in American Negro rhythm'n'blues." And I said, "Oh . . . Sounds very interesting. And he said, "John, it's going to be one of the biggest things that will ever hit this country." And I said—I was rather bored, in fact— "[yawn] Oh yes, Alexis. Would you like another cup of coffee?" My God, how true, how true, because that was the beginning of the whole rock scene in this country.

WILLIE DIXON: Well, it's just like anything else, you know? The majority of the black people have been underprivileged, and they don't have the amount of understanding they should have for the blues, because most of them feel like the blues is music that represents slavery days, and they feel like this is a reminder. You see, they don't seem to understand that blues is the truth and blues is the facts. Blues is the roots of all American music, so they'd rather listen to some other type of American music that's the fruit of the blues, on the tree of the blues, rather than the roots themselves, because the roots represent a bad time for the black people.

In the fifties the Blues wasn't sellin' much, and Memphis Slim and I left the United States in 1959 and went to England and Europe to help keep the blues alive. We had discussed it two or three years ahead of time and we was saying how the blues was dying and the people weren't accepting the blues and were callin' it "low-down music" and all this, and we made a decision that we were gonna try to uphold the principles of the blues and keep the blues alive, and we went everywhere. We went all down England, then we worked in France, then Scandinavia. At the time the only people that actually heard any blues were the record collectors and like that. They weren't making any albums of blues at that time.

Then we started this American Folk Blues Festival while Slim and I was over there. We were trying to find a way to get the blues out all over Europe, because in America they weren't accepting it. We were only working maybe one or two nights a week in Chicago, but after we got over there, and people started to hear the real thing, we were workin' every day.

Well, frankly, I want to tell you something. While we was in England, a lot of times it was a bunch of youngsters coming to the show and they were too young to come in to the various places where we was workin' so we'd let 'em come in the back door and they would listen to us and they would tell us they were gonna do this and do that. But you know what you'd be thinkin' about a bunch of young kids and their big ideas. Then when they'd come along later and tell you, "I'm so and so, and I gave you my picture when you were in England and I told you we were gonna have a group, and this is the group!" Well, I couldn't remember them because they were just kids then and when I saw them again they were twenty or twenty-five and they got hair all over their faces and how would I know who they are? And this was the beginning of those groups like the Stones and the Animals and Long John Baldry.

ALEXIS KORNER: The Roundhouse was better known in Chicago than it was in London because of all the blues players that came through. In the fifties a lot of blues players came through England, a really tremendous amount because they worked with jazz bands, and they'd do a spot in clubs of which we had a great many at that time. We're short on clubs now, but then we had a lot of clubs. And someone like Little Brother Montgomery or Speckled Red or Memphis Slim or Dupree or anyone like that would come over and they'd do fourteen, fifteen dates and then go back to Chicago . . . having made a lot more in fourteen or fifteen dates here than they probably earned in three months in Chicago . . . Having had an audience they really dug, and the audience dug them, they'd come back every year. It was great.

We used to get evenings where Speckled Red would be at the end of his tour, and he'd play the first set with us, and then Slim would just be arriving for his tour, and he wasn't starting until the next night, and he'd play the second set, so we'd have Speckled Red on piano for the first set, and Memphis Slim on piano for the second set. All they got was drinks . . . but that was because they'd been told in the first place by Bill Broonsey and then by Sonny and Brownie and so on, if you went to London, the Roundhouse was where you had to play. There's no bread there, but it's the right club. And they would go and play there, so we got the chance to play with every single important blues player that came through the country between 1956 and 1961.

DICK TAYLOR: We were called the Blue Boys or Little Boy Blue and the Blueboys. That was with Mick, Keith, me playing drums, a maraca player, no bass player, and two guitars. We sent a tape to Alexis Korner, which was the tape that eventually got eliminated. After that we started going to the Ealing Club, where Alexis was playing. The first couple of nights we went there we went, "Blimey, this is amazing . . . Wow! . . . Best thing ever." I must admit that after a little while we thought perhaps we could do this as well. I mean, these boring old farts were doing this [laughs] and we thought, "We can do this even better." It started off with Mick and Keith going up on stage to join the band. Before this Alexis had introduced Paul Jones and Brian Jones to come up and play. They were coming up from Cheltenham, where Brian lived.

April 1962.

ALEXIS KORNER: When people first became aware of us, we were calling ourselves a rhythm'n'blues band. We were the first band to say, "We are an R&B band. We are not a jazz band, we are not a pop band, we are an R&B band." We were called Blues Incorporated. Mick sent me a tape that he and Keith had made with a couple of friends in Dartford, and I thought, "Yeah, this is okay." It was the Chuck Berry, Bo Diddley side of it, not the side we were playing, because we were more into country blues than we were into rock'n'roll blues. When Cyril heard Mick, he liked him—he liked the sound on the tape, as I did. So I rang Mick, and Mick and Keith came over because Mick and Keith went everywhere together in those days. You never got Mick without Keith, which was fine with me.

You know, people come over and you start talking to them and then they come over again and if you happen to have an open house and they know how to get through the kitchen window and make themselves a cup of tea, they tend to appear at three in the morning when they've got nowhere else to go. So you get up in the morning to make a cup of tea and you find five bodies on the floor. Okay, so you make two pots of tea instead of one pot of tea. That's just the way it was.

I don't think of starting points and finishing points. It just happened that Mick and Keith used to come around. They used to come down to gigs and things, and Brian—whom I had met in Cheltenham when I working with Chris Barber—Brian came into the dressing room to talk, not about the band set but about the blues set. I gave him the phone number, and Brian—who didn't like being in Cheltenham at the weekends because he found it very boring—he used to just appear in town and spend Friday night, Saturday and Sunday sleeping on our floor. Then he'd catch the last train back on Sunday night to Cheltenham and go back to work on Monday morning.

Mick and John [Baldry] and Cyril were the regular band

singers. Mick used to sing an occasional Chuck Berry song and then he used to do a lot of Billy Boy Arnold Stuff. Mick was very much into Billy Boy Arnold, so we used to play that area of Chicago stuff. John would tend to sing the jazzier side of things, because he was very much into Lou Rawls and people like that, and then Squirrel would sing the Muddy Waters, Sonny Boy Williamson material. That's the first Sonny Boy, John Lee, not Rice Miller.

JOE JAGGER: My wife got a few calls from this man Alexis Korner. He had arranged for Mick to sing at a club in London and encouraged us to come down and see him perform. We never did go, but he was very encouraging.

GINGER BAKER: Mick used to hang around with the Alexis Korner band. He used to sit on stage in a chair all night and sing one or two numbers. First of all I wondered who he was and I gave him a real hard time [laughs].

DICK TAYLOR: When they started doing it, Alexis's band didn't approve of Keith. He was a bit too rocky for the likes of them, and so it went back to Mick, Keith, me, Brian Jones we invited along. Charlie Watts wasn't meant to be our regular drummer, but we used him quite a lot, and that was it, wasn't it? Keith, Mick, me, Ian Stewart on piano, Charlie and the other drummer, Tony Chapman. He was supposed to be our drummer but he was working and he kept being dragged off to Liverpool. I remember this cartoon we had of Tony, and he's in Liverpool on the phone, saying, "Sorry lads I'm in Liverpool."

We used to rehearse in a pub in Soho because by that time Mick was at the LSE [London School of Economics], so it was easy for him and pretty easy for us. Besides, we liked going up to London, and Brian was in town, and Ian, and Charlie as well, so we just all congregated in this pub in Darby Street. We used to rehearse once or twice a week. That went on for some time.

June 2, 1941. Charlie Watts is born to Lillian and Charles Watts.

KEITH RICHARDS: In those days I wasn't even considering a career in music seriously—it was just something to do. We'd spend the weekends up in town and Alexis would ask me to come up and do a song. Eventually when we got to know him, he asked Mick and I up to do a song together. So we played with them a bit. He'd say, "Now here's a couple of boys from just out of town, what'cha gonna play?" And we'd say, "Roll Over Beethoven," and Alexis would take a very large swallow and his Adam's apple would go down and he'd put his thumb pick through a couple of strings and say "Uh . . . terribly sorry, old boy, I've broken a string. I'll have to go and change it, I'll leave it to you."

When we first met up with Alexis and Cyril they were all coming from jazz, but their tastes had gravitated to the blues. So their approach and slant on the blues came from the jazz angle—Big Joe Williams, Broonsey, Leadbelly, half-folkies, half-jazz cliques of people—and they were generally getting on together. They were trying it from their angle, but they didn't believe that rock'n'roll had any connection with it—they didn't see the connection. It was like they missed the Darwin connection, the missing link.

The Ealing Club was great. Mick and I went there every Saturday and Alexis would be playing with his band: Cyril, Charlie on drums, and I think Keith Smith on piano, a bass player called Andy Hugenboom. Later it changed to Ginger Baker on drums and Jack Bruce on bass. And in the same way I mentioned that he'd ask Mick and I to come up and play a few numbers, Paul Jones used to also come and do a couple of numbers. One night he says, "We're gonna ask this guy from Cheltenham to come up and play some Elmore James." And we thought, "Oh yeah, here we go, here comes another one." And it was Brian. He sat down and played "Dust My Broom" beautifully, and so the minute he finished we cornered him: "Come here my son, what are you doing?"

February 28, 1942. Lewis Brian Hopkins-Jones (Brian Jones) is born to Louisa and Lewis Jones.

BRIAN JONES: I had quite a few jobs and didn't really like any of them. My real passion was for blues music. I was playing occasionally with Alexis and kept trying to get a band together but I was unsuccessful. Then I met up with Mick and Keith, and that's when it all came together.

KEITH RICHARDS: It was great in those early days because it was just Brian, Mick, and me. We were like a team going to take over the world. But even then there was something weird with Brian. He was always working with one of us at the expense of the other. Like he would be conspiring with Mick against me, or he'd take my money when I was out of it so he and Mick could get a drink. Then the next day he's whispering behind Mick's back to me. It was weird. Even then he was a little paranoid or a little jealous of the thing Mick and I had.

July 18, 1938. Ian Stewart is born.

IAN STEWART: When I was a kid the only music I liked was jazz. Rock'n'roll was virtually nonexistent apart from the black acts like Chuck Berry and Fats Domino and people like that. But the white rock'n'roll I couldn't stand, I just hated it. Those people like Buddy Holly and Eddie Cochran were awful! To this day I still can't see what anybody sees in Buddy Holly. It gives me a toothache.

Brian was a bit of a crusader and he came up to London with his eyes shining, determined to form a very ethnic R&B group, a Muddy Waters kind of thing. He was hunting around for guys that liked the same kind of music as him and he ran across Alexis. He was always trying to rehearse with different people, and I think it was Alexis that put him in touch with Brian Knight and Geoff Bradford. I read an advert in *Melody Maker* looking for musicians. I turned up at a rehearsal room in Soho and met Brian, who seemed to be the leader. About the time I met him, Brian and Geoff were around as well as other people who would turn up. We weren't a band, we were all just keen on rehearsing.

It was a lot of fun in those days but it was also very serious musically. Nobody ever thought that they were going to form a rock'n'roll band that was going to make a fortune. They were interested in copying the sound on those old blues records. That wasn't really my interest—I was more interested in the records of Louis Jordan with all the saxes and the boogie-woogie piano, but I was quite happy to carry on with what Brian wanted to do.

JOHN GEE: My nights were the jazz nights, because I am a jazz-oriented person. We put in a guy to just manage the club on Thursday evenings, but I did go down one evening, and I was absolutely amazed at the noise, the volume of noise. Compared to today's standards it was just a whisper, but compared to the jazz scene it was astronomical. I was deafened. These little speakers, but it was all amplified. Cyril Davis's *harmonica* was amplified. Charlie Watts, I remember the night I was down he was sitting in on drums. So it was in the jazz tradition, in that the sets were improvised and musicians used to sit in, and Mick Jagger used to come down and do some vocals. So it was a very free and easy bluesy atmosphere. But as I say, the difference between that and the jazz sets was the volume of sound.

GEOFF BRADFORD: My love of blues came from listening to American Armed Forces Radio from Europe. I heard Bo Diddley and I thought, "I must have some of this." I got into it from there. I was in the skiffle scene as well. And after getting into the blues I wanted to have a band, so I put an ad in the *Melody Maker*: "Anyone interested in blues . . . blah, blah, blah . . . ring me up and we'll have a blow." And these guys turned up, one of whom was a piano player named Keith Scott, who had an incredible record collection, and he said, "Look I play at a club, why don't you come up and have a blow?" So I went up to this place, which was the Roundhouse on Old Compton Street. I got up there and there was a guy playing twelve-string who sounded just like Leadbelly. I couldn't believe it. He was fantastic. Cyril Davis this was. I did a number and it went down all right, so I got to know Cyril. In the end, Cyril and myself used to be a duo.

Cyril formed his own band with Nicky Hopkins in it and they were tremendous. I formed another band called Blues By Six, or helped form it, with a guy called Brian Knight, and we played the clubs. We were doing a club one night and this fellow came up to me and said, "My name's Brian Jones and I'm thinking of forming a band. Do you want to be in it?" And we said, "Whatever, we'll have a go." And we assembled this crowd of people: Ian Stewart, Brian Knight—who was the vocalist with Blues Classics—myself, a bass player named Dick Taylor. That was the bare bones of it. We rehearsed in a pub called the Brick Layers Arms in Soho. Then Brian brought Keith Richards in. I wasn't really into Chuck Berry at the time. Keith was though, and that's the way they wanted to go, but we wanted to stay on the really countrified stuff, and that's where we sort of split.

BRIAN KNIGHT: We were playing a gig, and Brian came up and asked me if I wanted to join his band and play harmonica and sing. So I said yes. At first things were good, but we had a difference of opinion on the material. I wanted a more purist type of R&B, that's why I left. Then Brian got Mick Jagger and Keith Richards and that became the Rolling Stones.

KEITH RICHARDS: Geoff was the guitar player that was in the room the first time I went to a Stones rehearsal. There was Stew, Brian, Geoff Bradford, and this other guy, Brian Knight, who is still out and about. It was an impossible mixture. They were purist country blues, and if I'd walked in with my hair dyed green I couldn't have made a worse impression. So after the first rehearsal it was decided that Stew and Brian would go their way. It wasn't clear if they'd ask me back for another rehearsal.

A lot of these guys we met in the first few months were great guys, great players, but they just didn't have the other ingredients that you suddenly need if you're about to be thrown into Beatlemania proportions, which is what happened to us.

IAN STEWART: In the beginning, Brian didn't think Keith should stay with the band and Mick was in the opposite corner. At the time, rehearsals included Keith, Mick, Dick Taylor, and Geoff Bradford, led by Brian.

NICKY HOPKINS: The first time I met Mick and Keith was in a club. Cyril's band was doing the Marquee every Thursday and packing the place out, and the Stones were our support band. When we went off for a drink, they'd come on for about twenty minutes, and so I got to know them. Then in '63 I got sick for a couple of years, and during that two years they went from a relatively obscure band to incredibly famous internationally.

MICK JAGGER: We were a blues band, very serious. We were like students—you know how students get really serious about things? Well, that's how we were, and we discussed— almost like theological discussions [laughs]—how it should be, and most of it was really goofing off, as they say. But yes, we were a very serious blues band. When we started playing in ballrooms we played a lot of blues, basically because we didn't really know what else to play. We were used to playing blues clubs and then we started playing in ballrooms, where people were playing popular tunes of the day. They would be dressed up in uniforms with red blazers and they'd play whatever was a hit record that week. We would be playing as the other band, and all we knew was blues, so we very quickly had to learn to "pop" up and lighten up, so we started doing ballads and things. We'd always liked those songs, it was just that we didn't think we should do them because we were about the blues. So then there were a lot of arguments: "How many ballads should we do?" I never thought we should do too many ballads.

ALEXIS KORNER: In July of '62 we were asked to do a jazz show for BBC, and they wouldn't pay for the extra singer, because they said, "Well, Cyril Davis sings, and you sing if you have to, so we're not prepared to pay for an extra singer." So we had a band meeting in the band room at the Marquee with everyone there, including Mick, because Mick was part of the band, and we said: "This is the situation. They won't pay for you, Mick, to sing. And if we take the gig we lose the Marquee, because Harold Pendleton has already told us, 'If you leave this Thursday to do a broadcast, I will not guarantee you your gig back the Thursday after.' On the other hand, we think it will do a lot of good for R&B if we get a broadcast, because no R&B bands had been offered a broadcast up till then of any sort."

So we sat down and talked about the whole thing, and it was finally decided that Mick would hold down the Marquee with Keith and Brian, and Stew and whoever else was there. John was going to headline it as "John Baldry and his Kansas City Boys." And we would do the broadcast. That way we would keep the Marquee gig open on Thursday night for R&B and we would still be able to do the broadcast. And that's how the Rolling Stones did their first London gig on July 12, 1962.

IAN STEWART: When the advert went in about the Stones playing support for the gig at the Marquee the night of the BBC broadcast, it said that Mick was the leader. Brian was really upset by that.

September 1962. Dick Taylor decides to leave the Rolling Stones to concentrate on his art college education.

DICK TAYLOR: I think I was getting just a little bit done in by it all. Rushing up to town for rehearsals and trying to do these things for college. So it got a bit into just seven loads of things to do at the same time and trying to concentrate on one or the other. I think I was also pissed off with playing bass. There were loads of factors that came into it.

October 24, 1936. William Perks (Bill Wyman) is born to Kathleen and William Perks. He meets the Rolling Stones for the first time in December 1962.

BILL WYMAN: My band the Cliftons was named after Cliff and Tony Chapman. They were playing black R&B and rock-'n'roll—Jackie Wilson, Little Richard, Fats Domino, Chuck Berry—which gave me that little bit of help when I first joined the Stones because we had something in common there. Most people were playing instrumental stuff at that time in South London, so we weren't doing that well. We were trying to be a bit funkier than the average "Shadows" type band, so when Tony Chapman, our drummer, answered an ad in one of the music papers for a drummer in an R&B or blues band, it sounded promising. He came back the day after, and I said, "What are they like?" And he said, "Quite interesting, very slow stuff, very easy to play [ha ha ha] and there's no bass player either, so I suggested you come up. Why don't you come to the next rehearsal?" It was in three days.

It was snowing that day, really horrible it was. But we went to this terrible pub called the Weatherby Arms in Chelsea. I'd never been to Chelsea before because it was a long way away from my house and we were living quite poorly. I did not travel very much. In those days you didn't have your own car or anything, you just went up on the tube and trains and buses and things with your amplifiers in the luggage racks, which the bus conductors didn't like.

Anyway I dragged them along to the rehearsal at this pub and met these four kind of strange people.

They didn't talk. I went in and said hello and nobody took any notice. It still happens, but you're used to it now. You just speak when necessary, it's that sort of thing—so you don't waste any energy, I suppose. If you don't have to speak, then don't. If you don't have to stand up, sit down. George Bernard Shaw always said things like that: "If you don't have to run, walk." I felt a bit lost, and they looked slightly beatnikish. They had longish hair and scruffy clothes and no money, but they had something to concentrate on, which was music in their case, instead of poetry or art, like the other beatniks.

And then Mick spoke to me—Mick and Ian Stewart. We were chatting away quite friendly, but Brian and Keith were having a beer, and they didn't really speak until they discovered that I smoked and that I had some cigarettes, and then it was, "Give us a fag, mate." Then it was like chat, chat, and, "Wow, you've got a big amplifier, haven't you?" So I was kind of voted in instantly because I had some good equipment and they didn't. They really needed some and had no money for it. Then it was a matter of me slotting in really quickly—before they found someone with a bigger amplifier, I suppose [laughs]. Which I managed to do over December of '62. And then we started to do quite a few gigs like the Marquee, and the Ealing jazz club, and the Ricky Tick Club at Windsor and places like that. Then they finally discovered that Tony Chapman wasn't a particularly good drummer. He sped up and slowed down and was very erratic, and didn't quite fit, so they asked Charlie to join in January of '63.

Charlie had already played with the band on odd gigs when they couldn't find a drummer. He was playing in two bands, I think, at the time, and he used to sit in if he was free. They liked him the best but he wouldn't join them because he was much better off with the bands he was in because we weren't making any money. Charlie was working at the time, and I don't think he wanted to become a professional musician. He was a graphic designer and he was doing very well and was getting a very good salary at the time. I think it was eighteen pounds a week when the average working wage was around eleven. I was also working, as was Stew. Mick was at the London School of Economics with a grant that sustained the three of them. Brian and Keith weren't working and they lived on Mick's grant and anything that we brought in, like fish and chips and food or if we put money in for the heating and so on.

They were really on a starvation diet when we met them, living in this terrible apartment. You couldn't find a chair with four legs—they only had three legs. You couldn't sit on anything; there were broken milk bottles on the carpets [laughs] and you stayed in bed all day because it was the only way to keep warm. Brian and Keith used to stay in bed all day long with their coats over them because there was no heating in the place. It was pretty bad and they used to get food parcels from Keith's mum. It was quite frightening actually, and I thought, "Is this for me?" *But there was something about the music.* It was quite interesting, if kind of hypnotic—a very slow blues. I only knew Chuck Berry's slow blues, like "Confessin' the Blues" and things like that. I liked it but I didn't really know much about blues.

Keith and Brian used to sit all day long and practise. When they weren't in bed in the cold they would sit and just practise note for note. Every Jimmy Reeves song they could hear, every Elmore James, Chuck Berry. Note for note they'd do these amazing, intricate patterns between the two guitars, one going down the scale and one going up, and they would work hours and hours. They really perfected that. They could play any of those things. Little Water and all the harmonica things.

When Tony Chapman said, "Okay, well, let's go back and re-form the old band," I made the wisest decision in my life and said, "No, I like the music, I think I'll stay." So he went back and re-formed his band, and a couple of years later, became The Herd with Peter Frampton.

It wasn't money—in fact, I was making less money with them than I was with my own band before that. Then at least we were getting ten or fifteen pounds a week. But with Mick and Keith and them I was getting, like, five shillings on a good night, and I was mostly out of pocket, what with travelling in buses everywhere. It was crazy.

Charlie eventually was persuaded to join in mid-January of '63, and that was when the band became Mick, Brian, Keith, Charlie, myself, and Ian Stewart.

BRIAN JONES: I like playing guitar, especially slide guitar, and for about two years now I've been playing a lot of harmonica. With the harmonica it's all about how you bend the notes. You don't just play them straight on. It's difficult to explain and I could never teach someone to play. It's just something you mess around with until you get the feel, like all the great American blues players, like Sonny Boy Williamson and Little Walter.

KEITH RICHARDS: Those were pretty Spartan days. We had nothing in those days, and Edith Grove where we lived was a pigsty. There was very little to party with because we had no bread. There might be a little bit of grass turn up occasionally, but our high then was just playing.

Mick was still a bit torn because he was at the London School of Economics on a grant and really didn't want to give up that security. Brian and I had packed it in already. College was happy to see the end of both of us. Brian and I would go out and look for empty beer bottles, which we could sell back for the deposit. One day I went out and when I came back Brian was playing harp. He said, "Listen to this." And he played the bluesiest shit, man! It only took him one day to get into the soul of the harp. So for a while he dropped the guitar and started blowing blues harp. He just had it in him.

ALEXIS KORNER: Charlie [Watts] was a visualizer for an agency, and he was quite the fair old drummer, too. But when we decided we were gonna go pro because there was simply too much work to cope on a semi-pro basis, Charlie wouldn't go with us, so we got Ginger [Baker] in. Charlie just didn't reckon on going pro. He didn't think it was a good idea . . . He didn't think it was very secure [laughs]. I quote him: "Well, I mean Alex, I don't think it's a very safe job [laughs].

KEITH RICHARDS: When we first met Charlie he had just quit Alexis's band. We were both playing the same club and he was playing in the other band. After our set he came up to us and said, "You guys are really good. You just need a really good drummer." We said, "We'd love to have you, man, but we can't afford you." He said, "That's okay, I'd rather play with you guys." You see, as much as money was important to Charlie, he really liked playing with good people. So he told the other band to fuck off and hooked up with us. As soon as we had Charlie, it started to take off. We were a real band then with great players.

January 17, 1963. Charlie Watts joins the Rolling Stones as their drummer.

CHARLIE WATTS: We used to live in Edith Grove—that's Brian, Keith, and me in this ridiculous household. Brian and Keith used to be hilarious together. It was actually Mick's apartment so it was usually on his head whatever we did . . . Funny how things don't change much. It was more of a family than a band. I'd never been in a band longer than three months. When the Stones asked me to join they talked in terms of a band—a commitment, in other words. I thought, "Oh, this will go on a year, and the next year, fold up."

January 31, 1963. The Stones play the Marquee club for the last time, until 1971.

HAROLD PENDLETON: Cyril took over the residency of the Marquee on the Thursday night when Alexis went off to the Flamingo, and he needed a guest group. One of them was the Rolling Stones. Ten pounds a night we paid them. I'll always remember one night I came out of the Marquee with Cyril, and the Stones were packing their stuff in a little van or something, and I shouted "good night" to them, and they were *arrrrrgh* . . . I said, "What's the matter with them?" Cyril said, "I've just fired them." "Oh, what for?" He said, "They're not very authentic, they're not very good." Which

I always thought, looking back in retrospect, was one of the funniest things of all time.

Cyril fired them because they weren't a terribly good R&B band. And they were picked up then by a friend of mine called Georgio Gomelski, who gave them a gig at the Station Hotel club in Richmond.

February 24, 1963. The Stones play their first gig at the Crawdaddy Club.

GIORGIO GOMELSKI: I had shot a documentary about the Chris Barber band and had started my own club called Piccadilly Blues Club. I heard the Stones playing at a small club in Sutton and they were fantastic. I arranged for them to play at the Station Hotel in Richmond. I became their manager and helped establish them at Richmond.

BILL WYMAN: It was very early in 1963 and we were doing a few gigs in the intervals with people like Cyril Davis. Suddenly people really started to catch on to us. The top band used to get very offended because we started to become more popular in our fifteen-minute spot than they were in the lead spot. So we got thrown out of that and then it was impossible to find anywhere to play, no one would book us. We were the outcasts. We were like the black sheep of all the club things going on then. In the end we met Georgio Gomelski, who was almost a kind of a manager at that time, and he found this place that did have music—a pub in Richmond called the Station Hotel. The band that was playing there previously just packed it in for some reason, and he said, there's an availability there, so we took that over in about February of '63.

I hadn't been to that part of London—Richmond—and the student thing was going on. They were the people that started to follow us, and it was very very different and a bit special in a way. I knew something was happening. I didn't quite know what it was, but I knew I wanted to be in on it.

It went from nobody the first night, just six or twelve people, to a point six or seven weeks later where there were four hundred jam-packed in with a fire regulation total of one hundred and sixty. And the local council and the police got excited and the newspaper the *Daily Mirror* wrote an article, and it really became big. Like, "What's happening in Richmond?" And then we got thrown out of there.

I used to have a great big amplifier about the size of a door. We used to call it the wardrobe. It was so big that you couldn't stand it up, so I used to lay it on the floor on its side and sit on it in the back. We used to sit on rusty old stools we stole out of some old club somewhere. We would sit almost in a circular way facing each other, just play like we were rehearsing at the pub in Chelsea. We'd sit around, play a number, then we'd have a beer and a smoke, and then we'd play another number. We didn't really take much notice of the people, but then this Richmond thing started happening and suddenly we'd see these kids stripped to the waist, swinging their shirts around their heads and on each other's shoulders, and up on tables, and it started to get really mad.

They started to invent dances for our music, which had never been done before . . . only like in cha-cha and twist and things like that. Kids didn't dance separately to music until then, so that was quite interesting. The *Ready, Steady, Go* people, the TV people, they heard about it and they sent their people down to find dancers for the show, and while they were doing that they found us as well, you see, so that was how our relationship with the *Ready, Steady, Go* people happened. It was an accident. We were great friends with them from then on, and very popular on the show. It was the kids from the art colleges all around that area, the art students that were our fans. They'd follow us from club to club.

VICKI WYCKHAM: We used to go and look at acts in clubs, and we started to hear about this group playing down in Richmond. So we went to the Crawdaddy on a Sunday night and saw the Rolling Stones. They were absolutely extraordinary and the kids were going crazy for them.

March 11, 1963. The Stones record five songs at IBC Studios with Glyn Johns.

BILL WYMAN: Another place we played was the Red Lion Pub in Sutton, which was a suburb of London, very near to where Ian Stewart lived. And Eric Clapton lived in that area, and Jeff Beck, all those people. The back-up band that used to play with us the same night was a band Glyn Johns used to sing in. Glyn was an engineer for IBC Studios in London, and he said one day, "Why don't we try to record?" We never thought about making a record in those days. We never thought about going to America or being on TV or having a pop record. It was just playing the music, and if people wanted to hear it and you could make a few pounds doing it, that was the ultimate. So we said, "Yeah, but what do we do?" And he said that we'll kind of select some songs that might be interesting, maybe make a record . . . *Wow* . . . It was really so far out of the norm that we couldn't relate to it.

So we went up there, and he booked a three-hour session, and we cut five tracks live on two-track, and then Glyn said, "I think they're fairly bluesy." And when you listen to them now, you'll understand that these days they would be totally acceptable, but in those days they were so uncommercial, because no one knew that music. The record companies weren't interested, and we were very disappointed, 'cause suddenly we were excited about, *"Wow . . . we could make a record!"* And then suddenly we were disappointed because people didn't like it. Seven record companies I think we went to. Cost about a hundred pounds, that session. We bought the tapes back later, because we were really scared about . . . and then we lost them . . . It's very typical [laughs].

IAN STEWART: There used to be a coffee shop called the Harlequin, and Glyn used to go in there, and when I got involved with Brian and the others I remembered that Glyn had his own rock'n'roll group. I got to know him then. He was learning how to become an engineer at a studio called IBC, and he knew all about the Stones from the earliest days because we had played the Red Lion a couple of times by then. So it was just a case of "Hey, let's sneak into your studio when nobody's looking and see what it sounds like."

The original idea behind the recording was to play it to a BBC producer called Jimmy Grant, who had a program on Saturday mornings. The BBC had a policy that they wouldn't allow anyone to play unless they passed an audition. We knew we'd never pass an audition, but we knew this guy Jimmy had a good set of ears on him and liked the blues. My idea was to get us down on tape, take it to Jimmy Grant, and say, "Bollocks to the audition, listen to this. Can we please be on your radio show, sir?"

GLYN JOHNS: I used to sing with them on occasion just for a laugh, and we started to run this club every other week, every other Friday night, mainly for somewhere to play, and we had a very large circle of kids in the area who went out together, so we'd all go down to this place on a Friday night, and I used to charge them five bob to get in [laughs]. Pretty good. Anyway, we booked the Rolling Stones. All I know is that the deal was we used to split whatever we took on the door, and we only took thirty shillings. I actually paid the Rolling Stones thirty shillings [laughs]. I think five people would turn up, but I was completely blown away by them.

I'd already been introduced to Jimmy Reed by then, and no one else had ever heard of him other than the Stones. The Stones were the first people into R&B, and I happened to know an American guy, a young teenager whose father was working in England. He had a collection of Jimmy Reed's stuff and so I was into this stuff. It had a sound that was completely different from anything I'd ever heard. I remembered these young, long-haired idiots playing the same stuff, so this was just too good to be true.

The studio I worked for had just been bought out, had new owners. I was the senior engineer by this time, and I went to these guys and I said, "Look, you just bought yourselves a studio. I want to start producing records. I haven't got any money. It seems silly if I work for you that we shouldn't do something together. Why don't you let me produce for the studio?" And they said, "Well, that's a great idea. We have no objection to it, but of course we'd want to do all the business." Well, that was fine, because I don't know anything about money because I was only a kid anyway. All I wanted to do was go and do it. I didn't care about anything else. And the first act that I took in there were the Stones—unbelievable, isn't it?—who of course leapt at the opportunity to do a recording session.

We cut five things in one evening. "Road Runner,"

"Bright Lights, Big City," "Come On," I can't remember what else. The tapes were handed over to the people at the studios the following morning. They had no idea, they were so far away from the popular music. I think the man who owned the studios knew somebody at Decca—that was probably the worst record label in those days. The guy he knew was in the classical department. That was his connection, but I didn't know any of that, I was just a kid.

So days go by, and the guy tries to get a record deal for this bunch of—as far as he was concerned—long-haired, filthy, dirty individuals. In the meantime, Eric Easton and Andrew Oldham appeared on the scene and saw them play. Andrew Oldham had never had anything to do with the record business before. He hung around the fringes of it, but he'd not been involved. He'd visited sessions of mine before, with other people. Andrew came and hung around but he didn't know anything about it. So he'd gone along and said, "Okay, come with us, we'll make you stars. I'll get you a record deal."

BILL WYMAN: When we couldn't sell the tapes, we thought we should try to get on the radio. Maybe we should try doing an audition for BBC. So Brian wrote a very good letter about us being a real, authentic blues band, very similar to the real Chicago stuff, and thought it would be applicable. In February or March we made an audition, and we were turned down. BBC said the band sounded reasonably okay and we could be used as a support band for visiting Americans, and jazz people, but the singer was too black-sounding and would never, never make it.

I don't think we played on the BBC radio for probably almost a year after we formed. They really did not like us, and we had many confrontations with them over the years, over cancelling of shows and being banned, and all kinds of things.

KEITH ALTHAM: I saw them at the Station Hotel in Richmond in the days when they were just beginning, so to speak, and hadn't had a record or anything, and people were hanging off the rafters down there. They followed the Beatles in, really, and used the Beatles as sort of the yardstick from which to work. They very swiftly realized there was a virtue in playing an almost opposite game to the Beatles. As the Beatles became more and more respectable, the Rolling Stones tried to become less and less acceptable.

GLYN JOHNS: It wasn't only the sound, although the sound was completely different from anybody I'd ever heard. It was the way they looked—the whole attitude . . . that was completely and utterly revolutionary. I'd never seen anything like it before. I can remember seeing them for the first time and being completely shattered, shocked, absolutely shocked. And if you look at a photograph of them in those days, they look like they're on their way to Sunday School [laughs]. It's funny, isn't it?

CHAPTER 2

Oldham Days

April 14, 1963.

BILL WYMAN: We were playing away one evening, one of those shows in the Station Hotel, in among this mass of people, probably after four or five weeks, in March of '63, and we looked up and we saw four shadowy figures standing facing us in the audience. Not dancing, just standing there in leather coats. And we looked, and we turned away, and we did a double-take. "That's the bloody Beatles! Standing there right in front of us, two feet away watching us!"

They were going to do some big concert or something in London—Albert Hall or something big—and we were invited. I think three of us went—Mick, Keith, and Brian. The rest of us were working. Anyway, [the Beatles played there] and got attacked for the first time by kids, and [our guys] said, "Right, we gotta be more commercial now." That's when the Stones first thought that we've got to start doing commercial material. The only commercial material we knew at the time or wanted to play was the Chuck Berry kind of songs, the fast Chuck Berry stuff. Certainly not pop music as such.

Then a few weeks after that, came along Andrew Oldham

and Eric Easton. They'd been tipped off because Andrew used to work for the Beatles—he was tipped off by one of the Beatles, I don't remember which one. And he came down with Eric, who was a booking agent, very businesslike. Andrew was a very artistic type, and they kind of chatted to us, and Brian went 'round the office the next day and signed a contract for us. I think he was under age at the time—I think he was nineteen or twenty. He signed the contract. And suddenly we had management, and a very good guy in Andrew Oldham. He really knew the media and really knew how to exploit our image. Many people think that image was created by Andrew Oldham, but the image was *there*. We were the only band I ever saw in those days and for at least a year afterwards that didn't wear stage clothes, that had long hair. The Beatles had a different hairstyle, but they didn't have long hair, just top of their ears, I think. Ours was down to our shoulders, it was, especially Mick and Keith's.

GIORGIO GOMELSKI: After we saw the Beatles at Albert Hall, Mick really pushed me for bigger clubs and to get them more exposure. So I approached Peter Jones at the *Record Mirror*.

PETER JONES: Yes, Georgio was a record producer in a very small way in those days. We knew he was involved in the basic R&B emergence in this country. He rang me and said, "Look, I'm filming a band and I would like you to come over and see them." I said, "Fine, what day?" He said Sunday. Sunday was a day I definitely didn't want to go anywhere, but I did go over at lunchtime on a Sunday, right across London, moaning all the way. I really was a bit upset that he should impose on my time, and there wasn't a great deal happening there, because he was actually filming them and he was going to use them as an insert in a film on the basic rock'n'roll and rhythm'n'blues area in this country.

I must say they looked very good. They were working onstage and there were just a handful of people almost operating as extras, creating a little bit of atmosphere. Georgio really was loving this film director bit. It was only very much after that he said, "I'll get a couple of the boys to come round and talk to you." And they came out and we had a couple of pints. It was Brian Jones and Mick Jagger. They were hungry and they didn't have any money—it is really quite true. Brian had the wallet, the group wallet, and there was no money in the wallet. But there was a cutting from the local paper, I think it was the *Richmond and Twickenham Times*, a local weekly paper.

It was a piece about the apparent success and controversy this band was creating in its evening gigs. There were people waiting on the pavement, and this upset some of the local residents who had to step into the road and said "What were they all about?" There was the usual kind of . . . well, early Rolling Stones controversy, I suppose. And they really bemoaned the fact that nobody was showing any interest in them in terms of a recording contract or even taking any interest in them, or bothering to come and see them.

With that in mind, I went back and had another look in the afternoon. There really was something pretty special about Mick, although I see that people like Tina Turner have since said how much they've helped mould his onstage movements. But I really do believe that even in those days—long before there was any kind of record—he was a natural mover onstage. There really was something absolutely exciting about the way he looked, even compared to the way he sang. We talked about their taste in music and the kind of stuff they were trying to get across.

So as a result of that, I promised I'd do the very best I could do to help them, and I also guaranteed that the *Record Mirror* would be the first nationally distributed paper that would give them a story. It was then that I got Norman Jopling in. He was kind of our arch-priest of the basically black American music field. He wasn't in any way bigoted or biased about whether white people could do it or not, and he decided to go along, and he confirmed what I felt—that there really was a great deal of raw excitement about this band. So on my say-so he wrote the piece that went in. This was well in advance of them making any records, but they wanted this nudge, and they wanted somebody to take an interest in them.

NORMAN JOPLING: Peter Jones had been down to see them, but in his editorial capacity he wasn't going to write about them because they didn't have a recording contract at the time, and also their management was in flux. My memory might be slightly awry here, but he said, "You should go down and see them because they're in your bag." Everybody then was into rhythm'n'blues. So I went down there and I took my girlfriend, and they were fantastic. The great thing about them was they had the rhythm'n'blues sound. When they played Bo Diddley numbers they sounded like Bo Diddley records, and they looked good, so later we met the band. I'd never met them before. We went round to a friend of theirs—six of them then. Ian was with them at the time, he was a full-fledged member of the band. And afterwards Ian drove us home. He was the roadie as well.

I wrote the article, and it was one of the first ones we'd ever done on an act that hadn't got a recording contract. The day the article appeared, the paper hit the shops about one o'clock in the West End, and by four o'clock three record companies had phoned me and said, "Where can we get hold of these guys?"

I was friends with Andrew Oldham at the time; he was vying for management with Georgio. I wasn't sure of the exact situation so I just gave them Andrew's phone number. There was Phillips and Decca and I forget the other company, and that's sort of the long and the short of the whole thing.

PETER JONES: We had this man, Andrew Oldham, who really was a tryer, this one. Whatever craze, whatever phase there was, he would come round to the *Record Mirror* offices and he would be in on it. For a while he wanted to make a name for himself as a comedian, and for a time he was called "Sandy Beach," which we said was totally improbable. Then he wanted to call himself "Chancery Lane," and we listened through these things and said, "Yes, Andrew . . . okay Andrew . . ." The thing was that he had this kind of public school image—which is rather different here—public school is the upper-crust school where you pay a lot of money to go. He had that kind of image, yet he had this basic feel for music and the kind of music that he liked. He was a very sharp boy.

So I mentioned the band to him, and he agreed that he'd take an interest, and he had links with Eric Easton, who I have to say is, or was, one of the squarest of guys on the fringe of the pop music industry in this country. But he and Eric turned up, and in a sense the rest is history, because it was Andrew who persuaded Eric there was something worth doing here, something worth putting money in.

Eric Easton was literally dragged along to Richmond to see the Rolling Stones in action, and he told me afterwards of his total humiliation and embarrassment at finding himself standing in line with lots of young kids. He was wearing his heavy tweed suit and his heavy brogue shoes, looking rather the kind of country squire businessman. At the same time, however, he recognized instantly the value of this band, the power, the energy they generated, and he was amazingly impressed with Jagger. Jagger really was an absolute natural. Whether it was intuition working or whether he picked up ideas from other sources, or whatever, once onstage he really worked brilliantly.

KEITH ALTHAM: Well, he [Oldham] was quite conventional in many respects, really. He came from basically what was a fashion area. I mean, he'd worked with people like Mary Quant, and he came across from France. He did a bit of publicity for people like Mark Winter, and then he worked with a guy called Tony Calder, who was also doing early Beatles stuff.

I think Andrew's ideas were quite conventional to begin with, and I think that even the Stones were conventional when they first went out. I mean, he tried putting them into leather waistcoats and jackets and suits and things. I think that was because of the art school background, but even the Beatles had that. I don't know what it was. I suppose probably because Andrew was of a different generation to Brian Epstein—that was probably the key factor. Oldham had a bit more in common with the slightly bohemian attitude, coming from the art school areas that he did, than somebody like Epstein would have had coming from a conventional family music business in Liverpool and seeing things, really as a business manager. Andrew was much more one of the guys, and still in for a bit of hell raising, so to speak. And that was probably where the divergent camps [developed]. You were either a Beatles fan or you were a Stones fan in those days.

May 6, 1963. Brian Jones on behalf of the Stones signs a management agreement with Andrew Oldham and Eric Easton's company, Impact Sound.

BILL WYMAN: Yeah, they did get a good deal for themselves. They also did a contract for all recordings through Impact Sound or something. Impact took most of the royalties, which we didn't know about until much later. Even so, we were getting something like 5 percent. I think Andrew negotiated something like 9 or 10 from Decca, but the Beatles were only getting 1 or 2 percent at the time and we were at 5, so we were well happy.

GIORGIO GOMELSKI: When my father died, he had been living in Switzerland. So I went there for the funeral and to take care of his affairs, and I was away for quite some time. When I came back, I found out that the band had signed a contract with Andrew Oldham. I found out some years later that one of the reasons they decided to sign with Andrew was that I was a foreigner. They felt that they couldn't trust me because I wasn't English.

TONY CALDER: Andrew and I were both working as independent PR guys. I remember one night he said to me, "Come on, we're going down to see a blues band and I'm going to make the singer a star."

Brian was the leader of the band in those days, so all the early meetings were with him. After a couple of meetings I said to Andrew, "Look, this guy is not capable of running this band." Well, Andrew didn't care. He never liked Brian. He didn't understand him and couldn't relate to him. Andrew's interest was entirely centred on Mick. He believed he was going to be a huge star. It didn't matter about the group— Mick was going to make it no matter what. And of course Mick didn't need any encouragement in that direction.

The two of them would compete to do the most outrageous things. I remember being in Berlin for a concert and we looked out and we realized the audience was basically male. So Andrew told Mick to "goose step" across the stage. Well, Mick would have to take it one further. Instead of goose stepping, he raised his right arm in the Hitler salute. The most frightening thing was that the audience then stood up and started wrecking the place. Concerts weren't allowed in Berlin again for years.

KEITH RICHARDS: Yeah, Andrew and Eric screwed Giorgio because he had nothing in writing with us. Also, Giorgio was a club guy and didn't have it together for making records, which we really wanted to do.

PETER JONES: I think the Beatles' manager Brian [Epstein] actually was a really businesslike guy. I mean, he brought the Beatles in to us, and there was never a moment of relaxation. There was never a hint of "Let's drop the veneer for a few minutes and just talk amongst friends. Can you do anything to help these boys?" He did it all on a very straight, business-like basis, as if he was selling something he did genuinely believe in. With Andrew, the relationship was totally different, because with Andrew it was a kind of "wink wink, nudge nudge" kind of thing. And he knew, that I knew, that he was kidding along for most of the people. And he also knew that he could depend on me to maintain his image.

Andrew was pretty unscrupulous, really, I must say, in the way he got his own way over things. Brian Epstein was much too well bred, in a sense, to do anything even slightly shady. I mean he really was quite a gentlemanly guy, although a very tough guy over percentages. I don't think Andrew was too good on the percentages. I think he needed someone behind him to check the bottom line on any kind of expenditure.

NORMAN JOPLING: Brian was really the leader at the time. He used to come up to the office a lot and hang around. They knew more about rhythm'n'blues than anybody. I liked it a lot and knew about it, but they knew all the records, they were really into it. And they were also very good musicians. I remember being around a film producer's place and they all picked up different instruments—even Mick who wasn't playing onstage at the time, other than tambourine and harp—and that was very impressive. Their background was very impressive even then.

May 8, 1963. Andrew Oldham informs Ian Stewart that he will no longer be an onstage member of the band.

IAN STEWART: After quite a long time of scuffling around just amusing ourselves, playing around in various pubs, the thing just took off like a rocket, so someone had to be brought in to coordinate and manipulate it and exploit it as much as possible. It was quite obvious that the band was going to be as big as the Beatles—but obviously we weren't going to be bigger than the Beatles if all we were playing was Muddy Waters songs. Someone had to say, "Look, you've got to write your own material, and you've got to go here and you've got to do this," and so on. My face never really fit in, and I still can't play piano. I never was any good, and I'm no better now than I was. As soon as they started writing more musically complex pieces, I couldn't play it anyway. Nobody ever said, "You're out," but all of a sudden I was out. It happened one night when I went down to play a gig and there were five guys all in band uniforms and none for me. Also, there were no pianos in the places we played, and if there were, they were useless.

KEITH RICHARDS: Stew was originally a fully paid-up member. He was our piano player. We suddenly hit the charts and became famous and all of a sudden there are all these managers and record companies hanging around. They suggested that Stew just didn't look the part, and there was nothing we could do. So Brian talked to him, and Stew said, "Fine, I know I don't really fit the image, but I'll still stick around and drive you guys about." He's on a lot of our records, and he used to play onstage. He was a member in the way that he was most comfortable. I always found it amazing that he actually stayed, but he was a big-hearted guy.

KEITH ALTHAM: I think my initial impression of Jagger was of a slightly foppish individual. I didn't appreciate the resilient qualities I see now in him, or the fact he used a lightly dandified, almost decadent effeminacy at times to kind of convey a feeling of rebelliousness or something. He seemed to me a slightly foppish character. Keith was much more relatable, really, in those days—more of a man's man so to speak than Mick was. The two of them together, when you did interviews, were absolutely lethal, because they'd send you up like mad. But I used to get very good copy out of that kind of a situation, and I used to almost encourage them to do it. I used to enjoy it. It was always the people you were most scared of actually going to do interviews with that always provided the best copy.

Brian Jones was a different character. I mean, to be fair

to Mick, Brian Jones made Mick look like Burt Reynolds. Brian was even more foppish than Mick, or so he seemed at that time. Brian really was a very delicate figure, actually. I mean, the difference between Brian and Mick was that you felt protective toward Brian because you felt that he was totally vulnerable. You felt that he was made out of porcelain, like he was going to fall over and shatter at any moment. Even in the early days he was a mess of nerves and loose nerve ends, and Mick somehow had a kind of arrogance—which was attached to his dilettantism, if that's the word—that Brian never had. You knew that constitutionally Mick was gonna be okay, but Brian had all the earmarks of one of nature's victims.

HAROLD PENDLETON: Friday nights were the Yardbirds top of the bill. Georgio had discovered them to take the place of the Rolling Stones, who'd been stolen from him by other managers while he'd gone to his father's funeral in Switzerland. Georgio, undaunted, having a club, found the Yardbirds and stuck them in. They became a very successful band also and were top of the bill on Friday the following year.

GLYN JOHNS: Having signed an agreement with Andrew Oldham, the Stones needed to get the recordings they made with me at IBC back into their control. So the Stones came and had a meeting with George Clewson, who owned the Studio. I didn't know about this. I was walking back into the building after lunch and they were all together and they said, "Oh, we just came to see George Clewson." I said, "Really, why?" They said, "We want to get out of this deal we did with him, 'cause it's ridiculous. We don't want to have anything to do with it, and we don't want to make records anyway." "Oh . . . okay." So Clewson gave them back their contract for the cost of the studio, which was ninety-four pounds, and I asked Clewson, "Do you have any idea what you've just done?" [laughs]. And he said, "They don't want to make records. They're obviously a complete waste of time." So I said, "Okay, well, fine," but it was so obvious they were going to be enormous, it was written all over the wall in pink writing.

May 10, 1963. Decca's Dick Rowe meets Beatle George Harrison at a talent contest in Liverpool.

DICK ROWE: I was talking to George [Harrison] and I said, "You know I really had my backside kicked over turning you lot down." And he said, "I wouldn't worry too much about that. Why don't you sign the Rolling Stones?" And I said, "The Rolling Who?" He said, "The Stones." I said, "I've never heard of them. What do they play? Where can I see them?" He said, "You can find them at the Station Hotel at Richmond."

I left him right there on the spot and came down to London and picked up my wife and we drove to Richmond and it was late summer because the sun was very low round about seven o'clock in the evening, and we arrived at the back entrance to the Station Hotel and there was a small table and a bloke on the door. Because of the low sun I had dark glasses on and jumping out of the car quickly I forgot to pick up my other glasses, so I said, "I'm from Decca, may I come in and listen to the group?" He said, "Fine." So my wife and I went in and from this low bright sunshine into a dark room I couldn't see anything.

Gradually I began to make out what it was about. I could see the group, and then I noticed that the room was full of young fellows—there wasn't a girl to be seen—and they were standing in little groups of two or more talking to each other. No one was dancing, there were no girls, they were just listening to the music, and all the time they were up and down on the balls of their feet to the rhythm. I said to my wife, "What do they look like?" It was a bit ridiculous—I could hear them and it was a nice sort of earthy sound but I wanted to know what they looked like. She said, "The lead singer's very good." As always when I go to see anybody, I never let them know I'm there, and I never stay very long, no more than fifteen minutes. So I left, and the next morning I started chasing around trying to find out how to sign them, and I found Andrew Oldham. And that was the start of the Rolling Stones with Decca.

May 1963. Encouraged by the Decca contract and the recording they were about to do, Mick quits the London School of Economics. He explains to his parents that he is taking a year's

sabbatical from his studies to sing. The news is greeted with relief and cheers by the other band members.

ALEXIS KORNER: It was a difficult decision for Mick. He didn't want to risk his future and he didn't want to hurt his parents. His mother even called me one night asking if Mick had the talent to make it in show business. I told her he was the best singer I knew.

MICK JAGGER: They weren't well pleased. No. Rock'n'roll was just a lower-class thing. Obviously they wanted me to continue with LSE.

KEITH RICHARDS: When the band started out, the height of our ambitions was playing three or four sold-out club gigs a week in London. That was the height of ambition for the Stones because we didn't see any larger market for what we were doing at that time. Everything else just grew out of that. Suddenly it went from London, to England . . . and then just as suddenly from England to Europe and then it was America. Well, I had nothing better to do at the time, that's for sure.

June 7, 1963. Decca releases the Stones' first single, "Come On."

DICK ROWE: Yes, well, I put a young man in charge of their recordings called Michael Barclay, who was a fine producer.

He made some fine records for us and he later set up the pattern for the Moody Blues, but he couldn't work with the Rolling Stones. He was a very artistic young man, and delicate in his appearance and everything, and they didn't really hit it off. He brought back the results and it was ghastly and everybody knew it was. He knew it was ghastly, the Stones knew it, and Andrew knew.

So Andrew then took them to the cheapest Studios in London on Denmark Street, and they made this very raw record, and I remember taking it up to Lewis [Sir Edward Lewis, Decca's chairman] and playing it to him. I wondered if it was too raw, but he was so annoyed that we had passed on the Beatles, he was determined that the Stones were going to make it. He hadn't the slightest idea what they were about—it was just a very intelligent gamble on his part. When I played it, he said "Fantastic," and I remember looking at him and thinking *fantastic?* Even if it had been fantastic, that kind of music would not have got through to him [laughs]. When he said *fantastic*, after that moment he had the entire company work as they'd never worked before to make sure it happened.

KEITH RICHARDS: It wasn't a great song but I remember the feeling of actually having a bit of plastic with our names on it. It was a real natural high. We were all like little kids jumping up and down and shouting.

BILL WYMAN: The "Come On" thing . . . we went in the studio and cut that one. "Come On" and "I Want to Be Loved" was the first single, which went out and sort of hung around the charts for three or four months. It got to about #20 I think, or #19, and then we had a problem of follow-up. There was the Chuck Berry song, which we didn't really like and we didn't play live—we thought it was too pop-y . . . "dud duddud" [he sings]. It wasn't what we were playing onstage. We wouldn't even play it onstage. It had been out about a month, it was in the forties or thirties or something, and Andrew came down to one of the gigs at the Scene Club in London, and at the end of the show he said, "You bloody idiots, you forgot to do the single!" and we said, "Oh, we don't play that," and he said, "What, you haven't been doing it on the shows?" and we said, "No, we hate that song, we aren't going to play that anymore." And we had this huge row with him about promoting this single in our live per-formance. In the end we relented and would pop it in and just get it over as quick as possible and go on to the things we liked.

After "Come On" was released and we were starting to get more attention in the press, they began to talk more and more about our appearance rather than about the music. We were accused of being dirty and having offensively long hair.

KEITH RICHARDS: We recorded it ["Come On"] because we had a recording session and we had to record something and they wanted something commercial. They refused what we gave them in the first place, so we said okay, and delved back and went through everything we were playing. I don't know, somebody—probably Brian because he was at the time considered the leader of the band as he kept the band's money under his bed—said we should do "Come On." It was a commercial song and that was our first compromise. You see, the baddest thing we wanted was a chance to keep on recording. "Okay, so they want something commercial? We'll give it to them." That's what the record business is about. It's no good making records if you don't sell them, so we thought we'd give ourselves a second chance by giving them something they wanted to start and then we'd take it back later, which we did. I think it was the one and only time we did anything the record company wanted us to do.

Then we refused to play it. Andrew Oldham almost went up the wall. "You've got a hit record and you don't play it!?" "We ain't playing that goddam thing . . . it's awful."

June 16, 1963

BILL WYMAN: We got kicked out of the Station Hotel because of the fire regulations. The pub got worried about all these kids in the street dancing, and the publicity, and the brewers came down on the owners and said, "Look, you're only supposed to have a hundred and fifty. You're going to be in dead trouble so you better fix it." So we got cancelled, and then we lost the one gig that was really happening again. There were a lot of things against us at that time. And then we said, "What do we do now?" And we moped around for a few days with Georgio. We went to his flat and talked to him, and he said, "I've found a place in Richmond. It's the Athletics Club and it's the clubhouse, and it can take six, eight hundred people, and I think we can get it." I think he arranged that through Harold Pendleton.

July-August 1963.

HAROLD PENDLETON: Georgio started off at the Station Hotel with the Stones and then the Station Hotel closed for refurbishment, and Georgio was desperate to put the band somewhere. The Richmond Athletic Association Ground was immediately behind and I'd already started my festival there. I'd been there one or two years, and they had a clubhouse on the ground, and I'd overcome the fears of the Richmond Athletic Association. They trusted me. Also helps to have white hair, which I had then actually. So I went to them and I said, "Look, a friend of mine's got this sort of music we have here now every year. He's got a club [that's being renovated]. Can he hire your clubhouse? I'll vouch for him and I'll guarantee it's all right. There won't be any problems." So he was saved.

I introduced [Georgio] to Commander Wheeler, the secretary of the association, and vouched for him, and he got

Friday nights or whatever to put on the Rolling Stones in this place. It's there that they began to collect their serious following, and they were growing and growing. Comes August I want to put the festival on and I said to Georgio, "Next month I take over." He said, "Hang on, what about my club?" I said, "Well, it closes, Georgio. While I'm doing the festival, I take over everything in the whole place." "Oh, Christ," he said, "can't you make a little pathway through to my club so I can still have the club?" I said, "I can't make a passageway—what are you talking about? I have a big festival on, Georgio." He said, "Oh damn, what can I do? I've got to *pay* them, I promised to pay them thirty quid." So I said, "Well, I'll tell you what I'll do, Georgio. I'll pay them that week. I'll take them off your hands. 'Cause I had no concept how important they were, because they weren't. This was the band Cyril had sacked from the Marquee, bugging about in Richmond—which incidentally is where I lived—and they were of minute importance, so I'll take them for thirty quid and stick them somewhere in a corner and forget them. I can now put my whole festival on and get on with things, and have them in a corner.

Between my agreeing to that and the actual event taking place, they became a hit . . . a record or something. When we opened the gates, a thousand little girls rushed in, and my security, mostly rugby players, were completely baffled about what to do about little girls. They packed into the room, the clubhouse I had them in, and it was frightening to look at—the window were bulging because there were all these little girls all pressed against . . . So I quickly took the band out of the clubhouse and moved them onto my number-two stage, which was in the big marquee, because there were a thousand of them and the clubhouse only held about four hundred. I quickly had to rearrange the festival to cope with these thousand little girls.

The next year I thought, "Well, the best thing I can do about this music, as they're so popular, is I'll make it Friday night." So I gave them a night of their own and I gave them a thousand quid to top the bill, so it was thirty pounds, then the following year a thousand, and they were top of the bill on the Friday night and I lost the Friday nights now to R&B. So it was R&B Friday, and jazz on the Saturday and Sunday.

MICK JAGGER: It was very exciting in those days because I was, like, really naïve as a teenager and then all these little girls are screaming at us. Then we started getting good reviews in the music press and eventually it went to the national press and television. It was good fun.

KEITH RICHARDS: Yeah, it was crazy. The Richmond Jazz Festival was an annual event and it was attended by all the old English jazz enthusiasts with their corduroy trousers and baggy sweaters. So they look 'round and there's all these twelve and fourteen year old girls screaming at the top of their lungs and it was like Martians had just arrived. The look on people's faces . . . They just did not know how to handle it. We were like pigs in shit [laughs].

August 23, 1963. The Stones make their first appearance on _Ready, Steady, Go._

MICK JAGGER: If it hadn't been for television shows like _Ready, Steady, Go,_ it would have taken so much longer to succeed. If the band hadn't been so good at doing TV in the initial stages, it would have taken much longer. This band really grasped the television style in those early days. I remember those TV things really started us off—more in Europe than in America, because radio is important [in the United States], and you can make it big just by being on the radio. In those days Ed Sullivan was a big shot, so if you were good on _Ed Sullivan_—which I don't think we ever were, as compared to how we were on _Ready, Steady, Go_ . . . it was a different kind of show. There are a lot of tapes of those shows around and they're very funny to watch. That's what got us off the ground in Europe.

KEITH RICHARDS: What did they used to say? "Is it a boy or is it a girl?" [laughs]. It was the question I heard most for about two years—"What is that, Mavis, a boy or a girl?" or [whistles] "Hello, darlin' . . . " Think back to '62, '63, and if you didn't have a haircut for a week, everybody would be going, "Oooh . . . hello, curly . . . " That's the way it was. If you didn't get your hair cut for a month, look out. If you look at the photographs back then, we weren't Ted Nugents [laughs]. No Ozzy Osbournes there, baby.

BILL WYMAN: We had to start to do TV shows. The first time we went on TV, Andrew said, "Look, they will not let you be on television dressed without uniforms. You have to have a uniform." We had big fights with him about that, and in the end we went down to Carnaby Street, which was almost unknown then, and he talked us into buying black trousers and houndstooth jackets—black and white with velvet collars—and what were later called "Beatles boots," which we found in Drury Lane. They were these Spanish black leather boots, and after we told the Beatles about them they went down and got some. After that they were called "Beatles boots" [laughs].

So, we had to wear these terrible uniforms to get on this TV show, which we had to do to be seen in the rest of the country. At the time we'd never played outside London—the suburbs was the furthest we'd go. We hated the suits, and after that one show we felt so ridiculous that we conveniently managed between us, one by one, to lose a jacket, and then someone lost their trousers, and two lost their shirts. And then we tried these much hipper, blue-leather waistcoats, which everybody tried to buy afterwards, and then one of us would wear the waistcoat and the trousers, one would wear the jacket. And suddenly we were back into nonconformist—no uniforms—and we got away with it. It was like Andrew said—"If you do the TV show once, then the next time we can tell them how we want to do it." And that's exactly what happened.

The image, really, was "getting out of the van and getting onstage." Three of us—Charlie, Ian Stewart, and myself—were working at the time. So it was a matter of when I left work, I just went up to town and went onstage in my working clothes, my jacket, and trousers. Whatever they had on when they went on the bus or got a lift from someone, that's what they would wear. Wearing uniforms wasn't thought about until that TV thing. It was that walking off the street and going on the stage that the kids related to. I think that's what endeared us to those fans in those early days. They could have been us, and we could have been them.

PETER JONES: I believe that [Andrew] had decided on doing the opposite of that which had gone before. He was involved with the Beatles early on—he did their publicity as well. And that image, the uniformed image, had to be countered in some way, and the Stones could never have been wrangled into any kind of uniform, could they? They just weren't that kind of people.

MICK JAGGER: Andrew had decided that the way we were going to break through was to present ourselves as the "anti-Beatles." They were wearing their nice suits and all that and we would just be the opposite. The funny thing is that the Beatles were quite good mates of ours and they were really just as cynical about the whole thing as we were. They really weren't any different. When you look back at the photos from those days you can see that we were just a bunch of sweet, innocent kids [laughs].

DICK ROWE: You see, Andrew and I worked very closely together. He and I knew what was going on, but our sales department, they said, "Why can't they be like the Beatles, nice tidy young men [laughs]. Why do they have to get up to all these atrocious antics?" Well, I tried to explain to them that it's Andrew's way of getting publicity. He believed if you can alienate the adults then the kids, they'll love it, and that's the psychology he used to establish them.

Andrew decides to drop the "s" from the end of Keith's name.

KEITH RICHARDS: Perhaps he fancied me more without the "s." I'll tell you why, because I know the labyrinths of Andrew's mind. He wanted a little bit of confusion between Cliff Richard and somebody in the Rolling Stones. He figured it could only work to our advantage. I'm sure that's the reason he did it. If you say Keith Richard, Cliff Richard, you might get a couple of extra paragraphs or lines in a gossip column, because people think you're somebody else. Knowing Andrew, that is the real reason. I still haven't been able to tag it back on successfully. There are always alternative spellings.

My name's Keith Richards. That's my name. There was a time around '77, '78 when I started saying, "There's an 's' on my name. You can take it or leave it, I don't really give a shit." What's one "s" with the problems we've got?

BILL WYMAN: It was a real grind in those early days. Eleven o'clock in the morning we'd do photo sessions, then we'd go to a rehearsal of a TV show in the afternoon, then in the evening we'd do two shows in Leicester, drive a hundred miles in a van and do two shows and the next morning you'd be in Southampton to do a TV show at lunchtime. Then you'd go back to London to rehearse for something else, and then do the show and after that you'd go and do the Richmond jazz festival. You had, like, three or four things going a day and it was nuts. We were always driving around late at night. In England there's nowhere to go for food when it's late so you were always hungry, you were always tired, always fatigued and with so much to do.

We used to travel in that van—we're back in late '63 now—all over England, and there were no windows in it. It was a Volkswagen van and one person could sit in the front with the driver and the rest sat in among the equipment, which used to fall on your head. Keith got knocked out once. Stew took a sharp turn one day and some of the amplifiers came down and knocked him out. Stew went to drop Brian off at his place and when he went round the back of the van to open it to let Brian out, Keith was still unconscious. It was really funny . . . well, not for Keith I suppose.

September 29, 1963. The Stones begin their first tour of England. In just over one month they perform in thirty-one different venues.

KEITH RICHARDS: When this band started it was totally non-profit-making and had an evangelistic "spread the blues gospel" mission. The height of our ambition was just to get three or four steady gigs in London. Then all of a sudden we got a record in the top 20 and we're out on tour with Little Richard, the Everly Brothers, and Bo Diddley. We learned more in those five weeks than we did in any other period.

November 1, 1963. Decca releases the Stones' second single, "I Wanna Be Your Man."

BILL WYMAN: Yeah, the Beatles were receiving some award, and we met them in the street. We were rehearsing in Ken Collier's club, and we were trying to find a follow-up to "Come On." We'd been to Decca and we'd tried. We'd done "Poison Ivy" and "Fortune Teller" in the studio and Decca didn't like them, and we didn't really like them either. Then Decca tried to make us use one of their producers, recut things, and we didn't like the results of those, they were too commercial. So we cancelled the releases of them (needless

73

to say, Decca re-released them later) and we were looking for a follow-up. So we really wanted a song. We tried all kinds of things. We were working much earlier on "Twist and Shout" and things like that.

And so it went on, and suddenly John and Paul, who we'd seen a little of—not too much because they lived in Liverpool and we lived in London—they said, "We've got this song, 'I Wanna Be Your Man'" [he sings]. It was quite pop-y the way they played it to us. I remember them sort of working out the middle at the same time as playing it. And we learned it really quickly, because there wasn't too much to learn, and Brian got his slide out, his steel out, and [sings], and we thought, "Ahhh . . . that's right . . . bash it out." And we kind of completely turned the song around and made it much more sort of tough Stonesy, Elmore James type of rock. That really did well—#9.

KEITH RICHARDS: Oh, we liked that song, and the fact that John and Paul came down to a rehearsal of ours and laid it on us was magic. We hadn't heard their version—we just heard John and Paul on piano, banging it out, and then we picked it up and it was just one of those things. They got enthusiastic, then we got enthusiastic and said, "Right . . . we'll cut it tomorrow." And that was it.

ROY CARR: You've got to realize the Beatles were establishment. The Beatles were never looked at as being, "Oh, I would never let my daughter marry you, Ringo." I would definitely not let my daughter marry Keith Richards. The Stones were really raunchy, but at that time Andrew Oldham was, what—nineteen, twenty, twenty-one?—and he just knew what the . . . He wasn't an old man trying to sell something. He thought it was a go-for-broke thing. It was either going to happen or they'd be just one, two, or three-hit wonders. People forget that when the Stones first went to America, nobody wanted to know them. They were schlepping around the South, playing to a hundred people a night. Same with The Who.

When you saw them in those early days it was like seeing the Sex Pistols when they first came out, that sort of energy. It was "Did I actually pay my five shillings and see that?" or "Oh, the Stones are playing . . . must go and see them." Because you actually thought they were going to burn themselves out like The Who, you thought The Who were going to burn themselves out.

This is a weird thing—that you liked the Stones and didn't like the Beatles, or you liked the Beatles and didn't like the Stones. It was really two separate camps. You went through periods where it was fashionable to like the Stones and unfashionable to like the Beatles.

I think the consistency of the Stones singles was fantastic. The whole thing was the Beatles were basically singers who accompanied themselves and the Rolling Stones were a bunch of serious, dedicated musicians who had sort of a half-decent lead singer. The whole big joke—and Jagger has always admitted it—is the vocal harmonies they did were always pretty rough.

December 20, 1963. American Gene Pitney releases "That Girl Belongs to Yesterday," the first Jagger/Richards song released.

KEITH RICHARDS: Yeah . . . well, that was because Andrew used to do Gene Pitney's publicity.

GENE PITNEY: The song didn't fit me melodically. I would like to know how they wrote it because it was the Stones' interpretation and I was having hits with ballads in those days. So I changed the whole melodic structure and rewrote it with them. Then I went in with the track they had cut originally, which is where it came from. It was not a big hit for me in North America but it did very well for me in other markets around the world.

January 6, 1964. The Stones begin their second British tour with The Ronettes as one of the opening acts.

RONNIE SPECTOR: On all the tours, Phil [Spector] used to send all the bands telegrams saying, "Please do not talk to the Ronettes." We could never understand why the guys in the Stones were so reluctant to have anything to do with us and wouldn't talk to us. Then my sister asked Mick, and he showed her the telegram from Phil. It happened everywhere we went—whether it was a tour or a club date, Phil would send a telegram saying, "They're here for a reason, not a season."

January 10, 1964. Decca releases the first Stones EP (four songs). It includes the Arthur Alexander song "You Better Move On."

BILL WYMAN: "You'd Better Move On" was the one that came out the most interesting on that one. We like the song, but we just thought of it as one of the four songs, a difference from the fast things. And suddenly that was the one that everybody was playing and liking, and different fans started to listen to that, and more grown-up people liked it . . . your mums liked it. And you thought, "Oh, no . . ." But it was a nice song, so it didn't sort of put you off like "Come On" did.

January 28, 1964. The Stones record "Not Fade Away," released on February 21.

GENE PITNEY: I was flying back to the States from France and I stopped for one day in London. Andrew called me up and said they were trying to record a follow-up to "I Wanna Be Your Man." "The band hate each other today," he said. "I'm in a little two-track recording studio in Denmark Street. What do I do?" I said, "I'll be right over." I had a couple of bottles of cognac from the duty-free in France so I brought them along and said it was a tradition in the Pitney family that if anybody had a birthday—and of course I said it was mine—everybody had to have a tall glass of cognac. They stopped working on the song, which was "Not Fade Away," and we drank the brandy and everybody loosened right up. We recorded a "B" side, which was just a blues jam called "Little by Little." Then Phil Spector came along in his big Rolls-Royce limousine and ended up as the percussionist on "Not Fade Away." He was playing the empty cognac bottle with a half-dollar coin and maracas. So the day turned out all right.

KEITH RICHARDS: It turned out like that because Phil was on it. What Chuck Berry was to me at that time, Phil Spector was to Andrew Oldham. It took us a long time to come to terms with that musically.

IAN STEWART: I mean, Phil Spector's got to be the most overrated producer of all time. His idea is to throw everything including the kitchen sink on the track and then add tambourine, handclaps, and some girl singers. And he's a pain in the ass. I mean, more by luck than judgment he's produced a couple of good tracks like "The Doo Ron Ron," but that's about it. Gene Pitney was a really nice guy, but as for him playing piano on a Rolling Stones track, that's just bullshit. He couldn't do it. That was Andrew's idea to put his name on the record. That's not Gene Pitney, that's me.

CHAPTER 3

American Nights

March 27, 1964. Andrew, Mick, and Keith meet Marianne Faithfull for the first time at a party.

MARIANNE FAITHFULL: I was at school in Reading, where I lived in a convent, doing my exams to go to university. I went to a party with a boyfriend I had, and Andrew was there, and Mick and Keith and some of the Beatles were there . . . all sorts of people. And I was seventeen and I was very, very pretty and Andrew asked my boyfriend if I could sing and would I like to make a record, and he said I could, and so they suggested I make a record, and I did. People said "As Tears Go By" was written especially for me, but no, the song had been written already and it wasn't suitable for them, so they had that song going. That's why it happened, I'm sure. They were looking for the right person to sing that song, and when Andrew met me he decided I was the right person for it, so we did. But I always thought it was a bit odd for me to be singing a song like that. It was really meant for a woman of about forty who is looking back on her life, not some innocent seventeen-year-old girl. It took a long time to take off—about three months before it got into the charts.

April 17, 1964. Decca releases the Stones' first LP, *The Rolling Stones*, which includes the first Jagger/Richards song.

KEITH RICHARDS: "Tell Me" was the first song that Mick and I wrote that we felt was good enough to give to the Stones. We'd written other songs before, like "As Tears Go By," which we gave to Marianne. Gene Pitney had covered a song of ours, but we'd never said, "Hey, we've got a song for us to play." Mick and I were kind of nervous when we laid it on them, but it turned out well. Everybody liked it. That's the roots of Mick's and my collaboration in song writing. It was the first song where we said, "The Stones can keep this one for itself."

MICK JAGGER: I was really naïve as a teenager, maybe even more naïve than most. I'd spent all my time at college and then working with the band on the weekends, so all of a sudden you're kind of thrown into what they call "show business," and I wasn't really ready for it. So we got ripped off a lot at first. Then we were told to start writing songs. We'd never thought about it and I never thought I could. So Andrew said, "Keith will write the music and you'll write the words," and I said, "Okay, I'll try." The first things we came up with were absolute rubbish . . . terrible. Then we finally got a good one and it really helped us out because it gave us a lot of confidence to continue. I guess Andrew deserves the credit in a way, but at the same time he was just looking for another way to make more money out of us.

BILL WYMAN: Lots of reviewers said that was probably the best first album by any band, ever. I don't know whether I can really agree with that, but we never, between us, throughout the years, we have never, kind of run [that album down]. We've run certain albums down, saying, "Well, I hate *Between the Buttons*" or "I don't think *Aftermath* was very good." But nobody's criticized that first album. It was our stage show in a way, or a lot of it. We just went straight in from playing these things onstage to just recording them, like in one day or something.

KEITH RICHARDS: Yeah, it's like a lot of people's first albums. They're great because all you're doing is putting your tried and tested, best stage numbers on record. It's very easy. You've got the material, you know it by heart, it should be great.

June 1, 1964. The Stones arrive in New York.

SID BERNSTEIN: What happened was that the next big group after the Beatles that came up quickly and in a very, very important way, were the Stones. I decided that since I'd brought the Beatles, why not go after the Stones? I made a call to Andrew Oldham, who I guess was their first manager and producer. He recognized my name because I'd just done the Beatles, and he said, "Yes, I'd like you to bring us to America." So I brought them to Carnegie Hall four months later. I believe that was June. We did the Beatles on February

12, 1964, and I think this was June something, 1964, and again, that was historic. I didn't bring them to Shea, but I brought them back four more times to the New York Paramount after Carnegie Hall threw us out because the Stones crowd was a little threatening and the paintings and the building shook a little.

KEITH RICHARDS: We were well aware that they'd lay on some hype in New York because of the Beatles thing. But we also knew it could backfire on us. When I say *we*, this includes Andrew Oldham, Mick, and myself, and to a certain extent Brian, but not so much Andrew and Brian because there was always a certain conflict. Andrew and Brian together would not share so much information and strategy if you can call it that. It's made up in the morning and done by the night. There was no sort of five-year plan. You had to improvise as you went along, but we figured it would be best to arrive in New York, use the hype from that, and start slogging because we also knew from our experience in England that if you can do it in one place, you can do it somewhere else.

The Beatles to us were always like . . . somebody knocks on the door, such as the gas man, and gets in, gets his foot in the door, and he's the salesman. They were the ones people would open their door to. If we had knocked at the door first, forget it, they'd have just put the other chain on. So it was like using the Beatles to open the door for us, and using the differences between us and the Beatles as soon as we could. In actual fact, they were the same kind of blokes as us, but the way they were projected meant that we had to make a difference between ourselves and them, which wasn't that difficult. In a way, we were encouraged, especially by Andrew, to be a little more outrageous than we even felt. Since then it's become a well-known scam [laughs].

BOB BONIS: I was an agent, and a friend of mine, Norman Weiss, who is the agent for Paul Anka and at that time was an agent for a lot of acts, asked me as a special favour—because I had a reputation for really taking care of troublemakers—to take care of these wise guys that were coming in from England. Boy, what a horrible reputation they had, and all that! And I said, "Come on . . ." I had my own management firm and I really wasn't that interested in going on the road anymore. I hadn't done that before. And Norman says, "You have to—they're great," and so on, and he pulls this article from *The Times* of London: "Would you let your sister marry a Rolling Stone?" or whatever that one was. I said, "What a great sales pitch! Thanks."

Anyway, I finally went with them and of course they were not the least of a problem. It's terrible for their image, I know, but they were really great, they were really a pleasure to be with and a pleasure to work with. Andrew and Eric Easton were both travelling with them on the first tour, and they were no problem—Andrew was particularly very helpful. Andrew was like another member of the group. He was more of a wise guy than the rest, actually.

When they arrived at the New York airport there were a lot of screaming kids—I suppose that should have warned me right there [laughs]—including a couple of English sheepdogs. At that time there was a hot PR guy with a big beard, and it was his idea to have them met with English sheepdogs, or anything hairy—it was very clever. The reception was unbelievable and everyone said, "Wow, what a great staged reception." But that wasn't staged. I mean, we were hoping to get them in quietly and meet with them and then go into the publicity end of it and everything, but the kids all found out about the arrival and stormed the place.

BILL WYMAN: Bob Bonis was great. We had a few other strange people we didn't think were so great, from the promoters, that big company in New York. We didn't like them very much, but Bob was great. He was like an American version of Ian Stewart, who'd become our roadie by that time and wasn't playing in the band, only on records and things. Bob was great and we toured around in places with guarantees. Three-and-a-half thousand guarantees every show, that was it—that was all we got, I think. Most of the shows we went to, nobody had ever heard of us, they thought we were copying the Beatles, and we went into ten-thousand-seat auditoriums, or sixteen-thousand-seat auditoriums with three hundred kids there.

They went nuts in a couple of places. It was packed out

in San Bernardino—that was the first one. We've always got a soft spot for San Bernardino because it was like three or four thousand kids went nuts, and it was exactly like England because it had become completely mad in England wherever we played. That happened in San Bernardino, and a couple of other places were reasonably good. There were some small places where we had like six hundred or eight hundred kids that went nuts, and then of course there was Carnegie Hall. We did the first show and the kids went so nuts they tried to cancel the second show.

So we had about three really great "ups" on that tour and we had about ten really bad "downs," and all the media things were downers—the interviews and the television show we did. We couldn't get *Ed Sullivan*, which everybody went on and became huge.

We were given a dub of the Valentinos' "It's All Over Now" by Murray the K. He said, "You should cover this record; this is going to be a hit. We played it and thought, "That's interesting," and we recorded it. It was a great thing that he did for us that time. That was our first kind of hit and our first #1 in England.

BOB BONIS: It was a strange tour. A guy at the agency, which is now giant ICM, was really enthusiastic and insisted on booking them. It wasn't a promotional tour—they were all live dates, all for money. We would show up in one place and you couldn't move, it would be packed. You'd show up in another place and there were three hundred kids there out of five thousand [capacity].

The only thing on the charts was "Not Fade Away," in the forties somewhere in *Billboard*, and the album was just barely making it into the *Billboard* charts. And everywhere they went, people would say, "Oh, there go the Beatles, there go the Beatles!" It was really terrible.

The first show, I think, was San Bernardino, and it was the first California show that the kids broke down a steel door trying to get in early. This was a whole new phenomenon to me, so I learned the hard way, and very quickly.

KEITH RICHARDS: It was the first time we went to Omaha that I really understood how heavy it could get. We were just sitting around drinking whiskey and Coke out of little cups before we went on, and the cops walked in and said, "What's in that cup?" "Whiskey, sir." "You can't drink that here, it's a public place. Throw it down the drain." "No." I look up and there's a loaded .44 pointed at my head. That's when we started to see the dark side of America and what could happen.

MICK JAGGER: We first played L.A. and it was great, and so was New York, but the bits in the middle . . . that was depressing. It was still segregation in the states and it was very repressive and prejudiced. It was all very narrow-minded in a way.

BILL WYMAN: Going to America the first time was great in a lot of ways but it was really disheartening to find the way you were treated. I mean, we were really badly treated and badly promoted. The record company was useless. We never really had a big hit in England. We had one great problem in those days and that was trying to record, and [finding] an engineer or somebody who knew what we wanted to sound like. We had a great stage presence but we could never put it on record, whereas most bands made very good records. The Searchers, the Hollies, and Billy J. Kramer, they were awful onstage. We were the opposite—we were great onstage but we couldn't get the records right. That was our biggest problem, and in the end we decided we'd go to Chess Studios in Chicago.

June 10, 1964. The Stones record at the legendary Chess Studios in Chicago.

BOB BONIS: Andrew left some time open and they spent some time at Chess Studios, because they wanted to record at Chess. The place was great, just the feel of the place. Then one of their heroes came walking in and everything stopped dead, and knees started quaking much the way as when the Beatles met Elvis Presley.

KEITH RICHARDS: That was the best thing we did in coming to America. [Chess] for us was the Mecca. We were doing things that people like Cyril Davis had dreamed of all their lives. "The Impossible Dream"—you know that song? Big intro and the guy never makes it.

By then we were cocky because we had this wave we were on. We weren't overawed by the situation. The intention was "if we get to America we're going to Chicago to 2120 and record." Giving ourselves a golden handshake.

It was important in another way. In England at that time, nobody really knew how to record the sounds we were trying to get. The Beatles' stuff was easy—vocal harmonies, neat and precise. That wasn't too difficult, but to try and get that dirty sound we were after, it was just the most obvious thing in the world to record it at Chess. And those are the records that started to make people listen. They'd wait for the next one, and we started to gather some audience.

We got to meet guys like Muddy Waters and Willie Dixon. Muddy was in a low period. I think he was fixing the plumbing or painting the place. The Chess brothers were no sweethearts, darlin'—if you weren't selling records you were painting the Studios.

WILLIE DIXON: No I didn't arrange for them to come to Chess. I had talked to [the Chess family] quite a bit about 'em, because I heard that they were doin' these type of songs. They didn't think the blues were gonna make it in Europe. That was one reason why I was so interested in them.

When the Rolling Stones came from England and came

to Chess, they had already recorded two or three of my tunes. I came over and we stood around and we shook hands and talked trash and that was it.

BILL WYMAN: So we thought, so let's go to Chess where all the records were made that we played. That's where Chuck Berry does all his records. That's where Howlin' Wolf and Muddy Waters are, and people like Buddy Guy, so let's try to go there, and they've got a four-track studio there. In those days that was still amazing. So we made inquiries and we asked for the same engineer that they all used, a guy called Ron Malo, and we went there, and instead of recording in a conventional way, we plugged into the wall and things like that and it was very strange. There were just sockets in the wall, so I plugged my bass into the wall and it was direct feed.

Chuck Berry came by, and Muddy Waters helped us in with the gear! He met us outside. He was our idol, and because they'd told him we were coming, he came along. And we were like, "My God . . . he's carrying our gear!" We couldn't believe it! We were nearly passing out. What a gentleman! Buddy Guy was also there and he helped us in with the gear. He just came along the street as we were carrying all the amplifiers in out of the van and he helped carry some mike stands in and a guitar.

We did a Muddy Waters song and a couple of Chuck Berry songs. Then we went in to listen back, and it sounded exactly like it should, the first time ever, and we were like,

"That's it . . . we've done it. Four-track, American studio, American engineer. That' s what we gotta do." So we spent quite a few of the next few years recording as much as possible in America. We found Dave Hassinger in Los Angeles at RCA Studios, where we cut things like "The Last Time" and "Satisfaction" and found people who really knew what we were trying to do musically, which we couldn't find in England.

IAN STEWART: Over the years my favourite stuff came from the sessions we did at Chess in Chicago. All those songs like "Around and Around" and "Down the Road Apiece." We did fourteen songs in two days. That's the way to do it, not spend nine months working on one record.

MARSHALL CHESS: The English kids were way ahead of Americans in terms of taking an interest in black music, particularly the blues. The Rolling Stones took their name from a Muddy Waters song. When they came here, they said they wanted their records to sound just like the ones we were making with Muddy and Howlin' Wolf and all those guys, but it ended up sounding different. It was the blues through the perspective of the white English kids. But it put a lot of the older blues guys on the map.

BRIAN JONES: We're only hostile when people are hostile to us. We're not hostile as a matter of course. I don't want any trouble. We don't believe in putting on this big showbiz face. If someone annoys us we just kick him out.

We've just come along at the right time with the right thing when something new was wanted subconsciously by the kids. It boils down to that. It's quite simple really.

There's one thing to be said about groups and that is there are usually four or five or even six in a group, whereas with a solo singer the girl fan either likes him or dislikes him. With a group she may dislike one but like all the others.

June 13, 1964. The Stones perform on their first U.S. network TV show, *Hollywood Palace*.

BOB BONIS: What's funny is that Norman Weiss's partner at the time was the producer of the *Hollywood Palace* TV show. That's how Norman got them on the show. Dean Martin came in and had no idea what he was dealing with. He was a little out of it. They made an awful lot of fun of the band. In fact, Norman's ex-partner gave me money to go out and buy the band uniforms, and I said, "C'mon, they don't wear uniforms" [laughs]. By this time I've been there four days, so I was an expert on the Rolling Stones, right? So, it was just the whole feeling, the vibe as we call it today, and it was just awful. Dean and I got into an argument at one point, and Keith, my new-found friend, was about to pop him one with one of those solid-body guitars. We got through it. Nowadays whenever I see highlights of *Hollywood Palace*, the Stones are always in them!

KEITH RICHARDS: You can't blame Dean, he must have been shocked. I mean, he had to introduce an elephant, then us. What are you going to say?

MICK JAGGER: We weren't expecting anything big to happen in America. I was just excited about being able to buy some of the records more easily, and if we were lucky, actually see some of them in person.

KEITH RICHARDS: America the first time really blew us away. We bought lots of records there and heard some amazing things. That's where we first turned on to Otis [Redding] and people like Wilson Pickett. Musically it was great.

June 1964. The Stones are back in England.

PETER JONES: I had links with the Stones right the way through, because we ran their monthly magazine, which was an authorized business. There was Sean O'Mahony, who was actually the publisher in charge of all this. Sean sold space initially for Robert Stigwood's organization, and after he was fired by Stigwood he set up a business just up the road from Stigwood in publishing and started a magazine called *Pop Monthly*. That became *Beat Monthly*, and then he started specializing in the various major groups. The Beatles were the first band that he took out of the mainstream and gave their own monthly magazine, and the Stones became the second one.

Because I was editor of *Record Mirror* in those days, I couldn't write for these magazines, I had to use a pseudonym. The reason was that meeting the Beatles every week as we did—and then later, when the *Rolling Stones* magazine started, every other week—I was in a kind of privileged position, because the big circulation music papers couldn't get to these guys very easily. I was with the smallest circulation, *Record Mirror*, so although I was allowed to go and meet Mick and Paul and John and so on whenever I wanted to for their magazines, from which they made money, the basis was that I couldn't use this material in *Record Mirror*. The big papers like *Musical Express* and *Melody Maker* would have resented this very much, so as far as the Rolling Stones are concerned I wrote as Pete Goodman, and for the Beatles, the information was used as Billy Shepard.

In the early days it was a matter of guarding certain reputations. Andrew Oldham was creating quite a controversial image for the Stones, as compared with the Beatles, whom he'd also been involved with, but for the first book we did, the first paperback called *Our True Story* or something, by Pete Goodman, it was necessary to fight the fight on their behalf as a band. In other words, "These boys are misunderstood by the parents." I was instructed that the only way I was going to get this book into print was to paint a rather saintly image of "St. Michael" and the others and say that parents don't understand them, that it's a generation gap, and so on. Later on, of course—I happen to know because I met Mick quite a few times later on—Mick owned up that he rather despised me for being so dishonest about what they really were like and he didn't want anyone fighting his battles.

As with the Beatles, really, I had this terrible clash in a way. Had I been allowed to write as editor of a national paper and a contributor to national magazines, I really think I would have exposed a few of the things that went on backstage, a few of the excesses—and there were excesses with the Rolling Stones in those days. But the only reason I was allowed to be there was that I was writing their fan club magazine, and it was understood that I was going to gloss over orgies, drunken meetings, whatever. It was a very, very difficult position for a journalist to be in.

I had the same problem with the Beatles. It was decreed that the Beatles should be portrayed as amazingly loveable, amiable fellows, and if one of them, without mentioning a name, decided he wanted a short, sharp orgy in the bathroom with three girls, I didn't see it. It didn't happen as far as I was concerned. I went for the best part of a year knowing that John Lennon, at the Beatles level, was married and that Cynthia was there. The absolute denial that he was married went on and on and on.

June 26, 1964. Decca release the single "It's All Over Now." It would become the band's first #1 record.
July 24, 1964. The Stones play the Empress Ballroom in Blackpool.

ROY CARR: You see, the whole thing is that the worst thing the promoters at Blackpool could have done was to put the Rolling Stones in at "Scotch weekend." What used to happen was that Glasgow or Edinburgh would close down for a week, and everybody would move south to Blackpool, it being like Britain's equivalent of Coney Island. They were supposed to have something like six thousand people but there was more like ten thousand.

In those days the Rolling Stones were looked on as androgynous, a little bit effete. The Scottish fans at this time liked very macho bands. They were very much into soul music, American soul music like Otis Redding. It was the guys that dug the music, and the girls just kept quiet and looked pretty. The last thing they wanted was their girl-friends getting overexcited at the Rolling Stones, which they looked upon as being a bit "faggy," especially Brian Jones. Those were the days when Brian Jones was very much the centre of attention.

My band, the Executives, had been on just before them. We were shrewd. We knew how to go down well with a Scottish audience. You found out what the popular record in Scotland was and it was something like "In The Midnight Hour" by Wilson Pickett. They'd just come down to drink and fight, so when you went up there, the first number you'd open up with was [sings opening of "Midnight Hour"] and then you were one of the lads. You'd go down a storm, and you'd also always end with that number. It sounds corny, really, but you were protecting your life.

So the Stones come on, and they were just totally self-absorbed in those days. And there's Jagger wiggling his butt at the audience, and in fact Brian is doing most of the dancing. The stage comes up to about chin level, and so all the booing starts, and the cans of beer are going and girls are throwing their panties at the same time. Jones is really egging the girls on, and he's being very, very "camp." Jagger's just dancing away, Keith is staggering around, and there must be a gang down the front there and they decide to start gobbing, spitting—they talk about punks doing it—they start spitting at Brian Jones. And instead of Brian going back and getting out of the line of fire, he's walking down the front there in a shower of spittle and it hits him on the face and hair. It's coming right from their guts, and these guys have been drinking whiskey all day so they have a good supply of the stuff. So Keith comes down to the front, and Keith's always been a bit of a hard nut, he goes down and says, "Stop it." Of course they don't—they just keep on until someone spits at Keith. So Keith walks down there and this guy's hands are on the lip of the stage, and his chin's right there, and Keith goes . . . *Boom!!!* . . . he stamps on the guy's hands and then steps back, and it's just like starting a football match—kicking the ball—he has his "Beatles boots" on and . . . *Whack!!!* . . . kicks him right in the nose and the teeth. It's a wonder the guy's head doesn't leave his shoulders.

So all of a sudden it goes dead silent. Then all of a

sudden—"*SCOTLAND!!! . . . SCOTLAND!!! . . .*" like a tribal war chant and they come onto the stage, and by this time the Stones have crapped themselves. Well, Brian has anyway. They go flying out the back door into a car and off, leaving all the equipment there. At which time the grand piano disappears. It's turned into matchwood. The amplification goes, the drapes, which are about sixty feet high, disappear. Everything just disappears. They start fighting among themselves, like pro-Stones fans against anti-Stones fans. How nobody's actually killed I don't know, because there are people just laid around.

The funniest thing was the next day the place was absolutely littered with girls' underwear. We went there to salvage our stuff, and there must have been at least thirty or forty bras on the stage and about two hundred pairs of panties!

KEITH RICHARDS: Blackpool? Are you talking about the Empire Ballroom? Oh yeah, the drunk little Scotsman with the red hair. Yeah, that's it.

The Empire Ballroom . . . we were just sort of making a name for ourselves . . . packed full of kids, about three thousand—huge ballroom for England. Through the doors, halfway through the set, comes this wedge of drunken Scotsmen, because Scotland goes on holiday all at the same time. They have two weeks and it's called Scots Week. All the factory workers in Scotland are down there, and their only aim in life is to get well and truly pissed for the whole week.

So about twenty or thirty of them arrive at this ball-room at the back and just carve a wedge through these poor little chicks who've come to see the Stones. They've just come in there for a drink and they don't like it at all, because the chicks are all going, "Aahhh . . . Mick . . . Aahhh . . . Brian . . . ," and they can't "pull" anybody so they're getting pissed off. They get to the front of the stage and this one obnoxious little guy—if I saw him now I'd still know him, red hair, green eyes—just stands there and starts spitting at me. So the show must go on and I ignore it for a bit but it goes on for ten or fifteen minutes, and he's getting closer and closer until eventually his head is just in range—like a penalty kick. And he does it one more time, it hits me, and I say, "Right." It wasn't a conscious decision, it was just that the leg went back and it went forward and he went the other end of the ballroom [laughs]. Then the rest of his mates go mad—that's it, England against Scotland—and they just about destroy the place. I know I got an amplifier back. It was a piece of wood with one wire hanging out of it, and Stew came and said, "Here's your amplifier" [laughs]. Yeah, they destroyed the place. We had to get out over the roof.

August 1964. Decca releases the Stones' second EP, *Five by Five*. The Stones do their first European concert.

KEITH RICHARDS: It was the Opera House in The Hague and they had this huge chandelier and halfway through the show—that one also ended in a riot—we look up at this chandelier and there's like a lingerie department hanging off it. Chicks had been throwing them up to the stage and they caught on the chandelier. I mean, I don't know what they think we needed with their underwear. What am I going to do with this? I haven't got room to pack it!

1964. On October 14, Charlie Watts marries Shirley Shepherd. They are still married. On October 24, the Stones return to America for a second tour.

SID BERNSTEIN: Back in June we went ahead with the second show just to avoid a riot. It was thought better to do it than to cancel, and it worked. Security was good, the kids behaved themselves, and it worked out, but I was barred from Carnegie Hall for a while, so we moved to the New York Paramount, and then we moved to what is now called the Palladium. It was then called the Academy of Music. So I brought them in the first five times. Each one was exciting, historic, a little different, a little more physical. But it worked and established the Stones here, and then right after that, the next group I brought was the Dave Clark Five, then the Animals, then Herman's Hermits, et cetera, et cetera. I was leading the British Invasion of America. I felt like a turncoat [laughs].

CHAPTER 4

Satisfaction

October 25, 1964. The Stones perform on *Ed Sullivan*.

BILL WYMAN: It was impossible to get into the bloody place, impossible to get out again. I think we drove round that place and in and out of the side streets around there about six times before we finally found a way in. Andrew broke down the glass doors in the front so we could get away from the kids. It was nuts, and he cut his hand and somebody punched the doorman 'cause he wouldn't let us in. They saw us and they would not let us in the building. I mean, we were getting murdered by these kids and then we had to pay cops off to stay outside during the day. They used to come once every hour and say, "We want so much money or we're leaving." In the middle of hundreds of kids outside! That was a real rip off. We didn't mind playing live in those days, of course. It was quite exciting, I suppose.

I've got a very nice touch here, an article written the next day. [Reading from his personal diary] It says in headlines: "Stones-Sullivan TV" by Nat Hentoff. "The Stones played to more prolonged screams than any British group had received. They did not impress this reviewer. Mick Jagger lacked fire, depth, and was otherwise unconvincing. They looked very unkempt. Sullivan was pleased with their performance and mentioned future bookings." There was negative New York press reaction, particularly on Jagger's appearance. TV columnist Jack O'Brian headlined his journal American review "The Slobs" and described [us] as "musical riff-raff." Finally we left the studio and fought our way out through the fans and back to the hotel.

When Sullivan read the reviews he changed his mind and didn't want us on again.

KEITH RICHARDS: I thought we always played very well on Sullivan. Very professional guys down there.

BOB BONIS: I remember a few funny highlights, like the time I went to get Keith out of his room and Keith, knowing I'm coming, hides two girls on the balcony. I've always been security conscious, so I locked the balcony door, and we went off to play a date about a hundred miles up the California coast. When we came back there are these two freezing girls still on the balcony. Keith didn't want to say anything, because he figured they'd get out. He didn't realize they were five floors up. He thought he saw a roof, but it wasn't that kind. Or when we were just watching some kind of movie about the Knights of Olde England and so on and a security guard from the Texas State Youth Fair called up and said, "Hey, I'm scared. How do we protect you guys? What do we do?" And I was looking at the movie screen and said, "Put up a moat." And that's what we had. This guy put up a gigantic moat about fifteen feet wide, the length of the stage, plastic lined, filled with water. A gigantic swimming pool in front of the stage. Sure enough, nobody swam the moat.

Those shows were raw and very exciting, really exciting. I don't know how they could hear. At that time there were no monitors or anything of that nature, but what was different was Bill had I guess it was a Vox bass amp that had two speakers, so one of the speakers was over on the other side, so he could be heard, and the guys could lean on him and of course Charlie was like a metronome anyway. They were better able to hear themselves than most, and of course Mick was Mick and it was just . . . the whole band moved except for Bill, who's like the local lamppost and a really fine bass player. Lately I notice that the rhythm section, Charlie and Bill, are finally getting the credit that they've deserved for ages.

Yeah, we had problems, but the band was well behaved—again, bad for their image, maybe—but we were not so much the problem as the kids were the problem. Actually, the Beatles were much more difficult to deal with. More kids would try to sneak in, and with the Beatles you'd have to take the whole floor and post people at the two exits and at the elevators for security.

Brian kept referring to me as his father image. I could probably get more out of him than anyone else. I don't know if he was frightened of Andrew or what, but many times when the band was recording at RCA and Brian was over sleeping, if we couldn't get him up, we just left him there and Keith would do both guitar parts. Brian was fine when he was together, he was a really good musician. Once he was just totally run down and I had to have him hospitalized in Chicago, and had a friend of mine look after him for ten days. You should have heard the band then. We didn't get a substitute, Keith just worked like crazy and the band sounded great.

BILL WYMAN: Andrew liked to be very secretive with the band. He tried to divide the band, which he did do, actually. He divided the band into Mick and Keith on one side and Brian, Charlie, and myself on the other side. Although we were still friends, there was a separation. They were the leaders. Mick became the leader of the group instead of Brian, who was the original leader of the group, and [Mick and Keith] became the writers of the group. Mick was the leader of the band, which he still is, and he slightly alienated the five of us, in a way. You didn't always hear what was discussed or what might have been a title of something or what the proposed artwork would be for an album.

October 27, 1964. The Stones' first recording session at RCA studios in Hollywood.

BILL WYMAN: [RCA] wasn't as funky as Chess, obviously, it was more commercial, but [Dave Hassinger] really had a good ear. He used to get us good sounds, and we experimented with instruments and experimented with other musicians like Jack Nietsche. People like that would just play an occasional piano or something, and we'd always get a good take in three or four shots. We could experiment in the studio for the first time ever. We used to mess with other instruments, anything that was in the studio. Brian would pick something up, or I would. For "Paint It Black," after I did my bass part I lay on the floor and played the organ pedals with my fists. And then we did marimbas on "Under My Thumb" and all those kind of things, glockenspiels and anything that was lying around, vibes et cetera.

October 28 and 29, 1964. The Stones play the TAMI show in Santa Monica, California.

BILL WYMAN: We didn't really want to be top of [the TAMI bill], we still hadn't had a real hit record. "Time Is On My Side" was just released then and we hadn't had more than like a top 30 record in America, but we had the adulation. The fans were going nuts on that tour in America, but we still didn't have a hit record. Suddenly they wanted us to be top of the bill to people like the Miracles and Marvin Gaye and the Supremes and James Brown and Chuck Berry and the Beach Boys, Gerry and the Pacemakers, and so on. All these great American acts, almost all the Motown acts at that time, and Chuck Berry and Ike and Tina Turner. We thought, "We can't be top of the bill! This is crazy—let James Brown be top of the bill." And James Brown said, "I wanna be top of the bill," and we said, "Good, you be top of the bill" [laughs]. It's what you say to a four-hundred-pound gorilla.

But they insisted that we be top of the bill, and James Brown was quoted as saying, "I'm going to make the Rolling Stones wish that they'd never come to America." And he went out there and did the most amazing show as we all know he does, and I love it, and then we had to go on. I think it was the only time in our career that the band as a unit had been nervous. You might get one person who was a bit edgy. Brian might be on one night, or Mick on one show, but the band as a unit doesn't generally get nervous. So we said, "Oh come on, it's only a show and you don't feel nervous anymore and you haven't for years." But that show, everybody was terrified, because we'd watched [James Brown]. Everybody that was involved in the shooting was in the room watching him perform on the monitor and they were all cheering. We were thinking, "God, we don't want to follow this."

As we were getting ready to go on, Marvin Gaye and Chuck Berry came over to the dressing room and Marvin Gaye said, "You guys nervous?" I said, "I'm terrified," and Marvin Gaye said, "Man, it doesn't matter. Forget it. You go out there and you do your best. That's what you do. They're not interested in you because you're better than them, or not as good as them. They want to see you do your thing and that's what you gotta do. Just go out there and forget James Brown, forget everybody." And Chuck Berry was the same way. They said just go out there and do your act and you're gonna be all right. So we went out there and it was great, and afterwards James Brown came over to us and said, "Great, man," and we became friends. We saw him quite a lot after that—he was quite nice. He kind of swallowed his pride and was a gentleman. But when I look at it today I still laugh.

KEITH RICHARDS: Ask Andrew Oldham why we were top of the bill. Maybe he knows. I would say by the time the thing had been shot and aired, we'd probably just come off a hit record or a fairly big one. We had the biggest record of the day of all the acts that were there. Still, Marvin Gaye and James Brown were selling more records than we were at the time. The Supremes, too, but that week we were hot so I guess that was the reason we were top of the bill. But you try following James Brown [laughs]. If the audience hadn't been our colour we wouldn't have lived through the show [laughs].

November 8, 1964. The Stones return to Chess Records in Chicago.

WILLIE DIXON: When they came to Chess the second time, in 1964, they wanted to do "Little Red Rooster." They had done it before but we got a much better recording on it when they came to Chess. And I worked out with them, and we got a pretty good recording going on. They had it before Howlin' Wolf did his version. The only version they had to work from was off of my tapes that I left there.

I liked their version because it was new, and it was a version liked by the youngsters. You see, most of the time before then, when youngsters sang the blues they did it because their parents sung them, but they never did know the meaning of the songs. You see, the blues to begin with started from work songs, and people used to do them just following the mule, or on the railroad or working with a hoe or a shovel or a pickaxe, or cuttin' wood or something. Then in the evening when they'd get away from work, they'd come and sit down with their guitar and just sing the way they feel, and in those days, how could you feel, especially if you were bein' a slave, but feelin' lonesome?

MICK JAGGER: We knew we couldn't go on just recording old songs forever. We knew as well as Andrew that we had to start writing. He just gave us the push.

KEITH RICHARDS: We had a great first album, like a lot of bands. The problem is what are you gonna do next? You've run out of material. This is the point where Andrew Oldham said, "Get in the kitchen with a guitar and I'll let you out in two days when you've come up with a song." Otherwise we wouldn't have thought of writing anything. Andrew in his naïveté thought that any musician could write hit songs. The fact that it came up trumps was sheer luck, otherwise every guitar player . . . At that time, songwriting was as different to being a guitar player as a bank clerk working in a store. It was a different job—you had songwriters and you had [bands]. We were well aware that most of the songs we did were written by the people that had played them in the first place, but we hadn't considered seriously that we could do it. Oh, no, I'm lucky enough to have a talent for playing the guitar a bit. Don't let's pile on the optimism and be songwriters as well. But really it's the case of necessity is the mother of invention. When you run out of material, you come with it. If we hadn't we wouldn't be talking now [laughs].

BILL WYMAN: I think it was a very clever thing for [Andrew] to do. I don't think they would have thought about it if he hadn't thrown it at them at the right time. He just said, "Look you've got to write your own material, otherwise it's do or die. If you don't come up with original material, you'll be forever searching for cover versions. That's Elvis's problem." So they sat down and started writing and like everybody when they first start they wrote some pretty awful songs, but suddenly they started to write some good ones and they've just got better. They seem to have perfectly captured what was required throughout the years, which is marvellous.

CHARLIE WATTS: It's not a big deal, I'm just playing with the Rolling Stones, I don't really think about it that much. I just play what they tell me to play or what I think seems to fit. I don't think of it as "the evolution of percussion effects" [laughs].

November 13, 1964. Decca releases "Little Red Rooster" as a single.

KEITH RICHARDS: "Little Red Rooster." Well, Willie Dixon wrote it, but we got it from Howlin' Wolf's version. Willie's always sending us tapes. Willie's a songwriter, he's a song plugger, and he's a darlin' [laughs]. Howlin' Wolf did it way before us. He did everything way before us [laughs].

January 15, 1965. Decca releases the band's second album, *The Rolling Stones No. 2*.

DICK ROWE: We had David Bailey do the cover photograph with no lettering on it at all. No way to identify who they were. It was Andrew's idea. There were terrible fights, and Lewis would say to me, "Can't you stop them? [laughs] They're ruining us . . . They're ruining *themselves!*" Of course I couldn't, and I knew that I mustn't say anything, because I knew what Andrew was trying to create and why he was doing these things.

MICK JAGGER: The first albums were recorded in mono and a lot of the mixes were pretty terrible. We didn't really know what we were doing in the studio, and of course neither did Andrew and he was the producer! We would do a take and then listen back. If we liked the take, that was the record, and if we didn't like it we'd just do it again. Mixing wasn't really an issue in those days.

February 26, 1965. Decca releases "The Last Time," backed with "Play with Fire."

KEITH RICHARDS: "Play with Fire" was just Mick, myself, and Phil Spector on a tuned-down guitar to sound like a bass and what was left of Jack Nietsche knocking a tambourine or something. That was it. You wouldn't believe the personnel on what people considered to be Rolling Stones records. The players are just whoever's left standing at the end of the session.

March 18, 1965. Bill Wyman is caught relieving himself against a gas station wall.

KEITH ALTHAM: I mean, it was absurd. I'm fairly much the same age as the Rolling Stones, so it is my generation, the one I grew up with, so it was absurd to me that anyone should make a fuss about anything as trivial as somebody, you know, urinating late at night at a garage when they'd

come back from a gig. As it was to most other young people
of that generation when there were other patently obvious
obscene political ideologies being put out in terms of wars
and various other things that were going on, that were
being treated as if they were some kind of monopoly or
chess game. All of sudden you had the Rolling Stones held
up—for a lot of very trivial incidents, really—as being the
demon kings who were going to undermine the morals and
ethics of an entire generation. You know, it was just too
absurd for words. I mean, my generation loved it, and so did
the generation that came behind me, and the generation
behind that. The Sex Pistols were the extreme extension
taken to the point of total anarchy, but without exercising
the sensible control that they should have done at the particular point where it becomes suicidal if you carry on.

**May 20, 1965. The Stones tape an appearance on the American
TV show *Shindig* with blues legend Howlin' Wolf.**

HOWLIN' WOLF: I was playing in Florida and Chess called me
up and told me to meet him in California. When I got there
he explained, "There are some English boys and they want
you to be on a TV show with them." I met them and they
said they wanted me because they liked my style of music
and that they played it. I thanked them for saying so. I certainly appreciate what they did for me and my career.

KEITH RICHARDS: I don't know how it happened. [Show producer] Jack Good was someone who knew all about Howlin' Wolf. He's no idiot. He may not have been very successful in the long run of what he's done, but Jack Good's undying love for rock'n'roll and blues . . . I think I was probably as much surprised as anybody to find Howlin' Wolf doing the same show as us. The only thing that sticks in my mind about it is Jack Good running around going [assumes a very effected British voice], "Howling, can you do that again? Excuse me Mr. Wolf." Howling? His name's Chester, you fucking jerk! [laughs].

BILL WYMAN: We knew Jack Good from England because he'd done a lot of very popular TV shows there. When we were invited to play Shindig we were asked if there was anyone special we wanted to play on the show with, so we said, "Yeah, Howlin' Wolf."

BRIAN JONES: One of the reasons we got involved in music was because of the music of people like Howlin' Wolf, so when we found out that we were booked to play with him on Shindig we were thrilled.

JOHN ROWLANDS: On the road they used British wired Fender Showman amps, and when the guys came on stage they'd turn them all up to ten with one sweep of the hands. They were also miked into the house PA systems or an auxiliary system offstage with a couple of column speakers. After the shows the equipment was cranked into black Chrysler station wagons. There were four or five wagons and three or four cars. In 1965 their first program for the North American tour was so hastily put together that Mick Jagger had Brian Jones's name under his photo and vice versa. It was a two-dollar program in sepia-toned black and white. It had some pretty rough-looking pictures that had been put together very quickly.

June 4, 1965. Keith gets an idea for a song, which will be released as a single on August 20.

KEITH RICHARDS: It was just a riff. I didn't think of it as anything complete or anything special. I woke up in the middle of the night, put it down on a cassette . . . It was great! . . . then went back to sleep. When I woke up I listened to it and it appeared to be useful as another album track. It was the same with Mick at the time. It goes *da, da-da-da-da* . . . and the words I've got for that riff is "I can't get no satisfaction." So Mick went away and wrote the rest of the lyrics and kept the same title, because a lot of times we don't end up staying with it. There will be a working title, it might be, say, "Auntie Mable's caught her left tit in the mangle . . ." Anything. Just something to sing along over the top of a riff. But we kept that one and by now everyone must know the story: I just didn't think it was very good. I thought it was an okay filler track for the album. I didn't see a single in it at all. Not even when we finished cutting it and it had turned out better than I thought.

Everyone was raving about it and Andrew wanted to rush-release it, and I'm going, "No . . . no . . ." mainly because I wasn't that impressed with it when I wrote it. At that time, if you didn't have a new single every eight to twelve weeks, it was "bye bye, baby." The minute you finished one you had to write another. You just didn't have the time to think whether that one was great. You just wrote it, tried it out in the studio, and if it made it through the process of recording and writing, then you had a track. Before you knew it you were out on the road again and someone was saying this is your next single. "No it ain't . . . Is it? All right, okay, put it out." You can't be right every time.

The success of "Satisfaction" was important to Mick and myself because the previous songs we'd written, we'd given to Andrew, who had sold them off to somebody else to do, or maybe we used a couple as album track filler. We never seriously considered writing part of our job. We ended up with "The Last Time" back in February because at the time the Beatles didn't have another good one ready and we'd rifled everybody else's repertoire. So we decided, "Okay, I guess we are getting good enough to write for ourselves." And we started to believe that we could do it.

It's really difficult now to realize how important it was to have a hit single in those days. If the last one didn't do as well as the one before . . . It didn't just have to be better. You could make a better record each time, but if it didn't do better than the last one, or at least as good, it was a sign that you were declining. So there is a real pressure to come up with a red-hot song that says it all in two minutes, thirty seconds, every eight weeks. It's got to be ready within eight weeks and released every twelve or fourteen weeks.

So we just finished "Satisfaction" and been wrong about it—it's an enormous hit. And you're going, "Wow . . . lucky me!" and you're taking a breather for a couple of days and then Andrew Oldham comes to the door and says, "Where's the next single?"

June 11, 1965. Decca releases the EP *Got Live If You Want It!*

GLYN JOHNS: What happened was that Andrew Oldham stole them away if you like, and immediately rang me up and asked would I engineer for him, and I said, "You're joking. No, I want to see you exposed for what you are. You don't know what the hell you're doing. You wouldn't know one end of a record from another. You certainly can't produce and why the hell should I do it for you so you can take all the credit. Sod off!" And of course he did, and he went on with it on his own, and made a reasonable job of it, surprisingly enough.

Some period of time went by. I actually tried to get them back at one point and failed. Andrew threatened violence and God knows what all. It was quite amusing. We became very good friends in the end. I suppose a year or so went by and I was working in IBC one night. By this time I was freelance, and the manager called through and said, "Look, we just had a booking for after your session. Everyone else has gone home, would you mind staying and doing it? It's a mix and it won't take very long." I said, "Sure, who is it?" He said, "It's Andrew Oldham." I said, "No way," and put the phone down.

To cut a long story short, I eventually agreed to do it. Andrew walks in and says, "Look, let's forget about our differences while we're doing this." "Very good idea," I said, "gimme the tape." I put the tape on and it took twenty minutes to half an hour and as we got to the end of the session he said, "What did you think of that?" I said, "Well, it's very good." He said, "You told me that the day I could prove to you that I was a producer"—because that was what I had said to him—"that you'd consider working with me. How about it?" So I said, "I'm not going to go on this. I need to hear more than this." So he said, "Right," so he rang his secretary up, got her out of bed, made her go 'round to the office, pick up two records that he'd made, and she brought them 'round or had them delivered, and we put them on and listened to them. So he said, "Right, now what do you think?" I said, "They're pretty good." He said, "So will we do the next Stones record?" And I said, "Yep, that's right."

So I think the next thing I did was in fact the live EP, *Got*

Live If You Want It! I think it was recorded in the city of Manchester, and I seem to remember recording in Liverpool as well. We obviously recorded three or four concerts. The sound in the halls was terrible, terrible, and of course you had the added attraction of kids screaming from the minute this band walked on till the minute they left. A full album of the same name was released later in America. I wouldn't know about what was included on that.

MICK JAGGER: Some of the songs [on the American version of *Got Live If You Want It!*] might not have been live at all. Yeah, they were just studio tracks with Andrew Oldham overdubbing audiences onto the tracks. A belated apology to everyone!

August 18, 1965. The Stones sign a contract with American accountant Allen Klein, who will co-manage the band with Andrew Oldham.

MICK JAGGER: Andrew wanted to stop being our business manager so he could concentrate on being a producer. So he introduced us to Allen Klein. And he kind of presented him as an American gangster who was going to go in and get us a much better contract than what we had, which was pretty awful. So he went in and he did get us a much better contract but the thing with Allen is that he took a huge percentage for himself and we're still tied to him today.

KEITH RICHARDS: I still think going with Klein was a good thing in the long run because he opened our eyes to how much the record companies were making from us and that we actually could get a bigger piece of it. He just said, "Stand behind me and don't say a word," and he tore into these English lawyers and came out with a better contract than the Beatles, which was the best in the world at the time. Sure, he was there to rip us off if he could, but so was everybody else. It's just the price you pay to be educated [laughs].

BILL WYMAN: Klein was really good as a negotiator and in the end got us a really good contract, but he was basically using us to make himself rich.

DICK ROWE: Oh, yes. Money was always a big item with Mick and Andrew. I can remember on one occasion when the first three years were up or nearly up—perhaps another six months to go—and we wanted to re-sign them, so we had a lunch with the Stones in Sir Edward's private dining room. He said to them, "Now what it is that you want?" And I think it was Mick Jagger who said, "Well, it would be fantastic if we could have a million dollars." I daren't say anything. Because of my financial background it didn't take me two seconds to know the answer, but I didn't dare upstage Sir Edward. He immediately said, "That's no problem," which I knew he would, because we already had about six hundred thousand dollars on the way to them from the United States. So it was only a matter of finding, say, a third of the million dollars to re-sign them. But at that time they didn't realize that six hundred thousand or more of it they'd already earned. So they re-signed with us.

September 24, 1965. Decca releases *Out of Our Heads*.

KEITH RICHARDS: We had ten days to record an album between tours. We'd go in and do what we could, do our best—there wasn't much you could do with four-track in those days. You could overdub a couple of things, but you really just knocked them out.

October 22, 1965. Decca releases "Get Off of My Cloud."

KEITH RICHARDS: That was a bit too rushed and I never liked it—I think we were working in L.A. and we needed another single. But I mean, how do you follow up "Satisfaction"?

1966. On February 4, Decca releases "19th Nervous Breakdown." On April 15, Decca releases *Aftermath*, which contains only Jagger/Richards songs. It was originally titled *Could You Walk on the Water*. Decca was not amused.

MICK JAGGER: Those songs ["Under My Thumb" and "Stupid Girl"] aren't really misogynist. Balls. It's a bit of a joke, really. Obviously I was going through a series of bad relationships at the time and it's a reflection of that, but no, I certainly don't hate women. Quite the contrary [laughs].

I don't put women on pedestals. I think women should be equals and pull their own weight. Women who work and support themselves are a lot more interesting to me, not just because they have their own money but because as a result they feel more together in themselves. I just can't stand those women who are just playthings and sit around painting their nails all day. They just want to get you into trouble.

MARIANNE FAITHFULL: I used to go round to Brian and Anita's flat in Courtfield Road quite a bit in those days. It was a centre for the bohemians of that time and really quite a scene. It was always a mess, with dishes piled up in the sink and posters peeling off the walls. We smoked an awful lot of marijuana in those days and then we'd go out and about. It was a lot of fun. I think Anita loved Brian very much but he was very difficult to love. There were strange things going on with him and between them. There were bruises on her arms and we knew it was Brian.

I started living with Mick after he split up with Chrissie [Shrimpton]. The two of them used to have terrible fights. They were quite nasty, really. You can hear the venom on their songs of that time like "Under My Thumb," and I'm sure she's the subject of "19th Nervous Breakdown."

Mick was really wonderful to me in those early days. I

was just getting over my marriage and he was very attentive and witty, terribly interesting and very affectionate. One of the great things, for me, was that he wasn't really into drugs. He'd do a little grass, the occasional acid, but he liked to be in control of himself. I hate to think if I were involved with someone more like me at the time. I probably wouldn't be here now.

1966. On May 13, Decca releases "Paint It Black." On July 18, while on their fifth tour of North America, the Stones play Cobo Hall in Detroit.

CHRISSIE HYNDE: I still like all that early Stones stuff. I listened to them a lot when I was between fourteen and nineteen. Somehow rock'n'roll music sounds different when you're just discovering the opposite sex and all that. Which I took a long, slow time in doing. I was just like a voyeur for years.

I saw them playing in Detroit in 1966 with the McCoys opening for them. Brian was wearing plaid boots, and Keith and Bill looked really cool because they were wearing half of each other's suits. So Keith had on the yellow trousers and blue jacket and Bill had the blue pants and yellow jacket. I remember Brian playing the dulcimer on "Lady Jane." I even made a dulcimer when I got to university, I was so impressed.

September 23, 1966. Decca releases "Have You Seen Your Mother, Baby."

KEITH RICHARDS: "Have You Seen Your Mother, Baby": I liked the track, I hated the mix. Mainly because there was a fantastic mix of the thing that was just right. But because they were in a rush and they needed to edit it down for *Ed Sullivan*, because we were booked to play our latest single, the mix was rushed and the essential qualities for me disappeared. It was just because of the lack of time. We couldn't be there to do the mix because we had a very important gig in Dayton or someplace and so there you go. You win some and you lose some.

January 13, 1967. Decca releases "Let's Spend the Night Together."

KEITH RICHARDS: Yeah, I played piano on "Let's Spend the Night Together," and then I overdubbed the guitar. To me that song was a progression from "Have You Seen Your Mother, Baby." It was like "Have You Seen Your Mother" was a step toward "Let's Spend the Night Together," because the chords and the structure of the song are very similar. And the fact that I'd wrote them both on piano, one was almost the same as the other.

January 15, 1967. The Stones perform their latest single with altered lyrics on *Ed Sullivan*.

KEITH RICHARDS: We went on *Ed Sullivan* and sang "Let's Spend *Some Time* Together." That's the old "give a little and take a little." Nobody is unbendable. If you want to do something badly enough . . . I love selling out! Shit . . . "Sold out"—I love that phrase. All sold out . . . especially outside theatres [laughs].

Those were some difficult times. All we were doing was playing all over America and then when we had any time we'd be in the studio recording. It was great for a while but it was exhausting. Brian was getting more and more distant with us, too. He'd be out partying all night and Mick and I were mostly just writing and working on things in the studio. When it was time for a full recording session he'd come in out of his head and pass out with his guitar. So it got more and more difficult working with him because we were always having to work around him.

January 20, 1967. Decca releases *Between the Buttons*.

BILL WYMAN: Yeah, that was a bit strange. I don't think Mick and Keith had time to write many songs. There was so much going on. We were so busy with travelling and all the craziness. I don't think they had much time to sit down and write more than a couple of songs for an album, and the rest of it was just filled in.

KEITH RICHARDS: When you write a song and you record it, everybody takes that as being the version, and in actual fact you've barely learned it. You're still exploring it and then

THE ROLLING STONES: An Oral History

you take it on stage. Suddenly you find all of these other possibilities and ways of changing it, adding different nuances and new ways of dealing with it. And you realize that you never really stop learning. I'm still learning "Satisfaction."

February 12, 1967. Acting on a tip from *News of the World*, police descend on Keith's country home searching for drugs.

KEITH RICHARDS: A bunch of us had gone down to my place for the weekend for a party, which we had done before a million times, it was nothing unusual. As it happened we'd all spent the day tripping on acid and we're just chilling out when the cops come banging on the door. It was pretty weird, all these police running around the house. Marianne Faithfull had just taken a bath and was sitting in front of the TV with a rug wrapped around her so it was deemed to be an orgy. That wasn't an orgy—they should have showed up at other times—but this time was no orgy. It was crazy. There was this dealer there I didn't know, I think he came with some other people. He had a whole box full of stuff but the cops let him go, even let him split the country. He wasn't who they were looking for.

In the end they could only charge me with allowing people to smoke dope on my premises, and Mick they nailed for having a couple of amphetamine pills he'd bought legally at a druggist in Italy. It was just our time was up. They didn't mind kids with lots of money fooling around, but we didn't pay them the respect they wanted. The Beatles put up with the bullshit and smiled nicely while they took their MBEs. We always said no to that sort of shit. So it was just time to try and shut us down.

Usually when you get busted it hits the papers the next day, but with us, not a word, so we knew something was up. Someone needed paying off, and we didn't know what to do, so we paid a lot of money, but obviously not to the right person. Eventually it comes out that we'd been busted and it finally comes to court and the lawyers are like "This doesn't make a lot of sense, they really seem to want to get you guys."

Marianne Faithfull: We had been out all day and down at the beach so my clothes and hair were covered in sand and leaves. I hadn't brought a change of clothes so after I took a bath I covered up with a fur rug and dried off. The next thing all these police are running about and when they saw me they immediately started fabricating these absurd stories about sex orgies. It was bizarre. There was no sex trip at all that day. I was there as one of the boys if you will. It was clearly a setup from the beginning with this strange guy from America and his briefcase full of drugs. He conveniently disappeared back to America with no questions asked. In the end Mick claimed responsibility for some of my amphetamine pills I'd bought at a druggist in Italy. It was very noble of him.

It was a very uncomfortable scene, not what you want to deal with after a very pleasant day tripping on acid. It was starting to get really tense in the room and then finally Keith put on Dylan's "Rainy Day Women #12 and 35" [Everybody must get stoned], at which we all burst out laughing. It broke the tension but confirmed the worst feelings about us to the police.

It wasn't until after the trial that Mick finally told me about the Mars Bar story. At first I thought it was hysterically funny but as it began to make the rounds it became very boring. It was just so far out and beyond anything we could have thought of. It was really the product of some twisted cop's fantasy of what people do when they're on acid. They were the ones that needed help and they were arresting us! When Brian got busted the day Mick and Keith got out of jail, that's when it hit me that this whole thing was a planned conspiracy. They were trying to save the morals of the youth by fabricating offences to get rid of a music group. In the end it backfired because it absolutely mythologized the Stones beyond anything Andrew could ever have dreamed up.

MICK JAGGER: I guess it seems like a bit of a joke now, but at the time it was really serious. I mean, we were going to jail! For what? And everybody's talking about it and the newspapers have it on the front page everyday and it kind of distracts you from the music which is what we were meant to be doing. So, it was a bad time for the band I think it's safe to say.

PETER JONES: Well, we had to report those matters. There were pictures of Mick in handcuffs and so on. We had to take the line that it was being overplayed, that this was authority struggling to remain in control. By then we had slightly come round to the point of view anyway that there was a bit of a gap between the Rolling Stones and the estab-lishment and that there was no point trying to pretend there wasn't. And we simply took the line that loyal fans stay with the Stones. That they are behind the boys and what they do in their private life, really that's up to them, but what they do in music is up to us.

The image that I was required to put across was that they were misunderstood. I think on the back of the book I wrote it said something about a lot of mud has been thrown at these boys, giving the impression that they are great, sort of puri-tanical lads at heart and now it's time for them to tell their side of the story. What I didn't know, having done this so duti-fully—but I must say anonymously as Pete Goodman—the truth of the matter is that within a couple of years they were openly attacking me for having failed to be honest in the early stages. So I really was caught between the two then.

I think that the reputation—which may have been built initially as almost a deliberate thing, to counter another kind of reputation—I think there is a great deal of scapegoat about the Stones. I really felt sorry particularly for Keith, I think, over the years, and I have no doubt that they were watched more closely. You could almost sense it at the concerts. There appeared to be more observing authority hanging about backstage than there ever was with the Beatles, and the Beatles were really just as bad. Or worse.

February 25, 1967. Keith, Brian, and Anita Pallenberg make their way to Morocco in Keith's Bentley.

KEITH RICHARDS: It was right after the bust and we just needed to get out of England for a while. Brian and Anita were living together and I spent most of my time there too. It was like the headquarters at the time. So we decided to drive to Morocco and on the way Brian got sick and had to be admitted to hospital in France.

I think he was going through a rough time with Anita because he wanted to be the star and didn't like the fact that she had a movie career. So there were problems. Maybe that's why he got sick in the first place. He wanted us to carry on and he would meet us in Tangier when he got out of hospital. So Anita and I continued on and we had a great time. When we got to Tangier there were all these frantic telegrams from Brian telling Anita to get him from the hospital.

MARIANNE FAITHFULL: Mick and I had just arrived on our way to Marrakech and Anita asked me to go with her to get Brian. I don't think she really wanted to be alone with him anymore. Anita and I were close at the time and we had a lot of fun together. Brian was in bad shape physically and mentally. You have to be in good shape to take a lot of acid and he really wasn't. He had deteriorated and I guess he knew he was losing Anita, whom he adored. I sat between the two of them on the plane and the tension between them was very disturbing. We broke the tension by reading from an Oscar Wilde play I brought with me and things got better. But when they got to their hotel Brian got angry with her and broke his arm when he tried to hit her and missed. That's when she took up with Keith. He was like her white knight who had come to rescue her. He was appalled at the thought of Brian beating her. He'd been secretly in love with her for years anyway but had never said anything to anyone.

KEITH RICHARDS: Anita said, "Sorry, Brian, you're just too much of an asshole to live with and I've got something good that's starting to happen with Keith." Well, two kids later I guess she was right [laughs]. She was quite capable of taking care of herself but at a certain point you've just got to say, "Fuck this, I'm taking you back to London." So that was it between me and Brian. He could never forgive me for that. I don't blame him in a way, but it was his own fault. You just don't hit a woman and expect her to stick around.

1967. On May 27, the same day Mick, Keith, and friend Robert Fraser are formally charged in court with drug possession from the February Redlands bust, Brian and friend "Stash" are arrested for drug possession after a raid at Brian's London flat. On June 25,

Mick, Keith, Brian, and Marianne Faithfull join the Beatles for the first ever global TV broadcast. The Beatles sing "All You Need Is Love." On June 29, after two nights in prison, Mick is found guilty of drug possession and sentenced to three months in "Her Majesty's care." Fraser gets six months and Keith gets one year. At the trial it emerges that the bust had been set up by the tabloid _News of the World_ after Mick sued them for running a piece alleging his involvement with drugs earlier in the year.

KEITH RICHARDS: I didn't really help the cause, I suppose, because when it came down to the trial and they started talking all this shit about the "orgy," I said something about their "petty morals being illegitimate," which didn't go down well. When they actually sentenced me to the year in prison the judge was calling me "scum" and "filth such as you." He wouldn't have said that to me in an alleyway, I'll tell you.

I think that's where the tone of it changed. Before that it was just, "Oh look at those guys thumbing their noses at wearing ties, the length of the hair." Once drugs became an issue, suddenly the screw turned. After four years of riding on the crest of a wave you find yourself in Wormwood Scrubs [prison]—it's a bit of a bring-down, quite honestly. Suddenly you realize the world is still there. But the idea that a couple of guitar players are a real threat to British society and they have to be leaned on tells you just how fragile society really is.

June 30, 1967. Members of The Who take out a large advertisement in London's *Evening Standard* in support of Mick and Keith.

"The Who consider that Mick Jagger and Keith Richards have been treated as scapegoats for the drug problem and as a protest against the savage sentences imposed on them at Chichester yesterday, The Who are issuing today the first of a series of Jagger/Richards songs to keep their work before the public until they are again free to record themselves." (They released versions of "The Last Time" and "Under My Thumb," recorded in just twenty-four hours.)

July 1, 1967. The conservative *Times* of London runs a leader condemning the sentences handed down to Mick and Keith as unfair: "Who Breaks a Butterfly on a Wheel."

KEITH RICHARDS: We received support from the most unusual places, like The Times. I hope they live forever. They saved my neck. A year making mailbags in prison was not on my itinerary [laughs].

July 12, 1967. John Lennon and Paul McCartney join the Stones to record "We Love You," released on August 18.

BILL WYMAN: We kind of lost touch with the Beatles a bit in those years '64 through to about '66–'67. We were always in other places. They were in Japan and Australia and then we were in England. Then we were in Australia and they were somewhere else. We were really working hard, both bands then, so we didn't cross each other's paths much. We did play a few smaller gigs in London, earlier on, together, in which they headlined and we kind of opened. Then they came to our aid, or support, during the drug bust in '67, when Mick and Keith were put in jail overnight and Brian got busted—three times that year, I think.

We were trying to finish *Satanic Majesties*, during which Andrew Oldham left us. It was really another one of the three times when the band could have folded up. John and Paul came and sang on "We Love You" to give us a bit of support. The Who also helped us during that time when they publicly proclaimed they would record our songs and release them just to keep our music in front of the public. All the bands at the time came to our aid, as did *The Times*. It was really a tough time, and the rekindling of that friendship was really important to us.

I knew Paul very well. I used to hang out with him quite a lot, and Brian and George Harrison were quite friendly. I didn't know John that well, but Ringo I knew quite well. There's been a continuing friendship, from afar because we're always working in different places.

There was always an impression created by the media that we were against each other. It was always the Stones versus the Beatles. They always tried to build a wall between us as the two top bands in England, but it wasn't true, because we were quite good mates. And they liked our music and we liked theirs, and it was completely opposite music so there was room for both bands.

PAUL McCARTNEY: Yeah, the press always wanted to see us as enemies, but really we were great friends. There was a lot of camaraderie and we would go to each other's shows and hang out at each other's homes and in clubs. We'd tell them what we were doing and I think there was always a little bit of friendly competition between us—you know, "Look what they're doing, we better top that" kind of thing. We were good mates.

GEORGE MARTIN: The Beatles were very aware of the Stones and actually used to see them quite a bit. The Stones were the much harder of the groups, the "punkers" of their day, or the "new wave" if you like. The Beatles were running the risk of becoming very elementary and conservative in relation to the Stones.

July 1967.

BILL WYMAN: Yeah, I went to the studio, Olympic Studio, with Glyn Johns. When I arrived, Glyn said, "The session's cancelled. Mick and Keith rang up twenty minutes ago but you'd already left home." I said, "What a drag . . . it was quite a drive for me, about forty-five minutes." He said, "Well, have you got any songs you want to mess around with?" Nicky Hopkins was there on keyboards. I'm not sure whether Charlie was there or not. I said yes, because I'd been messing with this song and it was what I thought of as spacey, kind of *Satanic Majesties* and psychedelic in a way. So I just used those players. Next door in the other studio the Small Faces were recording, and Steve Marriott came in with Ronnie Lane and they sang with me, 'cause I just didn't want to sing. That's why I used that tremolo effect on the voice, because I was really uptight about my singing, which I still am. We just used effects and we just tried all kinds of things and it came out quite nice, and we were reasonably satisfied with the experiment if you like.

The next day we got to the studio and we were just chatting and figuring out what we were going to do that night and Glyn said, "Here, hang on, Mick and Keith and Brian. Have a listen to this." And he put the tape on and played them a rough mix. They said, "That's really good, what is it?" He said, "It's called 'In Another Land.' Bill did it yesterday." They liked it and we put it on the album. It's as simple as that—it was an accident. Most good things are accidents, aren't they?

I think the whole album was pushed off as not being right. The album musically was very confusing. I loved some of the tracks and some of them I hate. They always tried to talk it off as a copy of *Sgt. Pepper*, really.

MARIANNE FAITHFULL: Well, they were always so jealous of the Beatles. The Beatles were, perhaps, a little jealous of the style and all the rest of it, but they were never really worried the Stones would take over. They knew who they were.

1967. On July 31, the conviction against Keith is overturned on appeal and Mick is given a conditional discharge. On October 31, Brian is convicted of cannabis possession and sentenced to nine months in prison. He is released on appeal the following day. On December 8, Decca releases *Their Satanic Majesties Request*. It is the only album arranged and produced by the Rolling Stones, and the first without Andrew Oldham. On December 12, Brian's sentence is set aside in favour of a fine and three years' probation.

DICK ROWE: You can imagine the problems we had when they announced that they wanted to use that 3D picture for the cover. By then there was so much fuss over the jackets for the records that Andrew was dealing directly with Sir Lewis. I really couldn't cope. It's the old story—you can't fight a war on two fronts very easily at the same time. I couldn't really fight with Lewis and then try and calm the Stones down, because although I understood what the Stones were up to, I thought one must have a little good sense about it. I think Lewis took the attitude that I couldn't cope with the situation, and of course he then came up against Andrew and Mick Jagger [laughs]. He really had nightmares, and he would just close his door. I think it was slightly embarrassing for him to have these two young men shouting at him. He was a very dignified man, Sir Lewis was.

GLYN JOHNS: I did *Between the Buttons* as the engineer, and *Satanic Majesties*. I certainly wouldn't claim to have been the producer on that. There really wasn't a producer for that album. Mick and Keith were more of that than certainly ever I was.

Recording *Satanic* was really boring, really boring. They were going through an acid phase and they were trying to do a sort of *Sgt. Pepper*. It really didn't come off. A couple of interesting things were on there. I've never listened to it since its release.

MICK JAGGER: We were just taking too much acid at the time and we got carried away thinking other people should care.

KEITH RICHARDS: I didn't like [*Satanic Majesties*] for years. There are a couple of things. First of all, we'd dropped from exhaustion so it was a labour to make it. It was definitely a culmination of that whole sixties, youth-oriented, drugs-and-acid thing. The Beatles and what they were doing was important, and we just wanted to lie on a beach for a year and forget it, but we still had to make an album. So it's a bit of a patchwork quilt. It's a bit of what we thought they wanted, a bit of "let's get out of here as quick as possible," and a couple of good things. There's more interesting stuff on there than I would have thought, looking back.

But then it always seems like that to me. They didn't think much of *Exile on Main Street* when it came out either. *Black and Blue* is another one that suddenly people are appreciating, and that's a knock-off album—it was us auditioning guitar players. But as far as *Satanic Majesties* went, on top of everything you take a year off and get busted. *Great* . . . So suddenly you had to deal with that. It wasn't just fun anymore—suddenly it was serious.

CHRISSIE HYNDE: The only time they went off the rails was on *Their Satanic Majesties Request*. I thought—when they started doing that "If we close all of our eyes together then we'll see where we all come from" stuff—"Don't tamper with things. Go back to the 'glue.'"

February 1968.

BILL WYMAN: Yeah, it was a strange time. I never took things like acid and other drugs and so I was on the fringe of it. I watched all this strangeness going on and I suppose Charlie and I remained very straight and normal. *Satanic Majesties* threw a lot of our fans off. I think everybody knew we had to get back to our roots. That's why we got Jimmy Miller as a producer and came out with *Beggars Banquet* and those kind of albums after that, which were about reverting back and getting more guts and what the Stones were all about.

GLYN JOHNS: Then I did *Get Your Ya Ya's Out*, which I was given credit for producing. God knows why—I was never paid [laughs]. Funnily enough, Mick did tell me that I'd produced "Honky Tonk Women," which is the most astonishing thing he's ever said and he's said some fairly astonishing things to me. But he did reckon that I had produced "Honky Tonk Women." Why he should think that, I don't know. I think it was probably because Jimmy Miller was in the studio hitting a cowbell and I was left alone in the booth.

Jagger and I at the end of our relationship had some pretty hairy disagreements based very much on the fact that they would never really recognize that I was a producer. They'd known me since year one as an engineer. I can understand that—they'd had such limited experience with producers—they'd been produced by *Andrew Oldham*, for God's sake. Then they made one record on their own and then they got Jimmy Miller, so really in all those years, they'd only worked with two people, other than me as an engineer.

They worked in America at Chess, and at RCA where they worked with great engineers. The guy at Chess, Ron Malo, used to get really good sound. He was perfect for them, but they never really understood what a producer did, and I don't think they really know now. I don't think they've got a fucking clue, I really don't. I got so frustrated because we're talking about the Stones as being five people. In fact, Mick and Keith made all the decisions. They really use people, you know, they're great users of people, and I don't think they're alone and I don't blame them. I think in their position it's very easy to adopt that attitude because people are constantly falling all over themselves to be involved, to sort of touch their garment as they walk by. So it's very difficult not to abuse that in some way.

I always felt that although I did tremendously well from my involvement with the Stones—and of course I don't regret it on any level—I deserved to do incredibly well because I actually put a lot of my life, and time, and artistic input or whatever else, into their thing. So we gained from it mutually. However, I did feel that I was literally some employee on the end of a bloody telephone, and was never really considered as a person. If they had a session booked for eight o'clock and they knew they weren't going to turn up until midnight, they weren't going to ring me and say, "Look we're not going to be along until midnight." They didn't give a bugger.

Not only that, but I was frustrated as a producer. I'd been an engineer for several years, and I knew I could bloody produce and I was frustrated not to do it. I knew they were never going to ask me because they'd already passed me over and got Jimmy Miller, who in fact I recommended [laughs].

Jagger came to me after *Satanic Majesties* and said, "We're gonna get a producer." I said, "Okay, fine." He says, "We're going to get an American." I said, "Oh my God, that's all I need. I don't think my ego could stand having some bloody Yank in here telling me what sort of sound to get for the

Rolling Stones." I had very little time for American pro- ducers anyway, and I thought, "Christ, how am I going to get out of this?" So I said, "I know somebody. There's one in England already and he's fantastic and he'd just done the Traffic album. His name is Jimmy Miller and it was a remarkably good record—the first record he'd made with Traffic. He's a really nice guy and I'm sure he'd be really fan- tastic for you." Anything but some strange, lunatic, drug addict from Los Angeles! So Jagger actually took the bit and off he went and met Miller and gave him the job and the first thing Jimmy Miller did was fire me [laughs], because he'd been using Eddy Kramer as an engineer and so natu- rally, he would use his own engineer.

They started that with Kramer, who'd been my tape op at one point, and they ran into a bit of a problem with him after a while and called me to finish the record and mix it and that started my involvement with Jimmy Miller.

MICK JAGGER: Yes, Jimmy Miller will produce our next single, and he'll probably make the next album too. Of course, it all depends on whether he can stand the pace of our recording schedule [laughs].

KEITH RICHARDS: We needed a producer like Jimmy because you can't actually hear what you're doing on the guitar if you're not in the control room. Unfortunately, I don't have a long enough lead.

CHAPTER 5

A Beautiful Guy

March 1968. Work begins on "Jumpin' Jack Flash," released on May 24.

BILL WYMAN: We got to the studio early once—I think it was a rehearsal studio, not a recording studio. There was just myself, Brian, and Charlie. The Stones never arrive at the same time. Mick and Keith hadn't come so we were just messing about and I just sat down at the piano and started doing this riff—"duh dum, da da dah." And then Brian started playing guitar and Charlie was doing a rhythm and we were messing with it for about twenty minutes, just filling in time, and Mick and Keith came in, so we stopped. They said, "Hey, that sounded really good. Carry on. What was it?" I said, "Just something we were messing with." The next thing I remember is that we recorded it, and Mick wrote great lyrics to it and it turned out to be a really good single, "Jumpin' Jack Flash."

June 1968. The Stones record "Sympathy for the Devil."

CHARLIE WATTS: "Sympathy for the Devil" was tried six different ways. I don't mean at once. It was all night doing it one way, then another full night trying it another way, and we just could not get it right. It would never fit a regular rhythm. I first heard Mick play that one on the steps of my house on an acoustic guitar. The first time I heard it, it was really light and had a kind of Brazilian sound. Then when we got in the studio we poured things on it, and it was something different. I could never get a rhythm for it, except this one, which is like a samba on the snare drum. It was always a bit like a dance band until we got Rocky Dijon in, playing the congas. By messing about with that, we got the thing done.

Now it took six days of messing around in the studio to get to that point. The argument against [working like] that is that you might not have got a track like "Sympathy," which is a very good record. It's very expensive, very time-consuming, and there's a lot of waste, but what transcends all that is the spirit and an atmosphere you create with it, and I don't know what that is. It's in the air.

NICKY HOPKINS: I remember the studio caught fire, which was quite interesting. We were cutting "Sympathy for the Devil" and we were trying to get it right for three days, or three nights, and they were filming it all. All of sudden we were doing one version where I was playing organ and I looked up, and on the ceiling there was a little ring of fire starting, because they'd covered all the regular lights up and put big fluorescent lights on the ceiling. They'd covered that with some sort of tissue paper and all of a sudden it just started, a little ring of fire, and within about a minute the whole roof was ablaze. So people were rushing around, hurling tapes out, saving tapes. It was pretty wild!

December 6, 1968. Decca releases _Beggars Banquet_. After Sir Edward refuses to allow the original album art—a graffiti-laden toilet stall—they use a white cover with fancy script.

DICK ROWE: Oh yes, [Sir Edward Lewis] couldn't believe it— he just couldn't believe it. He had good judgment, or correct judgment. As all of us get a little older, it becomes just that much more difficult to understand the younger people, even if you have a young way of thinking. What really disturbed him more than anything was the fact that [the original sleeve] had no sales potential. He said, "How could it possibly help sell the records? People would not want to stock the records because of the sleeve." He could see all the wrong things about it, which is understandable.

KEITH RICHARDS: We found this wall—I think it was me and Mick and Anita—and we thought, "This looks pretty funky," so we had it photographed and it looked great. Decca couldn't believe it. They hated it and just wouldn't budge, and we were like, "Fuck you, that's the cover." They weren't backing down, and it dragged on for almost a year and it was like they didn't care if the album never came out. Eventually we put it in another cover, but we started to look into having our own label so that could never happen again.

BILL WYMAN: It was a nice idea, taking that photo of all those animals in that old house [used on the inside of the jacket]. We're all sitting at the banquet table with legs up and knives and sheep and things. It was the original idea for the cover. I really liked it.

We were always having problems with Decca over the album covers. Yeah, we had tremendous rows about them. Then about four years ago Decca released a compilation album after we'd signed with another label and used that cover. That was typical of Decca—turning things down, and then using them at a later date. They did that with "Fortune Teller" and "Poison Ivy" and album covers and all kinds of things. They weren't the best record company to be with. [Banquet] is one of my most favourite albums.

KEITH RICHARDS: Revolution was the thing at that time. Everyone taking to the streets . . . "We're gonna change the world" and all that. Mick used to go to the demonstrations and got busted. That's where "Street Fighting Man" came from.

December 12, 1968. The Stones begin shooting a TV special, *The Rolling Stones' Rock'n'Roll Circus*, at a studio in London. Over two days they perform alongside friends The Who, John and Yoko, Eric Clapton, and Jethro Tull.

MICK JAGGER: When will it be released? Never. Next question.

April 23, 1969. Some members of the band contribute to an album that will become *Jammin' with Edward*.

BILL WYMAN: It was really out-takes. Ry Cooder came to play, and I think Keith was a bit uptight about it. No disrespect to Keith—that happens to everybody. We're all competent musicians in these bands, but if Jimmy Paige comes to a Rolling Stones session, Keith or Mick Taylor might be a bit uptight. Not so much these days, but back then, if Paul McCartney came to see us, I felt uptight, and if Keith Moon came, Charlie felt strange. It's your fellow musicians on the same instrument. You always kind of felt like they're thinking "Oh, he ain't that good." If you go to other people's sessions you notice it as well. I know that Jimmy Paige is uptight if Jeff Beck's there, and Eric Clapton doesn't like it. All in all, you're all mates and you love each other's music, but there's always that feeling. I think Keith was uptight about Ry Cooder being there because he's a brilliant slide player. So he just found an excuse not to be at the session. So we couldn't record songs. We did a few things—"Sister Morphine" he was on, and another one I think, and then we just jammed. There was a lot of nice playing, so Glyn Johns said, "There's some good stuff, why don't you try to put an album together?" And everybody said fine, if you can find enough material. I didn't think there was enough material, but I liked some of the things we did. That was *Jammin' with Edward*.

June 5, 1969. Mick, Keith, and Charlie visit Brian at his home to tell him he is no longer in the band.

BILL WYMAN: Yeah, [Brian] had deteriorated as a musician. He was playing less and less guitar. He never fit anymore. He could never get anything going on a song, whereas I'd say, "I think the bass line should be like this," and I'd play that and Charlie would do a certain kind of matching rhythm. Brian would never find anything that fit, and he'd wander from instrument to instrument trying to get something going instead of sticking to his guitar. And he would play something pretty awful on some instrument, which would then be wiped off the tape. And he got more and more paranoid and uptight. In the end it was mutually agreed that he should leave. We separated quite friendly. I think he knew it had to happen. It was like waiting for a divorce to come through, when you know the relationship isn't working anymore, but you hang on for the sake of the kids. It was that kind of thing.

Then he got all excited and he used to come to the sessions just as a friend, and say, "Hey I'm getting this band together, and I've spoken to Korner and I've spoken to so-and-so and we're gonna form a band and play real blues." Because he wanted to play blues again. He was very excited about it for about three weeks. We saw him quite a lot then.

KEITH RICHARDS: We had to go and sort it out with Brian because we really wanted to tour again and we knew he wasn't up to it. So we went down to see him and he said, "I just can't do it anymore. I can't take another tour." So we said, "That's cool, we understand how you feel." Then we asked him, "Do you want to say that you've left?" and he said, "Let's say that I've left but I may come back in the future." Two weeks later he was dead.

ALEXIS KORNER: I thought Mick and Keith handled it very well, actually. Brian had been having real problems for several years and was in a terrible state. They didn't tell anybody outside about the problems or put him down publicly and they were actually very patient in hoping he would eventually get through it before they started thinking about getting a replacement.

June 13, 1969. The Stones introduce new member Mick Taylor at a press conference in Hyde Park.

MICK TAYLOR: I started buying rhythm'n'blues records and jazz records when I was about thirteen, fourteen. That's when I started to take an interest in playing on the guitar myself. I mean, I've always had an interest in music. The enthusiasm for music was already there, but it wasn't until I was about fourteen that I started to channel it in a positive direction.

They knew John Mayall and I think they asked him if he knew any good young guitarists, and he just said to Mick, "Well, you can have my guitarist because he's just left us." Yeah, it was as simple as that. Mick just called me up and said come down to a recording session we're doing at Olympic Studios—they were recording some backing tracks for *Let It Bleed* at the time. I went down there and played and that was it.

They had obviously been thinking of trying to find a replacement for some time, because they wanted to get back out on the road again. They wanted to reactivate their career. They'd done a very strong album, *Beggars Banquet*, which was really good, but they hadn't actually toured for about two or three years before I joined them, and I think basically it was because they realized that Brian couldn't do it anymore.

GLYN JOHNS: Mick Taylor was a brilliant guitar player. All those things he did on record and particularly onstage were fantastic. I mean, the power from his guitar was incredible. It was the first time when anyone else had that influence, that heavy rock'n'roll influence, other than Keith. I mean, the band was always known for Keith's rhythm playing, wasn't it? And all of a sudden there's this other monster sound coming out of Taylor. Fantastic. Incredibly fluid playing, and it had never happened before. It changed the band considerably.

1969. On July 3, Decca releases "Honky Tonk Women." On the same day, Brian is found dead in his swimming pool at Cotchford Farm. The coroner calls it "death by misadventure."

BILL WYMAN: One day I'd come back from a session really late. I was at the hotel and I'd just got off to sleep when I got a phone call from Charlie. He said, "Bill . . ." I said, "Why are you calling me? I was asleep." He said he'd just heard that Brian was dead. I couldn't believe it and I couldn't get back to sleep for hours, and the old lady was crying and I didn't know what to say. It was just so alien . . . such a shock. We were two days away from the Hyde Park free concert with half a million people. We didn't know what to do and we sat around in hotel rooms and the studio just talking about, well, do we cancel Hyde Park or do we carry on? What do we do as a sign of respect? And Mick was getting ready to go to Australia to do *Ned Kelly* with Marianne Faithfull. It was all a bit crazy.

In the end we thought we'd go ahead with it, and we put a photo up at the back and Mick read "Adonais," that great poem by Shelley, which was a very nice thing to find. I don't know how he found it in time, but it really fit, it really felt like Brian was there, it really did. It's a stupid thing to say, I suppose, but his spirit was at that show, and we all felt really good about doing the show when we finally did it. Then of course Mick flew off and Keith, who was very upset, locked himself away in the country somewhere with Anita, who used to be Brian's girlfriend.

Charlie and I went to the funeral, and we were the only two people who actually went, and it was horrible, that funeral. The priest was talking about drugs, and "Maybe you'll be forgiven." Then we started toward the cemetery and the whole of Cheltenham—which is the town he lived in—turned out. It was like the Queen had come in. The streets were lined with people crying as the procession went by. It was quite moving, actually.

Then we went to the cemetery where they put the coffin in the ground and there was just the relatives, all sedated, and Charlie, myself, and my girlfriend, and Brian's old girl-friend, and so on and so on, and a few friends, and there were these terrible photographers and newsreel men just elbowing people out of the way to get shots of the coffin going down in the ground, and pushing his mother out of way and *click click click click* ... All the time the guy's trying to say the prayers. It was awful. There were fans yelling from 'round the edge. It was really strange.

I felt very close to Brian because we were mates. We'd hang out together quite a lot, especially on tours and in London. We used to go to the same clubs and we used to go out much more than the others. At that time, Mick and Keith and Charlie didn't really go out when we were on tour. They stayed in their hotel rooms very quietly and were gentlemen and behaved themselves. They didn't take advantage of all the groupies that were always around. They all had relationships. Charlie was married, Mick had a very steady relationship at the time, and so did Keith, and they were very conscientious about it. Brian and I were the tearaways. We'd be out there having fun with all the girls. It was great. There were only the two of us so we didn't have to share between the five of us. For quite a few years we were always going to the clubs in L.A. and going out to parties. So I got to know him really well.

He was a little bugger sometimes, Brian was. He was really sweet sometimes and sometimes he was *the* worst. He used to do terrible things [laughs]. When we used to be on tour, once, we were playing Middlesboro, which is three hundred miles from London, and he picked up a girl there after the gig, gave her a quick one behind the stage door or something, and then invited her to come back to stay at his place in London. So she jumped into the back of the van and we drove down to London and when we got to London, he changed his mind. He kind of thought, "Well, she wasn't that special." People didn't have transport or money in those days. So he arrived at his flat, and said, "I don't want her to come in. Get rid of her." And he jumped out and ran in his house and locked the door.

That left Stew and myself and Charlie and maybe Keith. We'd just dropped Mick off, and now we had to deal with the problem. We had to get this girl onto a train, and there was no train because it was too late. So I took her back to my wife, but first I said to Charlie, "For God's sake, don't go home tonight. Phone Shirley, tell her I need you. You've gotta come back with me, otherwise it will never be believed." We couldn't leave this girl in the street, and she couldn't sit at the railway station all night. So Charlie came back with me and this girl to my house, just to prove that it was one that Brian had left behind. Brian was always leaving you in those situations, and next day it was always, "Oh, sorry about that, man, I just couldn't deal with it." And he always had that way of being so you forgave him. He was no angel, Brian was, but he was very funny as well.

MICK JAGGER: It was a real shock when Brian died, I guess because we were all very close, especially in the very early days. But in a way it wasn't that surprising, really. You just knew if anyone was going to die it was going to be Brian. He lived his life so fast. Brian was a really sensitive guy. I mean, in the beginning it was a bit of a joke but he really took the criticism very personally and he'd get really upset about it. It was all that stuff about us being dirty and "they never wash their hair"—those kinds of things, which the rest of the band just thought was a bit of a joke and didn't take very seriously, he really did. Then when the bust happened it really brought him down.

When you're the singer in the band you tend to be the focus of attention, and that really bothered Brian. He was a jealous guy, but it's not like we kicked him out of the spotlight or anything. I know it's been said that he didn't feel that he ever had his fair share within the group and that we never did his songs and all that, but he never really said anything. He never played me a song that he had written and said, "This is for the band." I think he was just too shy to do something like that. I suppose we could have tried harder to bring it out of him, but certainly we never tried to stifle him in any way. We always respected him as a musician. He was the first person in this country to ever play slide guitar. I never saw anyone else. Of course, now everyone plays slide, but Brian was the first.

KEITH RICHARDS: It wasn't really a shock because I'd even said to him, "Man, you're not going to live to see thirty." But it did hit me pretty hard. He was just one of those people that's a little more fragile. All those times when we were touring every night all through America, people would be laying things on him just because he was in the Stones. He'd take it all. And it was bad for him. There was no time to sort it out because of the pace we were going at. When I first met him I thought he was pretty tough, but gradually he just became more and more fragile.

We were in a session and about midnight someone called up and said, "Brian's dead." We wanted to know what happened as much as anybody and probably more. We certainly didn't want anything covered up the way some people said. Nobody wanted to kill him, that's bullshit. It was just that nobody was looking after him. Everybody knew what he was like at a party, somebody had to be looking out for him. He wasn't in the band anymore, so none of our people were around that would know what was happening. There were lots of people there, plenty of chicks, and someone got rid of everybody before the cops showed up, so it's hard to know who was there and what actually happened. He didn't have a good "bullshit detector"—he couldn't tell the assholes from the cool people. Hendrix had the same problem. Brian was a really good swimmer, so it just doesn't make sense [that he drowned]. I don't suppose we'll ever know. And anyone that tells you they really know is full of shit.

Brian was a beautiful guy. He could be a real asshole at times but I guess we all are at times. He could really feel the music; he was really connected to that vibe inside him.

CHARLIE WATTS: It was really sad. I think what made it worse is that just before he died he got into a really good phase where he was excited about music again. I felt really bad because we had basically taken the one thing that really mattered, being in a band, away from him.

LEWIS JONES: We always thought that Brian was extremely happy and that being involved in popular music had a beneficial effect on him. I don't think it was the music or the pressure of fame, if you will, that killed him. I believe that the single biggest problem Brian had to deal with was the breakup of his relationship with Miss Pallenberg. He was very much in love with her and the breakup was a severe blow to him. His mother and I were quite shocked when we saw him. His appearance had changed and he had become very withdrawn and morose.

Throughout this tragic occurrence we were very encouraged by all of the love and support that was shown toward Brian by the fans here in Britain and from the thousands of fans around the world who took the time to write letters of warmth and sympathy.

PETER JONES: One of the most misunderstood people in the history of rock'n'roll is Brian Jones, because Brian was open to so many temptations, so many pressures, so many problems. It was a tragic end. Brian did a great deal more early on for the Rolling Stones than he has been given credit for. He was in the shadow of Mick, so he had that kind of additional pressure as well. Brian and I always got on very well. I think it would have been great if he could have still been around.

GLYN JOHNS: Obviously, the band's changed many times. To me the Rolling Stones with Brian Jones—as odd a character as he was, and I don't want to go into that, but he and I didn't really get on—he was a major influence on the band. I mean, in the first session, in those days, he was really the leader of the band. He came in the control room at the beginning of that session and told me the sort of sound they wanted. I didn't hear boo from anyone else.

RON WOOD: I was always with them from the beginning in spirit. I remember when Brian died, Ian Stewart rang up the Faces rehearsal room, which we were using to get the band together initially. He spoke to Ronnie Lane on the phone, and said, "Would Woody like to join the Stones now that Brian's gone?" And Ronnie Lane said, "No thanks, he's quite happy where he is." I didn't find this out for five years [laughs].

1969. On July 5, the Stones perform a free concert in front of three hundred thousand people at London's Hyde Park. The show, during which thousands of white butterflies are released, becomes a memorial to Brian Jones. Later that month, while in Australia with Mick who is filming *Ned Kelly*, Marianne Faithfull is hospitalized.

MARIANNE FAITHFULL: It was after Brian died. The stories always say that it was something to do with a heroin withdrawal, which it wasn't, actually. It was before I was into heroin. I took 150 Tuinal [a prescription sleeping pill]. I was just very unhappy and I tried to kill myself. I was out for six days. It was very lucky I did it in Australia, because I don't think they would have been able to save my life in most other places. In America, in Australia, and perhaps in South

Africa, but nowhere else. The sisters at the hospital were very good to me—they were wonderful. It's terribly hard to save someone's life when they are really trying to destroy it. It was an awful time because Brian had died and everything was going wrong and it was like living in a goldfish bowl. I hated it. Oh some people like it, lots of people live under that kind of pressure. All the stars you think of, both women and men, they love it. I'm not very good at it, I'm afraid.

November 7, 1969. The Stones begin their sixth tour of North America. The top ticket price, US$7.50, is considered exorbitant by some.

KEITH RICHARDS: I think we really need to do a tour and a lot of people would like to see us because we haven't played live in a while. A tour is the thing that really knocks a band into shape. Especially now as we have Mick Taylor with us. We really need to go through the paces again and get the band back in peak form.

GEORGE HARRISON: I think they really need the money. I don't know how much they're doing it for the idea of wanting to go on the road or whether it's just to make a bit of bread. Then again, for the Stones it's a whole new scene with their new guitarist, who is fantastic. That will put a lot of life back in the band, which is great.

B.B. KING: I was one of the opening acts on their 1969 tour. I remember when the tour got to Baltimore, Maryland, a white lady came up to me. She had some teenage kids that had come to see the Stones and for some reason they liked me. She said to me, "What's your name?" I said, "B.B. King." She said, "We liked you, do you have any records?" [laughs]. Well, I didn't want to make her feel bad, so I just said, "Yes, we have a few." And she said, "Can you give me the names of some of them?" And I said, "Just ask for B.B. King in the record store." I was shocked. I thought that if you made a good record people would want it. It wasn't until later that I learned how much politics was involved. Playing with the Stones was good for my career because it exposed me to the white audience. Before that they didn't know who we were.

December 5, 1969. Decca releases Let It Bleed.

MICK JAGGER: Those two albums [*Beggars Banquet* and *Let It Bleed*] were recorded about the same time and it was a good period. I wasn't taking many drugs anymore and was hanging around with a group of people like [art gallery owner] Robert Fraser and a bunch of directors and theatre people. Plus there was lots going on with everybody protesting Vietnam and the students in Paris. Yeah, it was violent, a lot of it, but there was a sense that we could change the world.

KEITH RICHARDS: I started to play with different guitar tunings just before we started recording *Beggars Banquet*. It was around that period and into *Let It Bleed*. I'd been playing the guitar every night, three hundred and fifty-five nights a year, for five years. I knew the damn thing so well the way it was set up that I wasn't getting the surprises and the accidents out of it, which is what I love. I felt I couldn't learn any more that way, not being Segovia, and I met a few people and got heavily back to country blues and stuff and [caught on] that half of this stuff was tuned to a five-string banjo. All they did was buy a guitar, take the bottom string off, and tune it to a banjo tuning. So that to me was like learning again, and it introduced the element of surprise again into guitar playing, which I'd kind of lost from just doing gig after gig, night after night after night after night. That was the main reason I got into that.

A song like "You Got the Silver" just *came*. It was an acoustic guitar and when it came to making a record of it, we just built it up, and then the drums came in.

"Country Honk" was the original way Mick and I wrote "Honky Tonk Women" and sang it. That was the song as far as we were concerned. Then we said, "Ah, that's great, it should be a single." So we cut it with the band and made if sort of funky, drums, organized it for the band. But we were still interested in doing it the way that we originally thought of it—a sort of Hank Williams, Jimmy Rodgers, early pre-Nashville sound. I always loved Merle Haggard. I saw him at the Lonestar recently and he's still wearing Jimmy Rodgers' hat. Merle is an Einstein on his own.

CHARLIE WATTS: "Honky Tonk Women": we never quite knew how to get it right. When I say *we*, I mean Mick and Keith were never quite happy with it and I agreed with them. You know, whether we should do this or maybe do it like *that*. So we had "Country Honk" as well. I only help them write songs, I don't actually write them.

NICKY HOPKINS: The very first thing I worked on was "We Love You," the single. I think it was about a month or two later we started on *Satanic Majesties*. At first it was very much just the band itself, and I would usually be the only extra musician on those sessions. Toward the late sixties, of course, that changed. On that first session I did in '67, Lennon and McCartney dropped by to put on background vocals and things like that. David Mason contributed quite a bit to *Beggars Banquet*. Then a few other people would drop in, and so on and so forth. Interestingly, at that point in time when I was playing with them, Ian [Stewart] didn't want to play. I don't know what was going with him because he has played pretty consistently on their albums, from the beginning right up to date.

MICK TAYLOR: I joined toward the end of *Let It Bleed*. They had recorded most of the backing tracks already and I did a few overdubs and participated in the actual making of a couple of backing tracks that ended up as songs on the album. It was very loose, very easy, very relaxed, and I sort of fitted in straightaway.

December 6, 1969. The Stones end their sixth North American tour with a free concert at the Altamont Speedway in California.

MICK TAYLOR: It was just meant to be a concert. We were in Florida when it was being organized by a bunch of San Francisco people and we liked the idea of doing a free concert in San Francisco, so we said, "Right, at the end of the tour we'll do this free concert." That's really as far as our involvement went. When we turned up that day, we just turned up to do a concert as we would any other concert. But as soon as we arrived I sensed a very strange atmosphere. There were lots of things going on. There were fights and Hells Angels members were throwing people off stage. That had been going on all day. I don't know why it was like that. Certainly it wasn't the Stones' fault, because we turned up there perhaps forty minutes before we went onstage, but in fact the violence was there the whole time.

MICK JAGGER: Altamont was a very nasty experience. I guess we have to take part of the blame because we didn't really check it out as well as we could, but it was left up to the people in San Francisco. They seemed like they were so mellow and nice and organized that it was going to be under control, but of course it wasn't. So I learned the lesson that you never do anything that you're not in control of. You've got to be so careful. Even though it wasn't our fault, it *was* in the sense that it was our show and we let other people make some important decisions. Still, it doesn't completely sully the tour for me because it was one bad show out of a whole tour.

Altamont was a big thing for a lot of people. They were blaming it on our image and it was some kind of "end of the innocence." They're still agonizing over it. "Did it mean something? . . . Does it really *mean* something?" [laughs]. It was pretty awful but I don't think it meant very much.

KEITH RICHARDS: The [Hells] Angels should never have been given the job. They were into this thing about, "Don't touch my chrome, man," but when you park your bike in front of a couple of hundred thousand people trying to crowd around a stage, you gotta know there's a good chance someone's going to touch it.

We just wanted to give a free concert, and we asked the [Grateful] Dead to help us because it's their area and they'd given a couple of free concerts, so we figured they knew. They put us together with these people who seemed pretty cool. We were in Alabama at Muscle Shoals working on the next record and left the arranging up to them. Then the municipal government or someone tried to shut them down and they had to move locations at the last minute. There just wasn't time to figure out the parking and the facilities. Once I heard the problems the [Jefferson] Airplane were having, I thought, "There's no turning back." Once the mood's gone bad, it's only going to get worse not better. Cancelling the show would have just made things worse still, so we did it.

In 1969 in America there was a potential anarchy going on. You had the war happening and the whole community was doing whatever it wanted. Hells Angels were running towns and counties because all the cops had been sent to the war. When I think of Altamont I always think to myself, "Thank God it was only that guy that died and maybe after all he asked for it." I mean, pulling a shooter out in front of acid-crazed Angels, you're asking for trouble. My big fear at that point was, "Is this going to escalate?" All I've got are these few lights and a mike and saying, "Cool it" [laughs]. And they did. They cooled right out, because otherwise the body count could have been really bad because there was nothing there to prevent it. Once it started, anything could have happened when you have half a million people there. So to me, it was a tragedy in a way, but at the same time it was kind of a triumph. Right there you were on the abyss . . . We were right there staring it in the face. That's why it was important that the movie [Gimme Shelter] came out, because everybody skidded to a halt right there and checked it out. It was almost like, "Okay, this is civilization." Either the veneer will come off right now and it could have been a bloodbath, or we'll get it back together. When I think about it, a baby was born, so there were the same number of people left that came in [laughs]. We'll never do anything like that again. Besides, rock just sounds better in a club with two hundred people.

SONNY BARGER: We were hired to keep people off the stage and that's what we did. When people start messing with our bikes, look out. Those things are worth a lot of money and when people start kickin' the most important thing in your life, you better believe we get upset. They're damn well gonna pay for it. They blame the Angels for what happened and that's crap. That guy Mick Jagger is full of shit. I would never work for those guys again.

ALBERT MAYSLES: We wanted to shoot the concert because we expected it to be a real love-in full of great music and people, but it turned out much different. Everybody started to blame the Rolling Stones for the problems and how it was their satanic image and all that nonsense. I know that they were all really affected by what happened, especially Mick.

July 30, 1970. The Stones end their relationship with Allen Klein. The next day the band's contract with Decca Records expires. It is not renewed.

DICK ROWE: At the time when we lost the Stones, I did say to myself, "I think we may have had the best of them," and I think we did. Certainly from a musical point of view we did. You see, none of us really knows what has gone on in the other record companies with regard to the Stones. How many records have they given away? How many have they returned? I don't think that when they left Decca any of the record companies made very much money. But the companies may have used them as a loss leader, because if you've got the Stones, then you can tempt other people to come and join your company. Lewis wasn't into that. He was not a great believer in losing money for any reason.

I don't think they're great songwriters in the classic sense. I doubt many of their songs will survive the centuries as well as some other writers'. They wrote for themselves and it was just that it was very right for the times. If they were great songwriters, by now it would show. Isn't there an expression—"You can't fool all of the public all of the time?" As far as the Stones are concerned, you wanna bet? [laughs].

September 4, 1970. Decca releases *Get Yer Ya-Ya's Out! The Rolling Stones in Concert*, its last Stones album (excluding compilations).

PETE TOWNSHEND: As far as I'm concerned, I think the Stones are really way back on top. I'm so knocked out. I know they probably lost two years of development, which would have made them just giants now, but it's so incredible that they can come bouncing back, which you can hear on their live album. I mean, it's not the greatest sound and it's not the greatest-sounding group, but there's all these dynamics and all those rough edges . . . the friction . . . The music is right there. I don't know how to put it, you just get the shiver up your spine. It's incredible. *Let It Bleed* is a masterpiece. It beats *Beggars Banquet*, which I thought would be very hard to do.

GLYN JOHNS: [The live album] was fairly straightforward. I think I recorded just the one concert at Madison Square Gardens. That was it for that album. I've recorded them all over the place, but I know that album was recorded in its entirety at Madison Square Gardens. It wasn't a mixture of different dates or anything. I was pleased with the results, yeah—it was good.

Jagger has always been an innovator when it comes to the live shows. He's the one that saw from almost the beginning that playing in these big halls could be a lot more fun if you dressed it up. Nowadays everybody does it and it's expected that you'll have a huge set and stage show, but Jagger was the guy that really pushed that. He always wanted the fans to feel they got a great deal more than just a set of music. It goes well beyond his obvious talent for singing or dancing.

September 18, 1970. Jimi Hendrix dies in London.

KEITH RICHARDS: I remember seeing Jimi in a club and he was brilliant, so I was really disappointed when his records started coming out and he was sort of stuck in "the English psychedelic bag" and then everybody started to expect that sound. I mean, that's what made him but it was also the thing that got him down just before he died. He just couldn't figure a way out of the expectations everyone had that he would do all these outlandish tricks onstage. He just wanted to concentrate on playing funky music, but he couldn't because it wasn't what people wanted to hear from him.

December 6, 1970. *Gimme Shelter*, the Maysles' film about Altamont, premiers in New York.
1971. On April 1, the Stones set up Rolling Stones Records to release all its future music. Marshall Chess from Chicago's Chess Records is the first president. On April 16, the company releases "Brown Sugar." On April 23, it releases *Sticky Fingers*.

JIMMY MILLER: Ry [Cooder] added a real polish to songs like "Love in Vain" and "Sister Morphine" that he played on. The Stones' rougher edges started to become less apparent around that time, and then Mick Taylor helped them keep in that vein.

Mick Taylor: Their degree of preparedness varied from album to album. On *Sticky Fingers*, most of the material had some shape or form before we went in. They never used to go into the studio without any ideas, but I can't remember any occasions when they would actually go into the studio with a completely finished song, with words and everything. Most of the time we'd just be jamming and playing riffs and the tape would be rolling and then we'd listen back to things and say, "Why don't we work on that and make it a bit different?" That's how a lot of songs developed. That's not how their best songs developed, though. Their best songs I would say were two-thirds written before they were even touched by the rest of the band.

Marianne Faithfull: I wrote the words to "Sister Morphine," so Mick produced a record that I made of it. It was banned immediately, of course, and that version never really came out, but I sang the B side on *Rock'n'Roll Circus*. It was very nice. Ry Cooder was on the session. It was a lovely, lovely record.

I spent a long time trying to get away from Mick. I kept sort of leaving and coming back and leaving and coming back. Then eventually I left, and withdrew completely from the whole thing. I went to live in the country with my son and my mother and I stayed there for years and years. I came back to London in about '75.

Keith Richards: *Sticky Fingers* was where it first hit me that there was a real change happening. When we started recording it was all about having, as I've said, a red-hot single every couple of months. We were really in the business of turning teenage girls on. Then the album became the centrepiece. It was the main thing, and singles were just what helped sell it.

"Wild Horses" was inspired by [son] Marlon. Yeah, it was time to leave for a tour of America and I really didn't want to leave him. He was just a couple of months old and "Daddy has to go off to work." I mean, it's a cliché, right, but it's still tough to go.

April 1971. The Rolling Stones become tax exiles from Britain.

Keith Richards: No, no, they didn't try to get rid of us for the good of public morality. They just priced us out. They said, "It's going to cost you a half a million pounds a year to live here." "But I was born here." [In a low American voice] "I'm sorry, son, you're too young to vote" [laughs]. Citizenship and residency takes a subtle shift in meaning. I have a British passport but I'm a nonresident. I'm a Jamaican resident—that's my residency.

But I guess you'd say we made the best of it. We had a great time. We were all on the French Riviera in these great houses and speedboats, lots of women around and we cut *Exile* [*on Main Street*] in my basement. Then we got our own plane for a tour, which sure beat sitting in the back of a van with amplifiers crashing onto your head. It was a pretty wild tour.

BILL WYMAN: That was horrible . . . I didn't really want to go, but we were advised that it was the only way to sort out our financial affairs, which were disastrous at that time. We'd been a top band for eight years and none of us had any money. None of us—I really mean it— and we owed money to the Inland Revenue. There was no way we could make enough money, because if we were going to earn the kind of money to get ourselves out of trouble, we'd be paying like 93 percent tax and there was no way we could earn enough to pay back what we owed. So it was essential that we went.

I remember the drive to the airport, leaving England, and it was spring and the flowers were coming out, and I was thinking, "Jesus, it's the last time I'm going to see this road for two years, and wow, I'm not going to see any English roses." Really silly things like that. It was horrible leaving, and I was really convinced I wasn't going to like France, and I was convinced that the moment I could, I would leave. I didn't like French people, and I went there with an attitude and I stuck to that attitude for almost two years. Then I started to make friends and enjoy the climate and the food.

JIMMY MILLER: I just did the same thing I did the previous summer with Traffic, where the band moved into a secluded cottage in Berkshire together so they could concentrate on their music. I would go and join them for a few days at a time and help them develop musical ideas. It was the same with the Stones. They just lived together and played together and developed their own musical ideas.

KEITH ALTHAM: [Keith Richards has] definitely got a kind of thing that he's got to live up to now, which is quite amusing, actually, because he doesn't have to with me. I still think of him as a human being rather than the "Keith Richard" caricature that is so pervasive. I mean, an awful lot of people have come to grief trying to . . . join in his lifestyle. First thing they don't realize is that Keith Richards has the constitution of a rhinoceros. The second thing they don't realize is that Keith has had a lot of experience in abusing himself in one way or another over the years and he knows now quite clearly how far he can go and what he should, could, and cannot do. There are people who seem to believe that anything can go, and they believe that's the way Keith Richards lives, and it's not true. Keith Richards is far smarter than they give him credit for. You've only got to talk to the man for ten minutes to know that you're not dealing with a vegetable mentality. He's very, very sharp indeed.

MICK TAYLOR: Before I joined the Rolling Stones I never really thought of myself as a lead guitarist. Nobody used to say lead guitarist or solo guitarist or rhythm guitarist in those days. I learned a hell of a lot about playing rhythm guitar and about accompanying other people from Keith. In fact, his style of guitar playing has rubbed off on me in lots of ways that I didn't realize at the time. Not so much in a technical way but in terms of feel and sound, and especially rhythm.

May 12, 1971. Mick marries the twenty-one-year-old daughter of a Nicaraguan diplomat, Bianca Perez Morena de Macias, in Saint Tropez. Among the attendees are Paul McCartney, Ringo Starr, Eric Clapton, Bobby Keyes, Steven Stills, and Nicky Hopkins. A musical jam lasts until 4 a.m.

EVA JAGGER: I hope my other son doesn't become a superstar.

May 12, 1972. The Stones release *Exile on Main Street* one month after releasing "Tumbling Dice."

BILL WYMAN: Critics always like to give the Stones bad reviews. One day they're going to be right. They just haven't been right so far, because we always manage—I don't mean to be conceited, but we always manage—to come up with the goods, and the public seem to like it and buy it. Then three years later the reviewers turn around and say, "Yeah, that was a great album," after saying at the time, "It was a load of old shit." Most of them did that with Exile, and came back and said it was probably one of the greatest albums or packages that the Stones had ever put out. So what? [laughs]. I don't care what they say anymore.

MICK JAGGER: It was a difficult period because we were fighting the tax department and Allen Klein as well. We recorded about half of it at Keith's place in the south of France. It wasn't the best experience for me. It was the height of the drug period and with everyone living in the same place it was too much. France was all right but it's difficult to keep in touch with the music scene. No bands ever come through, so you either like Jacques Brel or nothing.

KEITH RICHARDS: "Happy" was something I did because for once I was early for a session. Bobby Keys was there and Jimmy Miller and we were in the south of France. It was at the time of recording Exile, so there was nothing to do and I had suddenly just picked up the guitar and played that riff. So we cut it, and it's the record. We cut the original track with a baritone sax, a guitar, and Jimmy Miller on drums. The rest of it is built up over the top of that track. It was just an afternoon jam that everybody said, "Wow . . . yeah . . . Let's work on it."

June 3, 1972. The Stones begin their North American tour in Vancouver. The tour has its share of problems, some of them violent.

KEITH RICHARDS: The thing is that you do have to take responsibility, if it's the Stones tour . . . Anything negative that happens on that is—from a media point of view and from a mass point of view—attributed to you. It's like what happened in Cincinnati. God forbid it should ever happen again for The Who. "Oh yeah, it's The Who's job to take the can [blame] for that." What do they know about whether it's festival seating or there's plateglass doors or the crowd was wild? You expect the promoter [to consider all that], they've done shows there every week. They should know what they're doing, but at the same time you have to be aware of the fact that anything goes wrong, it's not Frank the local Mafia promoter that gets the crap, it's the name that's on the marquee, of course . . . You don't go out in the world and put your name on marquees without accepting that responsibility.

As far as I'm concerned, promoters are beautiful, but I'm sure they're not beautiful to every act. It's worth their while to be beautiful to me. Promoters are like the rest of the world, they're the best and the worst of everything [laughs]. To me, they're sweethearts. They might not be great to the first band on the bill, or the next act that comes along. We always see everyone on their best behaviour, fawning around us, but I'm well aware of that.

July 17, 1972. A bomb destroys part of an equipment truck before the Stones' Montreal show.

NICKY HOPKINS: I wasn't with them for Altamont, but after that I think everyone was a little bit hesitant that something like that might occur again. In fact, we did get caught up in something in Montreal—one of the equipment trucks was blown up. There was a bomb in it, but it had nothing really to do with the Stones, it was just because of the political goings on there at the time.

July 26, 1972. The Stones finish up their American tour at Madison Square Gardens. In celebration of Mick's birthday, pies are thrown onstage.

KEITH RICHARDS: Well, everybody else got hit. I'm all against slapstick humour even though there was a good excuse for it. The only notable point being that with all that crap flying around the stage, I didn't get hit by a single thing, if you may notice. We have a film of it. I said, "You dare throw one thing . . . One thing hits me baby, and that's the end of the show" [laughs]. Miraculously, things were flying around and nothing hit me. I was well happy, so I thought it was a great laugh.

The celebrations continue at a party thrown by Atlantic Records president Ahmet Ertegun at the rooftop lounge of the St. Regis Hotel.

KEITH RICHARDS: It was a party for the Rolling Stones. It was a gathering of New York socialites, some of whom I like, same as any other group of people, and some of whom I don't. It was an organized affair, and after you finished a gig you don't always feel like complying with the organization. That's nothing new. It's one example of me leaving a party early [laughs]. That tour was noted for celebrities hanging around. We had a great time "taking the mickey" out of them [making fun of them]. In fact, I would say we owed a lot of our initial success to the support from that stratum of society. They were the first ones who flocked to our gigs at Carnegie. I mean c'mon, you come over from England and one of the first gigs you play is New York's Carnegie Hall! You're like, "Wow . . . I've made it." It's like some comedian from Vegas getting to play the London Palladium. That meeting of society people had been going on for years. They thought we were very chic from the minute we got to New York in '64. We had them all over the place and it made us very blasé for a bit. All these rich meat-canning millionaires and their girlfriends— ". . . so I'll just take your girlfriend out and show her the sites, okay?" I mean, it was handy.

MICK TAYLOR: When I first joined them their career hadn't been looked after properly, their business affairs were in total disarray. Mick's always been a very ambitious person, and he wanted to get back out on the road with a new guitarist and a new band and make lots of albums, and reactivate the whole thing, because he felt they'd become a bit out of touch with the times, a bit stagnant. So, that's exactly what we did. I guess that by1974 they were beginning to think of themselves by their own standards as successful . . . financially, I mean. When I was with them, compared to other people they were wealthy, but still it wasn't enough for them. There were still goals to be achieved.

CHARLIE WATTS: At the end of the 1972 tour I said, "I've just had enough." I was tired of living out of suitcases all the time and it was a pretty crazy tour, so I just wanted out. I needed a break, and then I was okay again.

1973. On August 31, the Stones release *Goat's Head Soup* ten days after releasing "Angie." On October 24, Keith is fined £205 and given a conditional discharge for four drug and three firearms charges arising from a raid on his Chelsea home. Anita is given a conditional discharge. On December 2, work begins on "It's Only Rock and Roll."

RON WOOD: I got to know Mick and Keith because I had a studio in my house. Yeah, Keith was there more or less at the outset on my first album *I Got My Own Album to Do* in 1974. My ex-wife invited him back to the house because he was trying to avoid these people at a club called Tramp. She said, "Why don't you come back to the house? Ronnie's making his album." So he whizzed back, thinking whatever he was thinking, but he did stay four months . . . solid! And he worked diligently on the album and we put some good stuff together.

Mick used to like my basement studio in Richmond, because it was a good escape for him, a good change of scenery. And he knew it didn't cost him or me any money [laughs]. I think that's why I got into staying up so late, because I had the studio in my basement and I thought, "Why sleep?" Think of all the money in studio bills I'm saving just being in here [laughs].

Anyway, Mick and I worked on "I Can Feel the Fire," and after we'd done that, he said "Help me with this song I'm working on." So "It's Only Rock and Roll" began on the Tuesday evening with Mick and I. Mick sang a guide vocal and David Bowie and myself were on backup vocals. I overdubbed the rest of the instruments afterwards and it sounded like a good demo. The next night we wanted to put it into more presentable shape, so we got hold of Kenny Jones, who plays drums on the actual record. I ended up just with my acoustic guitar that I'd laid originally. Keith replaced—and rightfully so!—my electric guitar tracks.

May 1974. Bill Wyman releases his first solo record, *Monkey Grip*.

BILL WYMAN: It was just a fun album to make with some mates. It's frustrating having ideas and not being able to put them to any use, so I decided to do it on my own with as many people that I really admired that would come and play with me. It wasn't easy. It was done in and around other Stones' work.

1974. On July 26, the Stones release "It's Only Rock and Roll." On October 18, they release the album of the same name.

KEITH RICHARDS: Writing with Mick is getting easier again. In the early sixties we were writing face to face because we were always on the road or in the studio. Later on when the Stones had to leave England we started to live all over the world, so Mick and I had to find a new way to write, which took us quite a while. You can tell in the records, after *Exile* and *Goat's Head Soup* we had to get used to writing apart and then trying to put it all together when we got together. It was difficult. You couldn't get an idea and then just call up Mick and say, "I'll be over in ten minutes with something to work on." That's tough when he's three thousand miles away.

December 13, 1974. The Stones announce that Mick Taylor has left the band.

RON WOOD: I was there with Mick and Mick Taylor the night he told Jagger he was leaving. There was a party at Robert Stigwood's place [on December 4 after an Eric Clapton concert], and Mick came up to me and said, "Mick Taylor's leaving. What am I going to do? Will you join us?" And I said, "You know I'd love to, but I'm not going to split the Faces up." And he said, "I understand that—I don't want to split them up either." I said, "Well, what can I say, I'll try and help you as much as I can. I don't know who you're going to get, though. If you get really desperate, ring me up." A few months later, he found me in L.A. while they were recording in Munich, and he said, "I'm desperate, Woody." So I went over there and carried on the next stage of the recording with them.

MICK TAYLOR: I was actually getting very bored with the inactivity and lack of direction. The whole time I was with them, except for about the last year, we seemed to be touring all the time—I think it was three American tours, which really is quite a lot by their standards. If we weren't touring America we'd be touring England, Europe, Australia, or somewhere, or we'd be recording.

Then nothing happened. The whole band seemed to be falling apart. It obviously wasn't as bad as I thought it was, but for a whole year we just didn't really do anything. We didn't see each other, and nothing was happening. I think there were all sorts of things going on, that were absolutely nothing to do with the band and being on the road and making records, which interfered with relationships within the band. That was one of the reasons why I was looking for something else to do, and I met Jack Bruce and thought it would be good idea to get a band together with him.

Nowadays the Stones are a much more relaxed kind of band, and when they're together they enjoy it. They're in a position now to be able to get together whenever they want, and when they're not together they have their own lives and do other things. It wasn't really like that when I was with them. It might sound strange to say this, but it was a constant struggle to keep the band going and to keep the inspiration going and to keep doing the albums. Even though they'd been together so long and perhaps to other people they were living legends as they are now, and they'd made it, and they couldn't possibly go any higher or any further, they didn't actually feel like that. They had all sorts of financial problems and drug problems and goodness knows what else. They were struggling all the time. They really were, and it was hard to make some of those albums. It was a very frustrating period, but you see they've grown up a lot and they've got through that.

If I'd been a bit older, I don't think I would have left. I don't regret that I left, but because I hadn't been involved with them from the beginning, there was much more of a sense of urgency about me needing to do something else. Whereas with the rest of them, they always knew inside themselves, no matter how difficult or how crazy things got, they'd always be together and get through it.

CHAPTER 6
Woody

GLYN JOHNS: Quite obviously, Brian was very instrumental in the Stones' early days. When he was replaced by Mick Taylor the band changed tremendously. Although Mick Taylor was a brilliant guitar player, it was the first two-thirds of the Mick Taylor era that was fantastic. Then it really went downhill and I had no time for him. They changed him tremendously, or the situation changed him tremendously, from being a meek, mild, extremely polite, inoffensive young man with what appeared to be no ego whatsoever who always was as frustrated as I was by the amount of time recording sessions took. Taylor would come and hear a song and he could play it immediately, and that would be it. He wasn't used to sitting for three days being asked to play the same solo over and over again and everyone expecting it to be wonderful. The last time I saw him he'd become worse than any of them. Unbelievable. Spending hours and hours and hours on things and it was all about himself. He didn't think about the band at all.

The last thing I did with him was a mix—he'd asked me to come in and mix something for an album. He walked into the control room and the first thing he did was want to hear each of the tracks he was on, and I said, "Well, I'm not using the drums, for a start-off." And he said, "What do you mean, you're not using the drums?" And I said, "Well, what the fuck do I want to use those for? There's a drummer in this band, and I'm using him. I think you've got a damn bloody liberty overdubbing drums on a Rolling Stones record, when you've got one of the finest drummers in the world playing with you. How fucking dare you!" As you can imagine, that didn't go over well, and I said, "Well, either you fuck off home or I will, one or the other, 'cause I am not bloody doing anything with you in here." So off he went and I wouldn't use his bass either. What a liberty, what a bloody liberty!

RON WOOD: Yeah, Muddy Waters used to think I was a member of the Stones, way back when I was in my first group in England. I used to walk into a club called the Speakeasy on Margaret Street and Muddy would be in there and he'd come running over—"Hey, it's the Rolling Stones!"—and he'd pick me up and hug me. Of course, he thought I was Keith, as usual. That's not as bad as Junior Wells, though. I said hello to him three times in the same night. He said a brand new hello each time because he thought I was somebody different. Muddy always used to think I was in the Stones, and then I finally met him soon after joining and he went through the same thing, and I said, "Yes, I'm one of them now, Muddy," but he didn't get it.

We had a very sporadic chain of rare meetings. Each time I met up with the Stones they'd always give me a good feeling and I always felt tremendously powerful and confident.

Maybe it was all the women, but it was a good feeling. I remember one specific meeting the Stones and the Faces had at the Beverly Wiltshire Hotel, which is why I can't get back in there anymore. Not that we did any damage there on purpose. It's just the general wear and tear on the room during that night and day when Keith and Rod [Stewart] and I, Mick and Mack [Ian McLagan] and Ronnie Lane and Kenny [Jones] hung around. I didn't see Bill or Charlie—I don't think they were around, actually. I had this massive room with mirrors all over it, and I think everyone was so busy avoiding bumping into these mirrors, they didn't realize the amount of pile there was building up on the carpet [laughs]. It was like an expectant father's rug. It was a good excuse for the hotel to sort of get mad at us—"Well, look what you did last time you stayed here." I'm only harping on this so long, because it's the story of my life now, everywhere we go.

If there's more than a couple of us staying in the same hotel, not previously arranged for by a logistics expert like Alan Dunn, they just think, "Here comes trouble." If they just cleaned up first, then assessed the room, it would be all right. But the rooms do look kind of disastrous. I know Keith shouldn't share my rooms or I shouldn't share his rooms so often, because we both walk in the same direction and wear the same bit out on the carpet. Then there's the occasional stumble when we burn a hold in the carpet, or if we're talking and looking the other way, a big hole in the carpet [laughs].

December 1974. The Stones begin recording *Black and Blue* in Germany.

GLYN JOHNS: Yes, well, I'd already stopped working with the Stones three years prior to that after *Exile*, on which I only did bits and pieces. I'd left them and gone off and done my own thing for many years and I'd had a reasonable degree of success producing things for Steve Miller, Led Zeppelin, the Eagles, and others. So when Mick asked me to come back and work with the band, I said, "Fine, but I want to co-produce with you. I wouldn't presume to be your producer. I don't think anyone has ever been your producer in the literal sense of it. I would want to co-produce with you and I would want to write." And he said, "You're mad. Why on earth should we give you a royalty?" "Well, the reason is because in fact, I deserve one, and if you don't think so, that's fine, but don't expect me to turn up." He said, "I'll pay you," and he offered me some enormous sum of money, and I said, "No, I don't want an enormous sum of money, I want what is rightfully mine, which is a royalty, however small and it will probably end up being less than the amount you're offering me now." He said "no way" and I said, "Fine, goodbye."

Then I was sitting in Woody's kitchen one day after a Faces session and Mick came round, and he said, "Oh, I'm glad I'm seeing you—I was looking for you." I said, "Really. Why?" He said, "Well, I've got to go to New York tomorrow.

What are you doing? Can you come with me?" So I said, "What on earth for?" So he said, "Well, I've got do this black box album for Allen Klein and we have to go through all these old tapes and as you did most of them, you'll know them and you'll help me. Just three days." I said "okay" and I went with him and went through the tapes, and we went out for a drink in New York, and he started again about going back to working with him. So I said, "I'll tell you what we'll do, I'll do it without any kind of deal at all. If I don't finish the record you can have the record as a gift, but if I finish it, I shall want a co-production credit. I will prove to you that I can co-produce the band." So he said "okay" and I went and did *Black and Blue*.

We started the record in Germany. The night before we started, Mick Taylor left the band. As far as I was concerned, that was the best thing that could have happened, because I couldn't stand him anyway, and I knew he was going to be the one problem. Also, the five of us—as it turned out to be—getting back together as the original crew if you like, on our own with Nicky Hopkins and Stew, was fantastic. It was just like the old days without Brian. We cut eleven tracks in just under two weeks. We overdubbed on a lot of them. They got on quicker than they had done before. We had a great time, the material was pretty good, and then we broke for Christmas.

Then they said they wanted to continue in Rotterdam, with the Stones' mobile in some hall, and I foolishly agreed to go. I don't think I was being given any option. As it turns out, it was some deal aimed at saving money. That was when they started auditioning people. They were unequivocally the worst, most boring sessions I think I have ever attended in my life. They were going through the phase of turning up at two in the morning instead of eight, and I can't be bothered with all that. I didn't mind the fact that they were trying out guitar players—they obviously had to do that. I recommended Wayne Perkins, which was not such a clever idea, really, because although he's a great guitar player, he's not English, and it should have been an Englishman. It's the reason why he didn't get the gig. Anyway, one night I had a terrible row with Keith, and I told him to jack it up his rear end, and I split. I didn't finish the album and I've never worked with them since, and that's fine with me!

RON WOOD: In Munich they checked me into a room between Jeff Beck, Wayne Perkins, and Harvey Mandel—no, Jeff had already gone. He said he couldn't handle three chords all the time, but boy can he! I went straight into Musicland in Munich and got on with it.

Being chosen for the band was a great compliment for me, but I don't take it that there was any kind of competition involved. Wayne is a very nice, melodic player and a great guy. Harvey is a real amazing player and I'm not in his league, but I think the job demands other things. I knew what they needed, and that was someone who could play well when he's in the hot seat, and play really well when he's in an even hotter seat. Most important of all, though, was to be English and to be able to travel and live with them. That's the most important thing because you've got to be able to get on with each other.

KEITH RICHARDS: Well, it was just up in the air, not between anybody, it was just up in the air generally. As much as we liked Wayne [Perkins], we liked Jeff Beck. I mean, they were all there—even Segovia tried out [laughs]. *Black and Blue* is a record of all that, except it's mostly Wayne and Harvey [Mandell] apart from myself and a bit of Ronnie. The sessions were essentially auditions with an endless stream of guitar players. The fact of the matter is that Harvey and Wayne were there and we were all working together to see what would be best. When Ronnie came in, it was really Harvey and Wayne who said, "He's the one." It wasn't even the Stones. Everybody agreed, even the guys who were looking for the job. "It's obvious man—it's English rock-'n'roll, and you need that combination, that connection, and that closeness of where you come from to keep it really together." Everybody loved Wayne but we had this incredibly important thing and that is that this is an English band and the communication is a certain way, and the way it works is because everybody comes from within a radius of twenty miles of each other. And the minute Ronnie appeared out of the blue it was obvious that it had to stay that way. This is not a band that you can hire musicians from other parts of the world. You need that certain communication that doesn't have to be spoken, doesn't have to be explained. You can give somebody a wink and a nod in a certain way, and if you do it in another way it means something entirely different. It saves a lot of time and trouble and it still kept the Stones for what the Stones really are, which is an English band, for better or worse.

May 1, 1975. The Stones announce their upcoming American tour by driving down Fifth Avenue in New York on the back of a flatbed truck, playing "Brown Sugar."

MICK JAGGER: Charlie was telling me about the old days in Harlem where the jazz guys would sometimes promote their shows by playing a couple of songs on the back of a flatbed truck. So we thought that would be a great way to announce our tour.

RON WOOD: I learned a lot under pressure. We rehearsed for two months or more in Montauk, Long Island, and I remember learning about a hundred and fifty of their repertoire. I gave up trying to learn which key each one was in or the chord sequences to a lot of them. I did a lot of it by feel in the end. I had to—it's impossible to log all of those songs. Although I was familiar with them, and a lot of them were my favourite songs anyway, I'd never played along, I'd never sat at home and strummed along. The things like "Wild Horses" and "Angie"—any songs of theirs that had a minor, shall we say, deviation from the twelve-bar sequence—were quite complicated.

I think I knew where they were coming from. The whole approach of "nothing need be said unless it's real important"—in other words, the whole thing to being a part of the band, I suppose, is just sliding in and asking no questions.

KEITH RICHARDS: Oh yeah, that phallic balloon thing was like a millstone around our neck. Police chiefs were waiting for it all over America. [Southern drawl] "You blow that balloon up big and I'll throw the whole damn bunch in jail" [laughs]. It was like a dare. And we said, "We're not going to back down, are we?" Somewhere down in Texas—San Antonio, I think—they were going to pull the plug on us and ruin the show for everybody. So you give and take. Mostly take [laughs].

PETER RUDGE: It's almost like going in the army. You get into a routine that requires a discipline that doesn't allow you a chance to relax in a real sense. Consequently what happens is all these incredible stories one hears about smashed rooms and outrageous parties. These people really are in jail. It's almost like that.

You're completely under the microscope. Every time you step into the lobby there are fifty people waiting for you—

press, photographers, fans, groupies, whatever. The big thing is to find out where they're staying, find out under what name Mick Jagger is staying, find out what restaurant they ate in for the local columnist. It's a very uncomfortable feeling and therefore you start to look inward to yourselves. The only time you feel you can have any privacy is when you lock yourself in your room. It's very intense because a Stones tour is more than just a rock'n'roll tour—it's a social event.

February 28, 1976. The Stones announce that Ron Wood is a permanent member of the band.

RON WOOD: I remember doing three tours that year [1975]. I did a Faces tour in the early part of the year, then I hooked up with the Stones on June 1st in Baton Rouge, and after that I went back with Faces. You see, Mick and the boys didn't want to split Faces up, and I didn't want to split them up either, although the Stones were always my first musical love as a unit. Faces was a very, very enjoyable band, but my heart was always with the Stones. I was in Switzerland after the second Faces tour that year, deep in thought, and I was thinking, "What do I do, what do I do?" Suddenly I get an English paper and it says, "Stewart quits the band, and is forming his own group." So that was tailor-made for me to join the Stones.

KEITH RICHARDS: Ronnie had to inject himself into the mainstream of the Stones in the early days, but it was only temporary at the time. He did his Faces tour right after ours. Then Rod screwed him, and it was all over for the Faces— sorry Rod, you'll sleep better at nights knowing everybody knows [laughs]. Hedda Hopper speaking . . . [laughs].

RON WOOD: When you're touring, you don't have time to get ill. It's the last thing on your mind. You've got all these commitments and you gotta put a great show on even if you feel terrible. You have to pull it together and by the time you get on stage you feel brand new again.

I do remember one occasion in Dortmund [Germany] on the '76 European tour, I was really ill. I had this terrible kind of flu, the kind where you couldn't move, and it was my birthday as well, June 1st. You know those little chairs that golfers have? I wanted one of those badly, because I could hardly stand up. I remember we were doing "Midnight Rambler" and everything was a blur to me. I was just getting through the show, and "Well, you heard about the Boston . . ." and Mick gets that belt and goes "whack" on the stage floor, usually. The second break comes along and I had my eyes closed. Mick takes the belt and goes *whack* right across the back of my legs, and there's this excruciating pain, and I said, "You . . . !" And he said, "Wake up! I did it to wake you up." It sure worked, because I was so mad the rest of the show that it made me forget about this flu thing I had. When I got back to the hotel I just locked all the doors and fell into bed. Of course I had got champagne and everything laid on in the room. All these big trays of booze and stuff. So while I was asleep, being the nice boys that they are, Keith and Mick took my door off its hinges—because it was locked—and they came in and relieved me of all my champagne and everything [laughs].

1976. In April, the Stones release "Fool to Cry." On April 20, they release _Black and Blue_. On August 21, they play in front of two hundred thousand paying fans at Knebworth Fair. Rumours are circulating that this will be their final performance.

Ron Wood: It's a lovely country house called Knebworth Park. It's an old English mansion with beautiful grounds, and two hundred thousand people on that land is no sweat at all. When we [the New Barbarians] did it with Zeppelin in '79 there must have been over that each day they played there. The Stones in '76 were only the second group to play it after Pink Floyd played it in '75, right? It was nothing to do with the band's last concert. I'm surprised that so much weight was put on the "it's their last concert" at that time, because those kinds of rumours had been going on before then, all through the 1975 tour, and they continue today.

I think the band can only stay together. Otherwise everyone will get lonely, despondent, get into things they shouldn't be doing, form offshoot groups, make solo albums . . . [laughs].

KEITH RICHARDS: I was sort of busy on junk at the time "punk" happened in '76. I was sort of on the periphery of life. I just thought, "What else is new?"

February 25, 1977. While in Toronto for rehearsals in preparation for a club gig to complete *Love You Live*, Mick and Ronnie go on a reconnaissance mission.

PAT JOYCE: One of our doormen came over and said, "Guess who's in the upstairs bar?" I said, "Barbra Streisand," and he said, "No, Mick Jagger and Ron Wood." I said, "I don't believe you." Half an hour later I turned around and seated at the bar were Mick Jagger and Ron Wood. My knees started shaking and my heart started thumping because I'd been a fan for quite a few years. The amazing thing was that no one rushed them for autographs. People just looked at them and thought, "Could it really be them?"

February 27, 1977. Keith is arrested by the RCMP and charged with possession of heroin for the purposes of trafficking and possession of cocaine.

KEITH RICHARDS: They couldn't wake me up to arrest me. Yes, it's true. A couple of RCMP tried, then I think they changed shifts and five other guys came to carry on and try to wake me up [laughs].

That was really the bottom, in Toronto. Things were

pretty bad. You know—"What's going to happen to the band? What's going to happen to me?" And then the establishment holds out its hand and offers me a medical visa to come in and clean up. The last thing I expected was help from the government in America, but they came through and saved my ass.

Cold turkey's hard, but it's only three days of climbing walls and then you start to feel better. After that it's up to you, and what do you want to do with your life? I got off the junk after that. But after ten years on that stuff, it's not easy. You live in another world and everybody you know is a junkie. It's still everywhere and cats are still trying to sell you stuff again . . . My high for a while was watching their faces when I said "no." They'd be saying, "Hey, man, just have a taste," and I'd say no. They were like, "No? How can you say no? You're a junkie." Just watching their faces would be my high. Best thing I ever did.

March 4 and 5, 1977. The Stones play two surprise shows at the El Mocambo in Toronto to record more material for *Love You Live*.

REGGIE BOVAIRD: Friday afternoon we were still open for business to the general public, and I went to the fine wine store to buy all these exotic wines. When I got back I went upstairs to the main bar and the Stones were doing a sound check in the middle of the afternoon. I looked down toward the back and the rear door was wide open. Anybody could have walked in off the street. Peter Rudge, the manager at the time, came running up to me screaming, screaming, and he says, "Do you realize the back door is wide open and there's nobody there watching it?" I said, "I'm sorry but I can't be everywhere at the same time. I had to go get the wine." He says, "Okay, okay, I know you're trying."

KEITH RICHARDS: Yeah, that was enjoyable, except for the Mounties [laughs]. I was framed!

RON WOOD: One of the things I can contribute is perhaps to give them a kick up the ass with a reminder, like I did at the El Mocambo. I made them play "Come On," "Little Red Rooster," all their first songs, and lots of the old favourites like "King Bee" that I used to remember them doing. "Johnny Be Good," "Little Queenie," "Let's Spend the Night Together," "Time Is on My Side," "Play with Fire"—you name it. I felt very pleased with the fact that nobody said, "We can't do that one, it's too old." They just went straight into them. They knew the chords, the keys, and everything . . . If you didn't, you could refer to the manual.

PAUL McGRATH: None of us in the press knew what was going on until a couple of hours before the show. There had been some rumours on the grapevine but it wasn't until we were all called to the Windsor Arms Hotel and told where we were going that we knew what was up. We were driven in two limousines behind the police lines set up around the El Mocambo and up to the back entrance. The place was already packed. Within two minutes of the Stones' first chords every sacred El Mocambo rule had been broken. People were standing on the tables, beer was flying through the air, joints were flared up everywhere—I mean *everywhere*. It was the only time in ten years I saw the El Mocambo staff unable to enforce the code—there was nothing they could do. Even the cops seemed to understand—that if they pressed the button, anything could happen. And they didn't want to find out what it could be.

It truly was the world turned upside down for a night— a transcendent musical experience. The Toronto audience knew it but the rest of the world never will because the excitement that's captured on *Love You Live* is only a fraction of the spunk and the fire that was in the band for those two nights.

REGGIE BOVAIRD: When they did the shows the place was completely surrounded by police. You couldn't get near the building. They were on the roofs; the front of the building was cordoned off. It was amazing. I think they captured what they were looking for although the first night the crowd went so crazy it was total pandemonium. Nobody could believe it; they were just in awe. After the show a few people asked for autographs. They were very, very nice and congenial. A few vodkas later everybody was having a great time, and then they left and I waved at them—"Thank you, Mr. Jagger, for coming."

PRIME MINISTER PIERRE ELLIOTT TRUDEAU: So a woman [wife Margaret Trudeau] goes to a rock concert, and then visits friends in New York to do some photography. I don't think she can be faulted for disappointing the Canadian people or rocking the dollar. If that's the way the media react and the people react as a result I suppose that's too bad. I guess it's the price you pay for being in politics.

I certainly wouldn't tell Margaret not to go to a concert of the Stones or anyone else. Whether on some other front they're accused of kidnapping or drug trafficking or anything else. If she wants to go to a rock concert, that's her choice. We've been to several rock concerts together at the [National] Arts Centre. I don't expect her to stop going to concerts or to stop visiting friends in New York just because some people will be misled into thinking she's not behaving properly.

1977. On April 1, Keith Richards and Anita Pallenberg enter treatment for heroin addiction under Dr. Margaret Paterson. On September 23, the Stones release *Love You Live*, a double live album recorded at concerts in Europe, England, and Toronto.
1978. On May 14, Bianca Jagger sues for divorce. In early June, the Stones release "Miss You" as a single. A week later, on June 9, they release *Some Girls*. Singles from that album, besides

"Miss You," include "Beast of Burden," "Respectable," and "Shattered." Mick Jagger describes *Some Girls* as the best album they've done since *Let It Bleed*.

KEITH RICHARDS: Mick's got a big mouth, you might have noticed that. That's why we use his logo on the label. He'll say things like that [about *Some Girls*] and in a way there's a point to it, but I think we've done some things that are worth considering, between *Let It Bleed* and *Some Girls*. I love the way people say, "The band went through a fallow period in the early seventies," because at the same time you're talking about *Exile on Main Street* and *Black and Blue*. What they're really talking about is the way [those albums] were received at the time, rather than the actual content. If you look at the reviews at the time for *Exile on Main Street*, it got panned. Almost *en masse*. If you want to talk about bad reviews, you got it baby . . . in spades. Then six years later the same guys that wrote those reviews are mauling *Black and Blue* and saying they can't make 'em like *Exile on Main Street*. You flip back through the years and find this guy is the one that wrote the review on that and he hated that one too. So I love reviews. I'm like a kid with a comic strip with them . . . and then I go round and murder the guy [laughs].

The main reason *Some Girls* was so much better was that I'd kicked junk. We hadn't been in the studio for a long time and everybody, including most of the Stones, was thinking, "Oh, Keith's finally rode himself into the dirt." We got it together for that thanks to the incentive the Canadians [RCMP] had given me [laughs] to keep myself in the black. I did the necessary thing and then we just threw ourselves together. It's another one of those impossible things to put your finger on. It was a great studio—it was the first time that we'd worked with [Chris] Kimsey, who is one in a long line of Olympic Studios—that's in England, folks, for you that don't know—tea boys who have always been our best engineers. Keith Harwood was another but he didn't spend enough on tires for his MG and rubbed himself out on the M-4. Kimsey was another one in that tradition from Glyn and Andy Johns, and it all came together very nicely. Also, you've got to remember, it was Ronnie's first full album with the Stones. We'd had the experience of playing together on stage for a couple of years. We'd done tours in '75, '76, and Ronnie arrived for the last couple of overdubs on *Black and Blue*. *Some Girls* was kind of like *Beggars Banquet*. We'd been away for a bit and we came back with a bang.

CHRIS KIMSEY: The *Some Girls* sessions were good sessions. That was the first time that I'd worked with the band, engineering for them. I met them during *Sticky Fingers* when Glyn Johns was working with them and I was assisting Glyn. There were a few nights Glyn couldn't make it, so I would take care of doing the vocal overdubs and things of that sort. I didn't meet them again until *Some Girls*, when Ian Stewart called me up one day—I'd just arrived back in England from the States—and the phone rang and Stew said, "Mick and Keith would like you to come do the new album in Paris." That's how it started. Since then we've been working together all the time. It's a real good relationship now.

Yeah, there's a very special way that they work. A lot of engineers can't deal with it because the Stones just do and feel things when they want to. There's no reason why they should set a time limit to themselves or anything, and not a lot of people can deal with that. A lot of people are so regimented, like you have to record from ten until six, or from seven o'clock until six in the morning, but why? And if you tell the Stones that, then they definitely won't do it. It will be completely the opposite [laughs].

"Some Girls," the title track, was twenty-three minutes long originally. It was so long it took up a whole reel of tape! It just went on and on and on, and if you watch the master go by after I'd edited it down you can't see any black tape. You just see all my editing tape [laughs]. Actually, that is one of the things I really enjoy about working with the band. When they go in, they don't have a set format for the song. They'll have the verse structure, the chorus structure, and the bridge, and they'll keep playing them over and over, putting in extra verses here and there or doubling the bridge or the choruses. You'll end up with eight or nine minutes like that, and then chop it down afterwards, which is a real good way to do things.

KEITH RICHARDS: "Beast of Burden" just cropped up in the studio. It started off kind of faster and funkier and more shouted. When we decided to cut it and everybody else started playing, it became more relaxed and came down and sort of fitted into the mood of it more. It was done in one take . . . that was it.

SUGAR BLUE: I started playing harmonica on the sidewalk in New York City and I just went and took my thing across the water [to Paris], and it was a hell of a lot nicer 'cause during the winter, man, you can go down in the Métro. The subways are very much unlike New York City's subway, thank God. They're clean, they're large, they're spacious, they're well lit. It's a beautiful space to play for a busker musician. It's really heaven there, and people appreciate good music there. They look for it; they search you out. I'd have people that would come back. It's one of the greatest stages in the world, let me say.

I had met some people from playing around. There's a very beautiful community of musicians there, right? And these people were well off, more than well off. They'd throw a party and they'd invite every musician they could find and they'd have a jam session. You'd have quite a lot of people from the "upper crust" that would hang out with the Stones, and I met this cat whose name I can't remember who said, "Hey, man, we really like the way you play—why don't you come on over and play with the Stones?" I said,

"Sure, Mack . . . uh huh . . . give me the telephone number." The guy said, "Hey, man, this is no jive." I said, "Right, man, yeah. Give me the number." So the cat gave me the number, and I said, "Well what the fuck have I got to lose? I'll give 'em a call." I called the number and said, "Hey, man, can I speak to Mick Jagger?" A couple of minutes later a guy says, "Hey, mate, how are you?" He invited me down to the studio and that's the way it fell out.

It was a hell of an experience for me, 'cause when I was a kid and they put out *December's Children* and *Aftermath* with all that harmonica all over the place, I said, "Man, that's hip!" Because I hadn't heard of Willie Dixon and the Chicago blues. I mean, it was damn near an impossibility in the really early sixties to get to that stuff, especially in New York. The only people that they were into were the folkies. When the Stones and the Beatles came back over here, they gave a shot in the arm to the music business. Willie [Dixon] would ask me, "Where did you learn the blues?" Well, my first influence was literally groups like the Stones.

I really enjoyed playing on *Miss You*. The first time I walked in, you know I was on cloud nine. I'm sayin' "Jesus Christ, man, I'm gonna *make* it . . . I'm here in the stratosphere with the world's greatest known rock band!" I was out to lunch . . . forget it . . . far out! I'm with Mick Jagger, Keith Richards, millions of bucks, big, fantastic studios and all of the equipment . . . *Look* at this, you know? I mean really, I was *spaced*, man. It really was one hell of a time for me. They were nice to work with, they were damned nice to work with, because they were patient, they tried the best they could to work me into their material, and I picked up on what they were doin' pretty quick, because me, I play the blues. No matter what they played, I played the blues.

Another thing that I really love about playing with these people is they know where the roots are. They'll sit down and tell you and anybody else that would like to listen about the roots. I've heard Keith say, "Unfortunately, man, the kids don't wanna know about Muddy Waters." They've always lived, as much as they possibly can, in an environment of blues. I was on the road with them for a while, in Paris and Europe. I did a concert with them in Antwerp, and all I heard was the blues. Every spare minute they get, they listen to the blues.

June 10, 1978. The Stones begin a two-month American tour in Lakeland, Florida.

MICK JAGGER: Up to 1976 we were touring quite a lot, but after 1976 we collectively decided that we really didn't want to tour very much anymore, for whatever reasons there were at the time. One of us would say, "I really don't want to tour, I just want to do nothing," or "I just want to devote myself to other things," or "I just want to write, or to go away." All these years in rock'n'roll is a long time. I think we would have gone crazy if we had toured all those years in the seventies—like every year in America, every year in Europe plus Australia. I think we would have gone nuts. I would have left the band and done something else, or I would have been in music but couldn't have possibly stayed interested in rock'n'roll. So for whatever reasons we didn't tour for a while. We toured in '78 but we didn't do a very long tour. I thought it was long at the time, but when I look back on it, it wasn't very long, especially compared to the last tour we did.

ROY CARR: People have this impression of the Rolling Stones as being aloof and removed. On their '78 American tour I went down to New Orleans when they played the Superdome. That had been the biggest indoor gig ever and we were staying at the Royal Orleans Hotel, which was a block-and-a-half from Bourbon Street. I was talking to Keith and Ronnie one night and said, "Look, I'm going down to Bourbon Street to do a few clubs tonight. Why don't you come along?" They said, "Who's on?" I said, "Well, Clarence 'Frogman' Henry, the R&B guy." He's working this corner bar which is about twice the size of this room and you pay a dollar fifty for a beer. It's full of hookers and tourists, but he's great. He goes on and does about four shows a night, so I said, "Let's go down." So there was Ronnie, Keith, myself, and a couple of roadies and we go in there and sit in the corner. Keith goes up to the bar, buys a round of drinks, sits down, then it's my turn, and I go up and buy five beers. So these young kids come in and you could tell they were college kids, about nineteen or twenty, and they'd come down for the Stones tour, and this girl in the front says, "Hey, look, isn't that the Rolling Stones in the corner there?" And her boyfriend takes a good look and says, "No, they wouldn't be in a cheezy joint like this!"

When I went to New Orleans I went with Chalkie Davis, the photographer, and Chalkie went down in the evening to do a photo session. Jagger was down there and he was very unapproachable that night. He wasn't being nasty, he was just concerned the gig was going to be right, and he was down there until two or three in the morning checking that the PA was right, the lights were set right. He was doing his job. He wasn't leaving anything to chance.

June 19, 1978.

KEITH RICHARDS: We surprised a lot of people on the '78 tour by playing the Palladium in New York. We didn't realize really what we'd done to New York until it was all over, and then it hit us. We blew out the biggest market in America and played a three-thousand-seat theatre. But that's what we wanted to do—we felt we needed to do it and that the people that dug us would understand it too. It's a one shot, we ain't dead yet, we'll be back.

We did a couple of small theatres that tour. There was a theatre in Atlanta [the Fox] we did and a small theatre in

Washington [the Warner]. There are some great halls left in America. In fact the Capitol [Passaic, New Jersey] was kept alive by the fact of us doing that gig. Which is great because you can see some of the best shows in venues that size. To do the real big stadiums and the big auditoriums requires a very standardized approach. You don't have that much flexibility in what you do. You can't throw surprises at anybody because you're surprising the mixer outside, you're surprising the monitor mixer on stage, you're surprising the promoter, you're surprising the lighting crew. You're locked into a certain thing in the big halls, whereas in a small place, if you want to throw in something off the wall you can. You can be more flexible.

We've always been good in the small halls because we did them for so long. I guess in a way we're kind of testing ourselves. I remember the first shock in the opposite direction—coming out of two hundred capacity clubs and the curtains opening at the Victoria Theatre in London, which is a cinema holding three thousand people but to us was bigger than the Superdome. I still have the memory of that place. It just looked so vast and I felt so small. And I know the rest of the guys did too. After playing stadiums this size, going back to playing small places again is always like, "Come on, let's do it. We used to be great at it. We can really turn it on there." For one thing, you have a lot less problems. You don't have to worry too much about amplification because you can fill the hall yourself.

CHAPTER 7

Fight Nights

October 12, 1978. The Rolling Stones release a statement defending the lyrics to "Some Girls."

EARL McGRATH: It never occurred to us that our parody of certain stereotypical attitudes would be taken seriously by anyone who heard the entire lyric of the song in question.

October 23, 1978. In a Toronto courtroom, Keith agrees to plead guilty to a reduced charge of heroin possession. The next day he is sentenced to a suspended one-year jail term and ordered to perform a concert for the Canadian National Institute for the Blind [CNIB].

KEITH RICHARDS: I don't think it's Canada's fault at all. It could have happened anywhere. Mind you, you should do something about those Mounties [laughs].

There's this little blind chick who lives in Toronto. She's my guardian angel. She's totally blind but nothing would stop her from turning up at gigs. Can you imagine, all the insanity of a Stones show? I had these horrible visions of her being run over, so I'd say, "Give this chick a ride," you know, "make sure she's okay." So just before my sentencing she finds out where the judge lives and goes up to his house in Toronto and tells him her story. So I guess the light went on in his head and he worked out the way to get Canada and himself and myself off the hook by doing this concert for the blind, which I gladly performed. So my sweet blind angel came through for me, bless her heart.

April 22, 1979. The New Barbarians with Ron Wood and Keith Richards perform at the Oshawa Civic Centre outside Toronto in a benefit for the CNIB, to satisfy Keith's sentence for heroin possession. The unannounced Rolling Stones "close" the concert.

KEITH RICHARDS: Once you get onstage, the circumstances don't matter, it's just another show. I think it's a much more interesting form of justice than just fining someone or sending them to jail. A lot of people could do something more useful with the talents that they've got. I hope other people see the reasoning behind something like this.

RON WOOD: That's where we opened the Barbarians tour. That was great. It was a good exercise in the way I like to look at my albums, and when I do a gig outside the band. I like to show off combinations of musicians. With my first albums it was Andy Newmark and Willy Weeks and Jean Rousseau, and Mack, Keith, myself, and Mick Taylor. All good fusions of people. With the Barbarians it was Stanley Clark and Zigaboo, Bobby Keys, Mack, Keith, and myself. The group had no record, no background, but it caused a stir. It could have been a lot friendlier a stir if my management at that time hadn't let the papers carry on thinking there were going to be "extra guests" arriving [laughs]. But for a band that was put together for one purpose and that was going on a tour in style, it worked. I got the 727, the four-star hotels during the whole tour, and came out a hundred and twenty-five grand in the red. It was great. CBS records picked up the tab for me, which I'm now paying back, every cent. But that's cool. I didn't do it to make money or exploit anything—I did it to show that old fusion thing. It goes back to the old jazz days where you find great musicians together with other great unannounced musicians and everybody plays off everybody else.

CLIFF LORIMER: They called me on the Friday and asked me if I would emcee the first show, and I said, "Of course, I'd be delighted." And they called me back later and said, "Would you do the second show as well?" And I said, "Well, it is the Rolling Stones, I don't mind doing two" [laughs]. I went onstage and introduced John Belushi, who came on and introduced the New Barbarians. It was a lot of fun. Everyone treated me very nicely.

PAUL McGRATH: Keith looked much improved and much more chipper than the last time we had seen him. The show was okay—what one might have expected from a good solid band of professionals. But it had neither the excitement of the El Mocambo show nor the feeling that history was being made. It was a lousy venue, way outside Toronto, the equivalent of an airplane hanger. Lousy sound, and the chairs had to stay where they were so the hundreds and hundreds of blind people in the room didn't become confused. Not a great night, but for Keith it sure beat the hell out of jail cell.

1980. On June 20, the Stones release "Emotional Rescue." Four days later, they release the album of the same name. On December 8, John Lennon is murdered in New York City.

KEITH RICHARDS: If there was one guy that didn't deserve to go like that it was John [Lennon]. Just look at what the guy gave and then look at what he got in return. It's definitely not right.

MICK JAGGER: That was awful. It was very ironic as well. He was really feeling good about living in New York and the fact that he could walk around the streets very anonymously. He could walk into restaurants and not be mobbed; he could take a cab like anyone else. He had overcome the burden of being a Beatle and he was really happy. It was sad—I really liked him.

We had a good relationship, all of us in the band did. We used to hang out quite a bit. He was a really smart, really funny guy and he had a good perspective on it all. He didn't take it too seriously, he knew all the fame and adulation was bullshit.

He said very nice things about me, and the band in general, when he was doing all that promotion for *Double Fantasy*. I know he said some funny things about us and the image after Altamont. He was real sarcastic and stuff. He liked to be sarcastic.

1981. On August 14, the Stones release "Start Me Up." On August 25, they release *Tattoo You*.

CHRIS KIMSEY: For *Tattoo You* I spent three months going through the last four or five albums finding stuff that had been either forgotten about or at the time rejected. Then I presented it to the band and said, "Look, guys, you got all this stuff sitting in the can and it's great material. You should do something with it." That was a collection of leftovers, see, from about three albums—*Some Girls*, *Emotional Rescue*, and I think some of it was from *Goat's Head Soup* as well. "Start Me Up" was originally recorded the same day as "Miss You," and at that time "Miss You" won out over "Start Me Up."

KEITH RICHARDS: I was shocked. That was a throwaway track that had been in the can a couple of years. It's like "Satisfaction." I do what I do and we put out the best of what we think we do. Some of the best we don't put out because we don't have room for it. I'd stopped thinking about records and which one should actually go out. Singles were no longer the number one important thing in my life because I didn't have Andrew Oldham banging on my door every couple of days. I became less and less conscious of having to write hit songs. More and more I just wrote.

Writing . . . I don't know if you call it writing . . . I don't put a thing on paper. It's either up here or, if I get the chance, I put it on tape. I make records. That's what I do. To me, writing a song and performing it are just part of the whole process of making a record. Making a record is different from writing a song in that eventually it's got to come of those two speakers There's gotta be a song. It's not gotta be virtuoso playing, it's not gotta be fantastic . . . Gigli doesn't have to sing it, or Mario Lanza . . . or even Rod Stewart. It's about the basic sound that comes out of those speakers. And it's got to sound good in mono, too, for the radio. And that's what I do . . . I make a sound . . . and I'm good at it now.

IAN STEWART: Over the years they've put out some great albums and some that weren't quite up to par. I don't think *Some Girls* was very good because it was full of really simple two-chord songs and I think they went on a bit. There were a couple of albums like *Aftermath* that I liked. I wouldn't play them today but they were good at the time. I hated *Satanic Majesties*. I've never played it since it was released—in fact, I don't even think I have a copy of it. Then I quite like the period at the end of the sixties and the albums like Let It Bleed and the one with the zipper on the front [Sticky Fingers]. Those were things that Glyn did, and Glyn always makes things sound very warm and there's a lot of feel to his stuff. Then there's a couple of really duff records like Goat's Head Soup and some of the stuff that was done in Munich [Black and Blue], although I quite like It's Only Rock and Roll. Then when they moved to Paris for Some Girls and Emotional Rescue I didn't like those much, but the last one [Tattoo You] was good. Then again a lot of those tracks went back a bit.

September 25, 1981. The Stones begin a tour of America at JFK Stadium in Philadelphia. Partially underwritten by a perfume company, it is one of the very first sponsored rock'n'roll tours. It is not the last.

MICK JAGGER: We hadn't toured for three years so going back on the road did feel a little strange. We had to rehearse for a very long time. I was a bit nervous at first because we went straight from doing one club gig to Philadelphia, which is in front of all those people. Yeah, I was a little nervous until I got on the stage and realized that although it was a little sloppy we got away with it. I knew we could be together, the audience was with us and we were going to have a good time. It took us a few gigs to get into it—like about five, which were all huge gigs. We did two in Buffalo, and then went all over. It was a pretty difficult first week, I think it's fair enough to say.

[Full of sarcasm] Yeah, I'm in charge of absolutely everything. I control every last detail and I make fifty-three million dollars at least before tax! What was it in the *Rolling Stone* magazine? Oh God, Jann Wenner. Talk about accuracy. He's generally all right but he could have phoned me up and asked how much I made out of the American tour. He wrote a figure and he never asked anybody. It's obviously totally wrong. They didn't bother to check with us or ask my accountant. I don't know what the figures are, actually. I haven't even looked at them. They're still being tallied up. We did make a lot of money, but not anything like what Jann Wenner said. Yes, we made a lot, because that was the biggest tour ever.

Yeah, we spent money on it. That's one of the things, is that if you spend money on them, people say, "It's worth it." Other people say, "Don't fucking do it. It's only rock'n'roll," and that crap. I like to think that the money you spend and the time and effort you put into the staging, as well as playing and the combination of both, make people want to come back and see it. They say, "Well, the Rolling Stones . . . yeah . . . it's usually a good show," and they got their twenty bucks' worth, plus parking, plus T-shirts. Whereas you could do it much simpler, and I guess some people really wouldn't care. I know a lot of the band wouldn't care [laughs].

BILL WYMAN: I was really looking forward to it. I thought it was going to be a big tour. We were talking about a million to a million-and-a-half people coming. I thought that's an awful lot of people, and it was going to be eight weeks or something. First of all, it was going to be just twelve shows. The very first talk about it was New York, L.A., Chicago, a few big places. Then it became four weeks, and then eight weeks, and I thought, "It's getting a bit long," but it looked like we were going to earn some good money out of it for a change. You don't earn the amount of money that anybody ever thinks we do on tours. Only in America do we actually make money. In Europe you don't, and in Australia and places . . . So it looked quite good, because when you're not writers in a band, like Charlie and myself, you need the live gigs to keep you in that standard of living, because you don't get writers' royalties, you get record royalties. So on the road is always quite important to Charlie and myself financially.

So I was quite happy about going and I was looking forward to playing. We went out there and we suddenly found the tickets were going like wildfire, and instead of doing the one gig in Philadelphia, one in L.A., and one in Chicago, wherever it was, we were being asked for a second gig, which was also enormous, so it ended up we played to twice as many people as we thought because of all the second gigs that were added. It was quite phenomenal. We were getting messages like so-and-so had sold out in

Toronto in six hours. I couldn't believe it. It was just a really good tour. I don't think the band had played better together for a number of years. Everybody was completely, like, straight, completely dedicated, and took care to be on form.

KEITH RICHARDS: You see, Stones tours have always been a turn-on and they've always been successful. The only thing surprising about the '81 tour was just *how* successful. We could throw in stadium gigs with three or four days' notice and sell out. Everybody was just rolling on that tour. It was amazing, the response. That's when you start to reach for new superlatives. There's always an audience there and they always have a good time, but that last tour? *Aaahhh* . . . fairy dust.

We were lucky. The album was ready, and it took off. It's a matter of timing. Talent is 10 percent of it. You can have all the other ingredients, but there's still the variable which is that certain timing that comes along now and again where everything is *bang* . . . *bang* . . . If you tried to plan it, it wouldn't happen. Maybe one of the great things about the Stones and why they've managed to hang in there, is their flexibility. When they're cold, they think they're still hot, so they go on [laughs].

This is the area that is impossible for anybody to engineer, even the masters of manipulation. There are so many things that have to come together at the right time to make something like that happen. What can I say—that it's my beautiful face? [laughs]. C'mon, I'm playing guitar the same as always, I'm hoping I'm getting a little better, but it's impossible for me to say. All I can say is it's that timing.

ROY CARR: It becomes too easy for people to kick the Stones. All right, they've stuck around. Some people say they've outstayed their welcome. I really don't believe that. I think they've had their ups and their downs. I thought *Some Girls* was a great album. I saw the tour and I was moved, and I felt very excited. I felt as excited seeing the Stones as say, seeing the Clash, or the Jam.

I do come from the same generation as the Beatles and the Stones, but I don't wallow in nostalgia. Some people say, "Well, they're over the hill," approaching middle age. But nobody's gone to the kids in America and said, "Here are the Rolling Stones, you gotta buy their album." This is going to be the biggest ever rock tour in the history of music. This album has sold more than any of their albums, and everybody wants to see them, so there is something there. They've still got something to offer.

I recommend the new album. Half I think is top-quality Stones material. I know Jagger. I'm not going to say Jagger is my best friend and all that, but I know Mick Jagger as well as Jagger wants me to know him. I think there's a lot of people like that, and Jagger is suss enough that if he felt that either he or the group could not cut it, they would not be on the road. This may be the last time to go out. I would rather the Stones hang up their rock'n'roll shoes when they can't cut it, than go out and do Mohammed Ali on us.

PETER GODDARD: It was the first time that the two generations that are now rock'n'roll fans found a group they could agree on. Up till then, rock'n'roll had been a divisive issue, so that a Journey fan would attract one kind of fan and Dylan would attract another. These were totally different people who had nothing in common. But the Stones attracted both, and Mick Jagger is just as much a sex symbol as David Lee Roth in the sense of being in posters on walls. I think that was the key to the success and why it took people by surprise. I think people thought that rock'n'roll was a generational issue.

KEITH RICHARDS: He has a good feel for the audience, George [Thorogood], and he's doing it by his own lights. He's not gone the usual route. George is all right. He did a great job for us. Between him and J. Geils, bless their hearts.

There are certain people who are great to work with. We always used to insist on the best to open shows if we could. We would pull our weight and say, "It's our tour, we want Ike and Tina or Chuck Berry," because they're the ones who make you good, because if you've got somebody *that* good on in front of you, then you better be at least as good if not better. You may have the good will going for you, but they've just been on, and you've gotta follow them. The people who are dumb are the ones who use a bad act to start off with just to soften the audience up, because what you get is a soft audience. I want a good opening act to make me work harder.

RON WOOD: I was missing one day and Keith met my old lady and she was crying, and she had a go about me to Keith. He said, "That bastard!" He thought I was fooling around with other women because I was missing, and he also thought I'd gone over to these really shady people's place to do drugs. So he got this posse, a search party, and they're all tearing down the corridor and finally found me in a friend's room on another floor. I'd just had an argument with the old lady, and went and sat with this old friend for a few hours. I hear this posse coming down the corridor, Keith walks in and smashes a bottle and comes at me and I did a quick swerve on him and elbowed him in the gut [laughs]. Then there was a fist in the genitals, and fist in the face, and he nearly went out the window, actually. I was equally livid 'cause they'd got it all wrong! So it was just one of those misunderstandings on the tour where everything gets blown out of proportion for a bit. So he was dragged off and we were yelling obscenities at each other, and then a couple of hours later we were back to normal. I remember walking into the next room and Mick and Charlie were sitting on the floor talking and I walk in with this real bloodstained face because Keith had managed to get a couple of hits to the face, and I walk in and say, "Can you believe this?" I'm just covered in blood. And Mick says, "You know, in the middle eight of 'Summer Romance,' do you think we should . . ." And he just started talking as if nothing was happening, so I just started laughing [laughs].

MICK JAGGER: I think it's a good idea to keep tours short. Anything above twenty-five gigs, you're really asking for trouble. While you may be holding it together, other members start to get "the crazies." After about fifty gigs people really start to lose it and it affects everybody and the shows start to become automatic. You don't know what day it is or what city you're in . . . it's a very strange life. You're cut off from people on the one hand, and on the other you meet more people than anyone else because you're always seeing different cities. I've probably seen more of America than most Americans. I know people in each city. I know the best bars and restaurants, where the best girls are . . .

November 22, 1981. The Stones join Muddy Waters, Buddy Guy, and Junior Wells at Waters' show at the Checkerboard Lounge in Chicago.

MICK JAGGER: Yes, I like to do small clubs occasionally . . . I love it. I liked the one we did in Chicago with Muddy Waters recently. That was a good club.

221

WILLIE DIXON: Last time they were in Chicago they came out to my house. I wouldn't let 'em all in because there were too many people with them. They had a whole line of limousines, a block long of limousines, and all of them full of people, and they thought they'd get in my six-room house. It was never going to happen, so I took them over to where Muddy Waters was workin' which was a good big place, but even then it was too small, because people was linin' up and down the stairways and everywhere. But we had a ball over there. We got to jammin' and singin' and playin' together and like this, and we'd talk about these things, and have a ball. They were tellin' me to come onstage with them at their concert in the stadium, but heck it was so noisy, there were so many people. Ooooooh . . . *man*, the people was raisin' more hell than the Stones were.

December 18, 1981. The Stones celebrate Keith's birthday and the end of their American tour—the last show is the next day— with their first live pay-per-view TV special.

MICK JAGGER: Yeah, the band was tense about the TV show, but when they got out there they played very well. We were doing live TV, but once you get out there it's okay. It's all this thinking about it that screws you up. Keith was saying, "What've we got into? How did I get into this?" Then he'd try to blame me—"How did you get me into this?" Then when he actually got out there it's really the same as any other show. Except that there is the pressure that you've got to sing pretty much in tune. I know I should always sing in tune, but there's this whole thing where you can't do everything. If you want to do a lot of leaping about and fooling around, you can't expect every note to be note perfect. So the pressure's there to sing a bit better than you would normally and not to fool around quite so much. That's for me anyway, and I think for Keith too. On the live record we used quite a few tracks from that show and the playing is very consistent.

I think the band saw the results of that. Keith was watching it the other night and I think it's truly very good and I think it was well worthwhile, whatever the problems. Even though it didn't make a fortune of money or anything because it cost a lot to do, I think it was kind of worth doing, and a good experiment in more ways than one.

Spring 1982.

RON WOOD: That was a blast, it was great. It was a fantastic vibe on that tour, which I don't think will necessarily carry on into Europe. I don't think we can just go, "Wow . . . everything's great. We're riding the crest of the wave." Because in Europe they feel, like, "All right, then, you left us out, or you were going to leave us out, and now you're here finally after doing the States and giving them all your finest" kind of thing. They do feel a little blown out, so what we do is make it an extension of what we did in '81 but even better.

I was talking to Mick the other night about the English and European tour we're about to embark on. He was saying that he was trying to think of numbers that England would like. Or, as "Angie" was the biggest seller ever for the Stones in Europe, we mustn't forget to put "Angie" in the set. So we'll make changes, good ones.

Actually how different will it be? All I know is that from the playing, it's going to be red hot, or I'm not fit to be called a member of the Stones. I'm doing it for fun and I'm doing it to say "fuck you" to all of those that thought I was so doped out I couldn't keep it together. And "fuck you" if you thought the Stones couldn't do it anymore, because they're boring old farts that can't compete.

KEITH ALTHAM: I can actually remember, very clearly, getting into a Bedford van outside these offices on Old Compton Street [London]. It must have been nineteen years ago. Ian Stewart was driving and Keith was asleep in the back in a sleeping bag with the rest of us crammed into the broad seats that go across, and driving up the motorways to Aylesbury in the fog to do a gig with the Ronettes, and it doesn't seem that long ago to me, actually, and they don't seem to have changed that much to me. Of course they've been through an enormous amount of different experiences and things during that time, but I still think of them very much in the same way, as people. You know, basic personalities don't change.

It's a never-ending source of amazement to me that when I meet someone that I've never, ever met before, who is, like, a kind of massive "name," I always expect them to be completely different to what they actually are when I meet them. The media does this. It magnifies things, and when someone makes it to the national level, it magnifies it a hundred times over. With the Stones I think the basic personalities are still there.

The recent [1981] tour is just the most colossal thing I've ever seen. It's got to be the biggest box office that the world will ever see, in terms of an attraction of any kind, anywhere, from Mohammed Ali to the Pope. I don't care, it's just so vast. And it was very exciting to see archetypal people, like Bill Graham, wandering around the stage picking up Coke cans and tidying up his own stage in the wake of Jefferson Airplane after everything else that he's looked after over the years. It was great to see the Stones on stage again and working, with Jagger prancing around like he used to. He's almost ageless. There was a wonderful line in *The Sunday Times* this week that described Jagger looking as slim and strained by his excesses to keep fit on stage, as Richards was by his excesses in the other direction. There's a certain truth to that.

BILL WYMAN: I just moved back to England two weeks ago as a resident. I can't stay in France any longer. The thing that disturbs me now in France, is not the things I didn't like in those days. What it is now is, I can't keep up to date with today's music, new movies, and so on, and so on, the new bands, the live gigs. I miss the comedy, I miss the soccer, I miss the friends, and all my work is outside of France so it's silly to stay there anymore. There's nothing goes on in the south of France, there *are* no live bands—it's very rare, anyway. The Police will come one year, Elton John comes one year. You have to go to Paris and London to see Duran Duran or anybody else, so I thought I should get back to England and sort myself out because you have to keep asking people to send you their new album. You see them in the charts in *Billboard*, and *Melody Maker*, or whatever, but you never hear them down there. You go to record shops and they say, "Never heard of them." They have the third album back by that band . . . It's really out of date.

May 26, 1982. The Stones begin their first European tour since 1976.

MICK JAGGER: In Europe it's expensive to tour. They say, "Why didn't you tour Europe all the time?" Well, you can't make any money, is one of the reasons, and life is only so long. You've already toured fifteen years of your life without making any money—would you do a job with no pay? Well, you've got to go every now and then, I suppose. There's a little bit of money on this tour, but the Europeans, as soon as you start making any money they say, "Hey what is this?"

[laughs]. We just figure we should really go. If it's going to be only every seven years, we may never go again.

KEITH RICHARDS: Mick's famous for statements like that, saying we don't make any money. What he's saying is that you don't make anything like you do in America. But since we didn't start this whole fucking band . . . I'll rephrase that—we didn't start this band to make money, because we didn't see it as a money-making thing. We used to *pay* to play in this band. It cost money to get to a gig. You had to take a train to get there and you used the money you made to get the train back and to pay for a bit of food and guitar strings. That was all we were looking for. In a perverse way it may be why it's been so successful—nobody was really looking to make money out of it. It really did have an innocent and pure meaning to start with. It's probably the only thing about us that did.

IAN STEWART: In the early tours it was just me and the band travelling around. As the shows got bigger, especially in America we would start to get guys who would take care of the equipment and I would make sure the travel and hotel arrangements were together, and these days I tend to make the arrangements setting up the rehearsals with the musicians and for the recording sessions. I still play with them but I also have the logistics to take care of.

CHUCK LEAVELL: I had auditioned in '81 right before they went out on tour. I think they had the idea of trying some new guys, and they'd had some people from New York come and audition. Bill Graham was tour director at the time and of course the Allman Brothers was one of his favourite groups, so he remembered me and suggested my name to the band. I had a gig that weekend, a little trio I had in Macon, Georgia, at a club, and I had this call from a friend of a friend saying, "Do you know the Rolling Stones are trying to get you?" "Right . . . sure." I didn't do anything for a day, and then I thought, "Well, you dummy, at least you ought to give them a call." I called the guy back and said, "Do you have a phone number?" and he gave me a number and I got hold of a secretary and I said, "Here's my number and my name." That night Ian Stewart called back and said [proper British accent], "Right, we want to know if you would come up for an audition?" "Wow . . . I'm honoured. Of course I would. I've got a gig this weekend, could we do it Sunday or Monday?" "We were really hoping you could be here tomorrow." "Oh Lord, okay, hold the line." So I called up the club, explained the situation, and they said, "Sure, it's the Rolling Stones . . . go!" and they cancelled the gig.

I got on a plane the next morning and went up and auditioned and it really felt comfortable from the get go. You'd have to ask the guys exactly what happened, but I think there was a bit of a divided camp. Some of the guys wanted me to go and some of the guys wanted Ian McLagan to go. Mac had done the previous tour and of course was very close to Ronnie Wood, having played in the Faces. They decided to keep Mac on for the U.S. part of the tour. Then the European tour came up, and for whatever reasons they called me and said, "Do you want to do it?" I said, "Well, yes . . . I missed the other one. You're doggone right I want to do it!" That was the first experience.

English musicians, especially from that era—the sixties—looked upon delta blues, rhythm'n'blues, soul, and country music as something very precious. When they met somebody from there, like myself or others, they were very curious and very interested about them. I felt an immediate kindred spirit to the guys because of that, and they had a respect for where I came from. All I had to do was play, and be myself, and be natural.

After the European tour, Keith reunites with his father for the first time in twenty years.

KEITH RICHARDS: It was just time to leave home. I was about eighteen, and I felt, "This house is too small for one of us," and then everything just took off. The next year the Stones broke, my mother split up from my father, and the years swept away. After a while it became very difficult to get back in touch again. Eventually it happened and it was great. It was one of the best things I ever did, to make sure we met up again. He's a great bloke.

June 1, 1982. The Stones release *Still Life (American Concert 1981)*. The same day, they release "Going to a Go Go."

MICK JAGGER: Live albums are funny things. It's not the sort of thing I rush home to play, but it sounds pretty good. It's concise—it's like a telescopic version of a show. This one's from all over. I don't really know where it is myself. We didn't record every show—that would have been rather expensive.

[Q: How do you see yourself today?] At the moment, sort of functioning rock singers, but it's a very odd way of looking at it because I can't really take it seriously. At the beginning we were a serious blues band, but I can't really be serious about what we do anymore. At least onstage I can't, because they're all these big shows and as you say, it is twenty years and you can dip into the oldies and all the best songs. It's not like that when you're very young and all you have to play is these few songs. It's all you've got and you play them for all you're worth. It's very odd when you've got a lot of material to choose from.

It's still a lot of fun, but it doesn't seem as intense as it used to be to me. And the audiences aren't as intense. There was one horrible period when we got quite old people only. I don't mind old people, but now they're very young and there's no sort of intensity in it. I'm sure the young people sort of see us as some kind of curiosity but they seem to enjoy themselves.

February 1983. Hal Ashby's movie of the 1981 American tour opens in New York.

KEITH RICHARDS: I've seen some rough edits of the film, which was done mostly out of Phoenix. It's a happy marriage—we were playing well that night. The sound is good, it looks good, I'm happy with it.

HAL ASHBY: It isn't a hand-held film. The idea was to get the best operators and the best cameramen, talk to them, and get as good a look as we could. We shot two shows at Meadowlands and then a third show that was outdoors, at Phoenix. With three different shows we ended up with a really good selection. The terrific thing about it is that all the guitars are now wireless so they could all move around. Charlie and the keyboards are the only ones that are tied down. So there's a lot of movement, and of course Mick is always in motion. I love what a couple of kids who saw it said about it. They called it "awesome!" [laughs]. I said, "That's okay by me."

BILL WYMAN: No, I didn't like [the 1981 film]. We'd already done it twice and I didn't see the point of doing it for yet another tour, no matter how good it was going to be shot. It was still going to end up a Rolling Stones live-on-stage film, and that didn't really interest me. For what it was worth, I think it was a well-shot stage show and as good as you could do it at the time. The colours were great, but it just didn't really excite me. But that's me—I don't get excited and interested very much. I'm very boring actually. It takes a bloody lot to get me to jump and say *yeah!* When I'm in England and it's soccer or something or when I see my favourite comedian on television or something like that. I'm much more down home, basic working-class values.

There's this English comedian called Tony Hancock who I introduced Robin Williams to, and [Williams] flipped out and said he's a genius, he loved him. He made me sit there while he kept putting tapes on . . . more, more, more . . . He was absorbing it all. A lot of people knew him, he was a great comedian, but he's been dead since the sixties. He's not like a Lenny Bruce, but he has the same kind of cult following as Lenny Bruce has in America. He was fantastic and no one has replaced him. They never do replace those people—they're irreplaceable.

August 1983. The Stones sign a four-record deal with CBS Records, reputedly worth US$28 million.

MICK JAGGER: I've always hated the music business, it's just so full of phonies. Everybody tries to make like they're your best friends and they're making you millions of dollars. The fact is that they wouldn't have anything if it weren't for the artists. I just think it's a really nasty business and the way they operate is really cutthroat. You know, everybody thinks

I'm obsessed with money, but I just want to see artists get paid fairly. They never used to. The record company would make two dollars and they'd pay the artist two cents. It really was like that for the longest time. I believe that if the record company makes a dollar then the artist should make a dollar. That's not just for the big artists but for everybody. The worst part of all this was in the sixties all the money we made Decca went to support missile development, which they would sell to the Americans for the war. It just makes me crazy. All that is just so senseless.

November 1983. The Stones start recording *Undercover* in Paris.

MICK JAGGER: In 1978, we had gone into the studio and recorded loads of tracks, part of which came out on *Some Girls*. Then we went back in 1979 and recorded a whole bunch more tracks, along with a couple of the *Some Girls* tracks that we hadn't used for *Emotional Rescue*. On the *Tattoo You* album, we did some more recording with some of the old tracks.

These are all new for *Undercover*—they were all written this year or last. None of them are from previous sessions, but I don't think there's anything bad in using stuff from previous sessions. I mean, we recorded twenty to twenty-five tracks on this session and I'm just not going to throw them all away because we didn't use them. These are the ones we liked the best, and they made an obvious album to me.

We started working on it last year, a little bit before Christmas. Keith and I got into it a bit early and rented an eight-track demo studio in a basement here in Paris. I said, "Well, what have you got, Keith?" and we took turns at playing the drums and guitars. So we got to know the material that each of us had written during the past few months, and then we said, "That's a good one," or "I don't really think that's very much good." Or I'd say, "I really need a part for this," and Keith would say, "I haven't any lyrics for this one."

So when we actually got the band into the studio, we had a hard-core bunch of songs, which is most of the songs on this album. Of course, when the band comes onto the scene, they change a lot—the rhythm changes or the arrangements change—and sometimes I have to rewrite the lyrics because they don't fit anymore.

There are no love songs on the album, really—there's no poignant charm. Our original intentions were that we wanted to make it an uncompromising, tough record.

The Stones release "Undercover of the Night." A week later, on November 8, they release *Undercover*.

MICK JAGGER: On some of the songs, like "Undercover of the Night," I took the precaution of going in early with Charlie. We were in a room in some small studio somewhere, and there was just a tympani that someone had left there, and I had a guitar, and that's how that one started . . . *dumdadadum-*

dadadum . . . Charlie got into that one from the very beginning. I like to get Charlie involved early.

"She Was Hot" starts off very musically, like a real kind of Rolling Stones song. Stew's playing piano on it, then it goes into the minor changes and becomes quite a different song. It's really two definite parts, with Chuck Leavell playing keyboards on the minor parts and Stew playing on the boogie-woogie parts.

IAN STEWART: Most of the time what happens is we go in and the songs are just sketches or jams and everybody plays a bit and then they're overdubbed and reshaped so by the time the record actually comes out the things I did on the basic tracks are buried underneath sixteen layers of guitar.

This one, I think the songs are much stronger than in a while. Mick has come up with some very good lyrics, and his voice is great on it. There's a varied feel to the material and a good feel. Mick and Keith have done a really good job. The only fault I have with it is, again, they've spent much too long mixing the bloody thing and as a result the sound of the instruments is a little bit hard and cold. In the early stages when the tracks are still new, to me, a lot of it sounds better. Mick and Keith are not lazy. They work endlessly and they're both content to sit in the studio for months trying to get it right, but after nine months sometimes it doesn't sound as good as it did at the beginning.

CHRIS KIMSEY: Well, Mick called me early November and said, "I hear you're having a baby but I'd really like you to do our new album as well." I didn't know then that it took nine months to do a Rolling Stones album, the same as it took to make [my son] Joseph. We started in Paris in November and continued through till the end of February, took March off, and then came to New York to do the mixing and some of the vocals. Then we went to Nassau for four weeks, mainly for Keith's overdubs. Mick came down as well, did some vocals down there, and that's where we met Sly Dunbar and Robbie Shakespeare. They were working on their album with Black Uhuru, and Sly has really got the Simmons drum sound down. A lot of people spend ten hours just trying to get the sound out of it, because it can take a long time, but Sly has a set sound. He came in, put some dubs on "Undercover" and "Too Tough" and maybe a couple more. Robbie Shakespeare played some bass on *Undercover* as well, so we had two basses, Bill's and Robbie's. Then we came back and mixed it all at the Hit Factory.

For this last album, they got together a month or two before actually recording, which wasn't the case before. Normally we'd go into the studio and what songs would come up would come from being in the studio together. They'd all have ideas, riffs and things, that they wanted to do, but so far as sitting together and doing things, *Undercover* was one of the first times they went to a demo studio and sat down and demo'd them, which was great.

I don't expect anything with the Stones. It can take a long time but there's no reason to put a time limit on it anyway. It's just whenever everybody feels that it's finished and it's right. Even with this album there were a load more songs recorded than were needed. In terms of titles—not complete songs, just ideas and titles—we got up to about sixty-two [laughs]. So you can never really tell when you're going to be finished.

The last four albums have been recorded in the same studio, but EMI is about to turn it into offices so we'll have to find another next time. The Stones definitely like large studios to play in. It gives it a feel of playing live, and you don't feel as though you're stuck in a little box. And the Stones always attract a lot of people, so when you're recording, a lot of nights it's more like a gig anyway, because a bunch of people come down. Especially in Paris, a lot of girls come down and dance around. It's fun. It's a nice way to make records.

BILL WYMAN: Videos are necessary. I'd been pushing for three or four years for something a bit newer than what we'd done before. I'd been trying to get a different kind of director in there and I made many suggestions [based on] what had been done in England over the last few years on video. There's been some great videos made. I think the point was taken. Mick went out and checked on people, and we got together with these people who seemed to have a good idea for the script and everything. So we gave them a shot with one video. We were going to do three, and we decided to have a go with one and see how it came out. It looks very good to me—I quite like it.

I don't give a shit if the video's criticized for being too violent. I mean, the Rolling Stones are always criticized and always have been. It's the same old thing, isn't it? You can't show a woman's breasts—though it's perfectly natural—but you can see a guy get his head chopped off. I can't be bothered to argue whether the video is violent or not. This is what life really is like in some countries.

JULIEN TEMPLE: I really didn't want to do the video until I heard the song ["Undercover of the Night"]. I thought it had all the raw energy of the early Stones. That's what attracted me to them in the first place, that aggressiveness and "I don't give a shit what anybody thinks, this is what we've got to say." I wrote a treatment that I never thought they would consider because it was quite strong even in those days, which I thought suited the song. But they liked it. So we shot it.

KEITH RICHARDS: *Undercover?* I thought it was a little busy. It didn't hang together, although some of the individual tracks I enjoyed very much. Some albums, you can have some of the best tracks in the world, and they just don't hang together, track by track by track. It's the hardest bit to do sometimes because you have to choose the tracks when you just don't know anymore, because you're at the end of the whole process of making a record. If it sounds cohesive that's always a bit of luck.

December 18, 1983. Keith celebrates his fortieth birthday at the altar, marrying model/actress Patti Hansen in Cabo San Lucas, Mexico. Mick is best man. The following New Year's Day, Alexis Korner dies in London at fifty-five.

BILL WYMAN: I'm the one who's always trying to encourage touring. Keith, myself, and Woody are always up for touring. It's the other two that are reluctant. I was saying for three years, "Let's go to Europe . . . We've got to do Europe," and I've been saying we should go to Australia because it's such a great scene down there. Two years ago I was telling the guys, "It's really happening in Australia," before it took off over here with Men At Work and all that lot, and they were, "Nawwww . . . it's a long way." It's much easier for Mick to say, "Oh, Bill doesn't want to tour anymore," even if I do, when he might not want to. It's much easier for him to say, "Bill and Charlie don't want to," you see? But myself, Keith, and Woody are the ones who like to tour the most. I think it's harder work for him. I don't blame him, but why doesn't he just say it? Charlie isn't always that keen on touring either.

There were a couple of periods when things could have

gone wrong for the band, when it could have folded. *Satanic Majesties* was a strange album in strange times, although a couple of tracks from that are in my favourite top twenty Rolling Stones tracks of all time. The same with *Goat's Head Soup*, "Dancing with Mr. D." I really liked that, but I felt that was also a bit of a trough, where we dropped off a bit and the album could have been better. The time before that was in the early sixties when we had problems. But they're the only real times when I felt there were real serious problems. It was that period between '72 to '75 that wasn't looking too healthy, but then Woody came along and started bouncing his little coloured ball around and brought life back into the band. He's a maniac . . . he's great. We all love him, but we'd all kick him up the ass as well. He's the youngster of the band. We were all thinking, "He's only been with us eight years," and then we realized that's longer than Brian Jones or Mick Taylor were with the band. He's been the fifth member longer than anybody else. Strange when you think about it—two-fifths of our career he's been with us.

1985. On January 2, Ron Wood marries longtime girlfriend Jo Howard in England. On March 4, Mick releases his first solo album, *She's the Boss*.

KEITH RICHARDS: I was kind of surprised that he came out with such a commercial effort rather than indulging a burning desire to play Irish folk songs on a harp or something. But it kept him busy, kept him out of trouble.

I suppose it's easy to go a little crazy living in the bubble of the Rolling Stones, so I guess he just needed a break and I think it was a good thing. He went outside the band and had a look and thought for a while that he could live without the Stones. I think ultimately he'll come back re-invigorated.

MICK JAGGER: I took the bird [Jerry Hall] and we went off to Barbados for a while. I wrote all these songs very, very quickly, so I thought I should do demos of a couple and see what would happen. Jerry was expecting a baby so there wasn't an awful lot for me to do. So I went in and did demos of about twelve songs. They sounded really good, so I thought, "Maybe this is the time to finally do this solo record." I went over to the Bahamas and I figured I'd do two weeks and see how it goes. I started recording with Sly and Robbie and Jeff Beck and it went really well so I just carried on.

The band was a little surprised, I think, but I was the only one who hadn't done anything on my own. Keith had gone with Ronnie on the New Barbarians tour and had done a record called Run Rudolph Run. The thing they were really worried about was if it was going to be real rubbish. They said to me, "Don't make it too rubbish-y." I said, "Don't worry. Have faith" [laughs].

I really just needed to get away for a while and work

241

with some other people. I think that's good because then you bring that energy back to the original band and you're stronger. I don't think Keith took it that way and he created a lot of tension in the band that I think was unnecessary.

June 1, 1985. Bill Wyman releases *Willie and the Poor Boys* and "Baby Please Don't Go" to build on the success of the ARMS charity concerts benefiting Ronnie Lane and others with multiple sclerosis.

BILL WYMAN: I'd had an idea to do an album like this for two or three years because there were a lot of early records I liked and I wanted to go into a studio with some mates and record them. I just couldn't find the right vehicle to do this kind of music. I couldn't do it as a solo record and I couldn't think of a band to do it with. Then, after we did the ARMS tour of America and the shows in England, everyone was asking whether there would be an album. There wasn't because there were too many managers and too many record companies, so I thought, "Why not put a couple of the guys together, do the album I wanted to do, and raise some more money for the charity?"

July 13, 1985. The Live Aid benefit concert is staged in London and Philadelphia. Mick performs songs with Hall & Oates and Tina Turner. Ron and Keith perform with Bob Dylan.

RON WOOD: Dylan asks me if we can get together at my place and do some rehearsals for a gig he's about to do in Philadelphia. So I say sure, and I get Keith over an hour before and tell him that Bob is coming over to do some rehearsing for, as Bob puts it, "the gig in Philadelphia." I think he's just doing a concert. I don't realize that it's all going to snowball into that big affair—I just want to go along and play. So Bob turns up and he walks in and he says, "You guys going to the concert, or are you going to stay home and watch it on TV?" And Keith looks at me like he's about to strangle me. So Bob goes up to the toilet and I pass him when he comes out, and he says, "Do you guys think you'd ever play a show with me?" And I say, "Of course we would." "Would you do this Live Aid with me?" I say, "I thought you'd never ask. For God's sake, go and tell Keith." So he goes downstairs to Keith and says, "Will you do the thing with me?" And from there it was great—we had these great rehearsals for a couple of nights round my house.

December 12, 1985. Ian Stewart, an integral part of the band from its inception, dies of a heart attack at forty-seven.

CHUCK LEAVELL: Oh God, piano was Stew's passion. I think he was one of the ones that really wanted me to get the gig. He said, "I quite like that boy from Georgia. He's very good." We became wonderful friends during that first European tour. When we would go to London he'd say, "You're not staying in a hotel, you're staying with me," and we'd go there. He had two grand pianos and a marvellous record collection, and he would make me tapes of particular boogie-woogie songs that he thought would benefit me. People like Albert Emonds, Meat Lux Louis, James P. Johnson, and on and on . . . Montana Taylor, all these wonderful names. We were very close, and his loss in '85, when he had his heart attack, was devastating to everyone but equally as much to me, because he was my friend, and he really took me under his wing, so to speak, in those years.

I guess at that point my role in the band changed significantly, because I had apprenticed under him in a way. I think the reason they had other keyboard players through the years like Billy Preston, or Ian McLagan, or Nicky Hopkins, was because Stew didn't like certain things. He wouldn't play on slow songs. He'd say, "I don't like slow songs, they're boring. Why is there a minor in this? I'm not playing a minor chord." So they had to hire other people because Stew wouldn't play the minor chord! Now, Keith would tell you real quick, "This is a guitar band," but there is a great tradition of piano throughout the history of this group, which has played an integral part, and I'm honoured to have the seat now. I guess at that time Stew passed away, I slid into those shoes to some degree to do the boogie-woogie stuff and then whatever else was on the menu . . . the slow songs and the minor chords.

1986. On March 4, the Stones release "Harlem Shuffle." On March 25, they release *Dirty Work*, their first album with CBS Records.

RON WOOD: There has to be a bit of tension in order to get good music, but on that album there was no more than usual. Well, maybe loads more than usual [laughs]. Yeah, it was mainly because Mick didn't seem to be enthused at the beginning. He just wasn't himself. We'd be saying, "What's on Mick's mind?" He'd be sitting there reading a paper or something and we wanted to rip it out of his hands and say, "Get up here!" That's all he needed, was a little kick and a little bit of support from the band. At first there were a few cold silences when we got together, but he got into the flow of it and he pulled his weight real well.

Well, you know how Keith and I feel: we love to tour. But it's just putting everyone together that's the problem. I don't know why we should have to convince Mick, but it looks like he's the one we have to convince to get out on the road this time. He's still not over the novelty of making solo albums. Bill's doing one now, and no one minds, but just 'cause it's Mick everyone goes "Ohh . . . is the band splitting up?" He got a lot of pressure from doing that first album, mainly because he was late showing up for the beginning of the *Dirty Work* sessions and we had to wait for him. So Keith and I got all these songs shaped up before he showed. That's probably why it's such a guitar-oriented album, like with "One Hit to the Body" with Jimmy Paige helping us out. [Paige] rang me at the studio one night and said, "How's it going? Do you mind if I come and hear how the album's going?" I said, no, I didn't mind. He's a very shy guy. After he'd done that overdub on "One Hit," he left the studio saying, "I'm sorry, man, I'm sorry." I said, "Don't apologize . . . you did all right!"

Being a very shy guy, [producer Steve Lillywhite] comes on like he's almost holding back, and you think, "Come on, tell us—was that any good or not?" And he'll say, "Oh yeah, come in and have a listen if you want," and we'll say, "How did it compare to the last take?" He'll say, "Oh, that one was great," and we'll say, "Well, let us know next time!" Where I was really impressed with him was in the closing stages of the album, where usually everyone bundles around the mixing consul and says, "Don't forget this . . . Don't forget that . . ." We didn't have to remind him of anything. He was already there. He'd already beaten you to it. I always loved the drum sounds he got, like he did with Simple Minds and U2 and all that.

KEITH RICHARDS: I don't think there was really a lot of extra tension on this album. Maybe there were a couple of more incidents, mainly to do with the timing of Mick's solo album and so on, and Mick wasn't there very much at the beginning so there were a couple of misunderstandings. But nothing more than usual. It just seems everybody knows about our problems this time [laughs].

Ronnie was a much bigger factor than on previous albums. Mainly I think because Ron and I kept working together and playing together, because we lived very close to each other most of the time. He's just around the corner from me, so we didn't fall into another of those slow, "nothing happening" periods like we did after the last record. So we said, we're just going to keep playing, and I guess that's reflected on the album. There's a lot from that year of just banging away together in the kitchen.

MICK JAGGER: Keith really wanted to tour with that album, but I just thought it would be a bad idea and I'm sure I was right. It was a real low point for the band. Everybody was disagreeing with each other and arguing all the time. If we'd done it, it could have been the end of the band.

CHUCK LEAVELL: Then there was Dirty Work and, yes, it was a tough time. Mick and Keith were not getting along as well as they are now, but there was something about the tension that was healthy, too. The fact that they worked their way through it, that says it all to me. They worked their way through it. It's much like a marriage. All marriages at some point in time have some kind of problem, and you either call it quits or reach a brick wall and realize you're not going to get over it unless you dig a tunnel or throw a rope over the top. You work your way through it, and that's what happened in that time period.

KEITH RICHARDS: When it came time to shoot the video for "One Hit," I guess it was a little tense. The director thought this was great and wanted to get that tension on camera. I said it was fine by me, so the video is kind of accurate in a way.

December 1, 1986. The Charlie Watts Orchestra's first album, *Live at Fulham Town Hall*, is released.

CHARLIE WATTS: Most of the [jazz] masters are gone. There aren't many people with any personality left. In the days when you could see Coleman Hawkins and Ben Webster . . . they were so different as players. You mentioned that orchestra I toured with—well, the thing with those guys is they were their own person-players. All of them. One of the great players—I mean, they all were—but Don Weller is fantastic. He's unique. There's no one in the world that plays saxophone like Don.

There aren't really a lot of guys like that. Now it's different—there isn't the interest and there aren't the clubs like there used to be. You could say, "Well, too bad, so what?" But for me it's a loss, because it's an era that I loved and in which I was brought up. But for a twenty-year-old man or woman now, maybe it isn't a loss, maybe they think it's all old folks who are over the hill. To me it was the hippest thing in the world to see Miles Davis performing in a club. Perhaps he's not considered that hip anymore.

CHAPTER 8
Steel Wheels

September 1, 1987. Mick Jagger releases his second solo album, *Primitive Cool*.

MICK JAGGER: It's different from *She's the Boss* because that album was more city-fied. I'm not saying this is a country album [laughs], it's just a little more considered and a little wider range of music and lyrics.

1988. On March 15, Mick begins a ten-date solo tour of Japan. He will perform another solo tour in Australia in September. On September 26, Keith releases his first solo album with the X-Pensive Winos, *Talk Is Cheap*. Two months later, he takes the band on a fifteen-date American tour.

KEITH RICHARDS: I'd known Steve Jordan for quite a while and we'd become close friends. After *Dirty Work* went down, about the same time Steve left the [David] Letterman band, we were both kind of stranded on the beach looking for something to do [laughs]. Suddenly Aretha [Franklin] called up and the "Jumpin' Jack Flash" project came up. I looked at Steve and said, "You want some work? I know the tune!"

So we started work on that and it went well and then there was the Chuck Berry project, so we've been working non-stop ever since. I realized what a great player Steve is and what a great ear he has. Finding the right band members is the most important thing, and with Steve as the starting point I had the most important element, which is the drummer. Waddie [Wachtel] and Ivan Neville I'd known for a few years, so I knew if someone wanted me to produce a record I would want to get these cats involved. I just didn't know that the album would be my own [laughs].

The great thing about working with these guys is that you didn't have the problems of dealing with a bunch of superstars. These guys just wanted to kick ass. Over the years my role in the Stones has evolved, so that I lay it down in front and everybody follows me. So if we're rehearsing a take and I'm not quite sure what to do, I'll stop at the bridge and say, "I'm not happy with that." I'll stop and the Stones will stop as well. They'll wait for me to get it back together and that's the way the job has evolved over the years.

With the Winos, I did the same thing. I'd stop and start looking around for the cigarette or a drink while I'm thinking about what to do next. But they don't stop, they just keep going [laughs]. I look over at [Steve] Jordan and he's going, "Pick it up, man . . . pick it up!" And I realize that nobody kicks me anywhere else, and I need it as much as anybody. Just to be the leader and kicking everybody else is not necessarily a good thing! You need somebody to kick

you too, and the Winos . . . that's what they did for me—
"Oh, that hurt! Nobody does that to me! It kind of feels
good . . . I need that . . . okay." So that was good for me.

Steve Jordan and Charlie Drayton had grown up
together. They went to school together and I see a lot of sim-
ilarities in their relationship, as I do with Mick and myself.
When you grow up with a guy, there are certain tensions
because you know each other so well, so you're always
checking each other a little harder. I'm familiar with that
kind of relationship. In actual fact, it's like my American
band. I've been living in New York now for many years; it's
become my second home. The Stones are my London band,
and now I have one from this country, this continent . . .
which is amazing. It's a weird mixture of guys. Three black
guys, a Jew, and an Anglo [laughs].

**January 18, 1989. The Stones are inducted into the Rock and Roll
Hall of Fame.**

PETER TOWNSHEND: There are some giant artists here tonight,
but for me the Stones will always be the greatest. They epit-
omize British rock. Even though they're all my friends, I'm
still a fan. Whatever you do, guys, don't try to grow old
gracefully. It wouldn't suit you.

MICK JAGGER: It's slightly ironic that tonight you see us on
our best behaviour because we're being rewarded for

twenty-five years of bad behaviour. I am very proud to have worked with this group of musicians for twenty-five years. The other thing I'm very proud of is the songs that Keith and I have written.

I'd like to pay tribute to two people who can't be here tonight. Ian Stewart, a great friend and a great blues pianist whose odd but valuable advice kept us on a steady, bluesy course most of the time, and Brian Jones, whose individuality and musicianship often took us off the bluesy course with marvellous results. So on behalf of the Stones, I'd like to thank you very much for this award.

KEITH RICHARDS: It's your classic Frankenstein's monster situation. You made it, it's yours, and now you're working for it [laughs]! A lot of the eighties was really me having a really hard time dealing with that fact. That you're just the Rolling Stones, and you're really working for this monster you created, and it's not exactly what you want to do all the time. If that's all you do, you're gonna just be stuck in that rut. What the Stones found out in the eighties, painfully, was that in order to keep the band going and keeping fresh, you really have to do other things, and be able to work and bring in outside influences to keep it fresh. As usual, we learn our lessons the hard way.

March 15, 1989. The Stones sign the largest concert deal in history with Toronto promoter Michael Cohl. It is the beginning of a

new era of mega-concert touring. The guaranteed advance is estimated at US$70 million.

MICHAEL COHL: Steel Wheels wasn't really my first involvement with the Stones—it was my first *prolonged* involvement. As a local promoter, we'd done shows with them in Toronto and Buffalo and Montreal over the years. That big financial commitment . . . I know it's a big number from zero up, but I never thought it was a big number relative to what I thought the results were going to be. I know that at the time there was a whole camp of people—in fact, the vast majority of people in the promoting industry—that thought I was nuts. But to me there was no doubt. The Rolling Stones' '81 tour had been successful, and a couple of things happened after that which were very important.

First of all, I did the Michael Jackson tour for Chuck Sullivan, which was the tour when *Thriller* came out. So I was on the tour but I'd never done anything before on that level. The tour got into a lot of trouble, as everybody knows, and Chuck was losing a lot of money, so I took over the tour and it made money from that point to the end. It taught me a lot. It showed me what might happen in the right circumstances. Promoters at that time were used to doing one show in a city and here was Michael Jackson selling out two and three.

Chuck did some things very well. He had some deals with stadiums that I would have never thought you could get. So that was step one. Step two was the Pink Floyd tour in '87. I was part of putting that whole project together, and we ended up selling three nights at CNE Stadium after they'd been away for quite a number of years, just like the Stones.

Step three was the Amnesty Tour. I got a call from one of my production people when they were at Maple Leaf Gardens at about two in the afternoon and they were saying "Everybody's screaming at us, everybody's making it miserable for us . . . There's this guy [promoter Bill Graham] running around criticizing every single thing we do, barking and yelling." I said, "I'll be right down and try to calm everything down as best I can." I went to the hall and we got everything calmed down and straightened out, and I said to my people at the time, "Don't worry, you'll never have to work with him again." The next morning they all come into my office and say, "Hey big mouth, do you realize what you said last night? That means we're not going to work with the Stones ever again." All I said was, "Don't bet on it."

The next day, I got out a piece of paper, and I thought about Michael Jackson and Pink Floyd, and I went tick . . . tick . . . tick . . . I said, "There's got to be forty shows to make"— I can't tell you the money because we don't talk about it—"but there's no way the Rolling Stones couldn't do forty shows and make this amount of money, because there's no way they wouldn't sell out." I was going, "God, Pink Floyd did three shows, the Stones gotta be able to do four shows in Toronto, and Michael Jackson did three there, the Stones gotta be able to do four." And I was up to sixty shows in about an hour.

At the time, I didn't know Rupert [the Stones' financial adviser, Prince Rupert Loewenstein] at all, but I knew Steve O'Rourke and I knew that they had worked together, so I called O'Rourke and I said, "Will you introduce me to Rupert?" He said, "What did you have in mind?" And I said, "I have an offer for the Stones." He said, "I know Rupert well—what is it?" I said, "This is the offer," and he said, "Rupert will be talking to you very, very shortly." I got a call ten minutes later from Rupert, who said, "I understand you have a proposal for the Rolling Stones." I made it right then and there on the phone, and we arranged to meet in New York, and it all started from there.

Until it was signed it was never a reality, because I always knew that at a given point late in the process they would sit with Bill Graham. I mean, they had to, and I knew that, so I knew that at a minimum I was going to be a shill to get a better deal out of Graham, and at a maximum I would get it, and I was willing to take that shot. Three or four weeks into the process, which took about six months, I said, "What the heck, I should phone some of the other promoters and get a second opinion." I phoned three promoters—I never got past three—I phoned them, and two of them said they thought the Stones would do "okay" and the third one said, "They'll do all right but there's no way they're as big as they used to be." So I stopped phoning, because all they were saying was that they'd lost faith in the Rolling Stones, and I'm never going to believe them because I think they're nuts, and off we went. But they did think I was nuts.

The first great day happened when we were flying down to Barbados to sign the contract and I had this cheque in my sports jacket and it was like . . . I'd never had a cheque like that. I'd never even seen one that big. [Reputedly, it was for US$70,000,000.] Every fifteen minutes I would check it was still there—"Okay, I haven't lost it"—because I was sure I was going to lose it. In fact, in the room where we were signing the contracts and shaking hands and getting ready for this great journey, I must have checked it three times in fifteen minutes, because I figured when the lawyer said, "Can I have the cheque?" I was sure I wouldn't have it. But it worked out well, and then we had lunch, and everybody parted company, and I got on the plane to come home. Norman Perry was with me, and up to that moment I was supremely confident, 1,000 percent confident. I got on the plane and I don't know what happened. I sat down, turned to Norman, and said, "I've really done it this time . . . I'm out of my mind. I think I've just bankrupted us. It's over. We're the super idiots of all time. What have I done? And how could you have let me do it?" Then I didn't talk to him for the next three hours. I just sat there going, "I can't believe I've done this . . . You egomaniac, you turkey!"

I got over that very quickly. It took me about two days, but I got over it—"This is just emotion . . . Relax, you're not stupid, you figured this one out. It's going to happen, it's going to be right . . . you're okay." The first city we put on sale was Cleveland. That was the first proof, because this is all speculation until you put the tickets on sale and, in a sense, people vote. It's like an election. We only sold 30,000 out of about 53,000 and it was like, "Get out the Alka Seltzer, quick . . . Holy Christ . . ." That next week was a terrible, terrible week. It was like, "Is it Cleveland, or is it the tour? Cleveland ended up selling 53,000, it just had a bit of a different pattern than we'd expected. The next week we sold out four cities and it was, "Wow . . . we're okay."

1989. On June 2, Bill Wyman, then fifty-two, marries nineteen-year-old Mandy Smith in England. On July 11, the Stones announce plans for the Steel Wheels tour at Grand Central Station in New York. On August 29, they release *Steel Wheels* and the single "Mixed Emotions."

KEITH RICHARDS: I'm very happy with *Steel Wheels*. It combines the elements and the feel of some of our better ones like *Exile* or *Some Girls*. There's a real good feel to the playing throughout.

Having a deadline worked in our favour on this one. It's been a long time since Mick and I have been under pressure to finish a bunch of songs—and remember, some of our best songs came under that kind of pressure. When we first told people we were going to start writing together after Christmas break and then record and have the album finished by June, everyone had a good laugh and said, "Sure you will. Love to see it!" [laughs]. But we really got down to it and it worked well, I think. It just shows that with the Stones, if you give them a deadline, they'll make it. It's been a good year. We're on time, and let's face it, the fact that were here talking at all is amazing in itself [laughs]. It's really been a pleasure, and I can't wait to get on the road and tour this stuff.

MICK JAGGER: When we started working on this album we knew we had a deadline, and that's a good thing for us because sometimes we can work too long on a record making sure everything's just right. This one went pretty quickly, and I think there are a lot of good things on there. There are some good rock tracks like "Mixed Emotions," "Rock and a Hard Place," and "Sad, Sad, Sad," and then there's some ballad-y ones. So I think there's enough variety to keep you interested all the way through.

KEITH RICHARDS: There's a great new energy with the band. Taking a couple of years off and everybody doing their own projects has really contributed back to the whole band. We've all learned a lot. Playing with other musicians and having to organize the whole thing for yourself, you start to appreciate what it's like to be upfront in Mick's position. And I think for Mick's part he appreciates even better what it's like to be able to lean back on such a solid band as the Stones.

August 31, 1989. The Steel Wheels tour of America opens in Philadelphia. It takes in US$98 million.

CHUCK LEAVELL: When the Steel Wheels tour rolled around, there was a determination like I'd never experienced with the band. In '82 there was a casual attitude. Yep, we get onstage, we do our bit, and we go. The rehearsal was ten days long. Steel Wheels was eight weeks of rehearsal. The feeling was, if we're going to go out there and do another Rolling Stones tour, it has to be the best Rolling Stones tour that's ever been. We've reached this point and either we get out there and do 150 percent or we don't do it at all. So that attitude prevailed, thank heaven, and it was extraordinary, it really was. In the rehearsal period we went through the book. We probably did 85 percent of every Rolling Stones song ever written, to see how it would translate on the stage. Checking to see did it feel good to play, did it make sense, could we edit it, or rearrange it. If it didn't, it went quickly, if it went well, it got a check on the board. At one point in time we had something like sixty songs that we all felt pretty good about.

I remember Mick calling me up, because at that point he

began to have some respect for me in that capacity of helping with the arrangements, and helping with set lists and that sort of thing, and he said, "Let's get together. We have to do some serious work to figure this out. You write your favourite thirty songs and I'll write the ones that I like, and then we'll compare notes." There were maybe five songs different. Then we took that back to the band and the band of course had input and made changes here and there. Then we began to say, "Keith's got to change guitars on this song, and we can't put that song right behind it." So we really, really worked hard to logistically make that thing flow from beginning to end and to do some unusual songs—"Two Thousand Light Years From Home," that sort of thing, that the band had not done in a long time.

RON WOOD: Any musician will tell you that you can't go too far—if you're on the road especially—without somebody putting something under your nose all the time . . . or in your mouth, or in your ear [laughs]. I've always hated needles, so I could never have been a junkie, but I used to . . . I blew a lot of money on drugs. It was a crutch, that old cliché. You might turn it down many times and then one day you have a little sample, then before you know it you're in it, whether it's hash or coke or whatever. You think you're just having fun and not doing any harm, but I wouldn't recommend it to the kids. It's a real hard one to get out of!

1990. On February 14, the Stones begin ten sold-out shows at the Korakuen Dome in Tokyo. It is their first performance in Japan. On May 18, the Steel Wheels tour, now called "Urban Jungle," continues in Rotterdam, Holland. On August 18, during the European tour, the Stones play in Prague for the first time.

MICHAEL COHL: There are a lot of high points—it's hard to pick one out. Prague was a high point in that the Velvet Revolution had just happened. It was a matter of weeks and no one had ever been in there, and there was the president of the country, Vaclav Havel, inviting the Rolling Stones to be the first, and they went. It was an absolutely amazing experience. I remember one of the great things for me is that we went over to the presidential palace, where they lived and conducted the business of the government, and we had a little bit of a tour, some tea and juice at mid-day, and outside there's this big square—the palace is like a open rectangle—and there must have been ten thousand people. It was just packed from wall to wall, and we were sitting there and we could hear them chanting in the courtyard.

So the band and the president and his wife and myself and my wife went onto the balcony. They were just going to wave to everybody, and the people were chanting and chanting, and we asked President Havel, "What are they chanting?" and he told us they were chanting, "Thank you, President Havel, for bringing us the Rolling Stones. We love you for bringing us the Rolling Stones." Well, you could see

Charlie's eyes well up a bit. I couldn't believe it was happening. It was "Wow, is this incredible?!" That was a pretty good moment.

August 25, 1990. The Stones perform the final show of the Steel Wheels/Urban Jungle tour at Wembley Stadium in London.

MICHAEL COHL: Yeah, it was the biggest tour of all time, in every respect, not just money because sometimes it's hard to deal with the amount of money. It's like *Gone with the Wind* versus *Star Wars*. I think *Gone with the Wind* may have sold more tickets, but they were only a dollar then, as opposed to seven dollars to see *Star Wars*. I'm sure in terms of money the Steel Wheels/Urban Jungle tour was the highest grossing. But more importantly, I'm sure it had the most people. Over six million people.

Yeah, I still get a thrill every night . . . every night. I'll stop doing this when it doesn't happen. The pinnacle for what I do, as a promoter, is working with the Rolling Stones.

Listen . . . the Stones were *always* the pinnacle from the time I started in '69, through the seventies, through the eighties, into the nineties. Whenever I sit down with people and they ask, "What band would you most like to work with and where would you want to be financially? Where would you see the most challenge in finding out if you can do a good job and keep everybody happy?," my answer always comes out, "the Stones." If you asked any promoter,

"Who do you most want to promote?" almost every promoter would always come back and say, "Well, Jeez, the
Stones." Doing the Stones in '89 was the pinnacle. As soon
as it finished, I wanted to do it twice more. It was like win-
ning the Super Bowl. I still get a big thrill. The best way I
can describe it is I walk out on a field, the band comes onstage, the people cheer, and it's very exciting. There's always
this little line that goes through the back of my head—"And
they pay me to do this?"

1991. On April 2, the Stones release *Flashpoint*, **comprising
songs from the Steel Wheels and Urban Jungle tours, along with
two new songs. One of these, "Highwire," had been released as
a single March 5. On April 3, The Charlie Watts Quintet releases**
From One Charlie. **On October 25, the IMAX film** *At The Max*
opens in eight IMAX theatres around the world.

MICHAEL COHL: We were talking early on about "Make a film,
do not make a film, do a TV show, do not do a TV show."
And the recurring theme in the discussion, which spanned
months, was "We've done concert films, and we could do
another concert film, but isn't there something different or
better we could do?" And I said, "Well, there's this process
called IMAX and I've seen a couple of space movies, and
bringing that to the stage could be incredible. You should
take a look at it." In the back of my head I'm going, "I know
I've got the idea," but they didn't know anything about

IMAX. I wanted to put it together, so I threw out the idea— "You should look at IMAX, because I think once you look at it, and you let your imagination go, it could be a very special way to capture the show." And everybody was going, "The show was so great, we should have this somehow in the library."

I think we were playing in Manchester, and IMAX has this theatre about two hours away. So after the show we all got on a bus and drove for two hours and got there at three in the morning. We had the projectionist waiting, and he showed us a movie called *Beaver*, and we all sat there and watched it for about ten minutes, and then went, "Right! This will do it." And we went and made the movie. I think it's incredible for what it is. It's a movie—it's not like being in the stadium but it's as close as you're ever going to get without having them live.

MICK JAGGER: It was an interesting way to do a concert film because the stage we used in Steel Wheels was so wide that even in a regular 35mm film you wouldn't really be able to see it all.

The best thing for a concert movie is to have the smallest camera with the least number of people operating it, so you don't notice them, and the longest length of film. Well IMAX is completely the reverse of that. It's the biggest camera with the largest amount of people on the biggest dolly with the shortest length of film that you can have, so it's a bit cumbersome. I was very worried about how they were going to shoot it. But it turned out all right. I was very interested in experimenting with this format because I wanted to give people the sense of what it's like to be there.

August 3, 1992. Ron Wood releases *Slide on This*.

RON WOOD: I'm the typical musician type that is a very bad businessman. Most of the time I wouldn't ask for anything. Then I realized I wasn't getting anything, so I ended up getting managers, and I went through quite a few different ones that advised me on this, that, and the other. They were never popular with the Stones and most of them were driven away . . . by force sometimes! I remember Keith chasing one of them across a field with a .38 once [laughs]. A lot of it's in my own interest. Keith's like a big brother to me there, saying, "All right, this guy's okay."

October 20, 1992. Keith releases his second solo album with the X-Pensive Winos, *Main Offender*.

KEITH RICHARDS: It sounds good to me. It sounds more like what we should have done the first time around—it sounds raunchier.

I found out a lot about Mick's job by going on the road and doing my own stuff. I found out what it means being the front man all the time, what you have to do, and it's not so easy. I think Mick found out that you can't just hire a bunch of guys, no matter how good they are, you can't just get a band like the Stones. I think he found that out on his first couple of records. You don't get the service he relies on. He can feel confident with the Stones. He knows he can do anything he likes and we'll be there—that backbeat will be there and that riff will hang around for him while he climbs down from the tower or whatever. You don't get that overnight, no matter what kind of musicians you get to work with. So we both found out that we do need each other, and we found out a lot more about each other's jobs.

The great thing about working with bands is that when you go out on tour, the individual musicians begin to form into a cohesive band. That's what happened when we took the Winos out on the road last time—they became a band. So to record another album was easier because we knew each other much better than on the first one.

It's not so surprising that our solo records are coming out at roughly the same time, because we finished working with the Stones at the same time. Ronnie Wood's album came out last month—that's how long it takes to make a record. You stop work with the Stones and start your own thing because we're always locked into the Stones' schedule one way or another. Mick's album is coming out in January, which gives us breathing space. I really didn't want to go head to head with him. It's kind of stupid, you know, and so I got in first [laughs].

Yeah, the time off between projects is so destructive. The Stones got far too big for their own good as a band, and I guess that's what happened in the middle eighties. You can't wait around for the juggernaut to wind up, because after you finish a tour or record, there's two years of nothing to do, which for a musician is ridiculous. Then when the Stones do get back together for each new record or tour, we spend virtually six months in maintenance, just getting the rust off. You can't just walk in after two years off and be the "greatest rock'n'roll band in the world," especially when people are calling you that and you know you're not. It takes a long time, and so I think the greatest thing now for the Stones is that everybody's working. Charlie's working, Ronnie's working, Mick's working, and I'm working. I know that when we do get together next year that we can just go straight at it. There's none of that feeling—"We've got to go through incredible therapy and hard work just to get the band back to where it was two, three years ago."

In a way I don't feel that I write songs. I think you can get into a lot of trouble thinking you actually create these things. I kind of prefer to see myself as an antenna. I think all of the songs in the world are running around this room right now and if you just give me an instrument, I'll sit around and if I'm in the mood and they're buzzing up there I just need a little snatch of music or a phrase. Give me eight bars, six bars, and an interesting chord change and I'll recognize a song in it, whereas to somebody else it might just be a pleasant little passage of music. It'll click with me and I'll build on that. The thing is to recognize them and then you just grab hold of it by that tail and don't let go.

November 27, 1992. Keith and the X-Pensive Winos begin an eleven-day tour of Europe followed by twenty-two dates in North America.

KEITH RICHARDS: That's one of the reasons that the Winos exist. As much as I enjoy going out on the cutting edge in football stadiums with the Stones, if that's all you do it's a bizarre existence for a musician. It's crazy. This guy called God joins the band every night in the form of wind, rain, heat, cold, whatever . . . thunder, lightning . . . you never know. You don't have a controlled environment; it's not an even playing field. The wind's going across the stage and some guy you don't want gets the best sound in the world two miles down the road. So with the Winos it's very important to be able to play good rooms for the joy and the pleasure, and I get to keep my feet on the ground. Also, I know I can face my people, the crazy fans, bless their hearts. They're nuts, all of them, and they know it but I love them dearly. There's a special warmth and a special feeling.

These guys are working my ass off, if you pardon the expression. We go back to the hotel room and everybody talks about what wasn't right and how they can improve this or let me hear that thing again. Every night! It's like honing it down. It's a heavy fencing class. This band never lets you go. You can't cruise in this band, and maybe I'm spoiled. You see, in the Stones I have a cruising position. I can put myself out there in the front as much as I want to support Mick, or if the music's not right, I can hunker back down there with Charlie Watts and Ronnie Wood and say, "Let's pull our things together." I have an option. Here, being a front man all the time I think is good for me—I enjoy it. But these guys are killing me. No complaints, though. Hey, to have one good band in your lifetime is a miracle. To have two is, well . . . I'm blessed, really.

What I'm looking really forward to is seeing how one thing spills over into the other. There's no reason why it has to be pigeonholed—like, "This is for the Stones and this is for the Winos." I think that's kind of shown itself with "Almost Hear You Sigh" on "Steel Wheels," which Steve and I had basically gotten together and Mick finished it off because he loved it so much and wanted to do it. I think whatever Mick's doing, whatever Ronnie's doing, is great. We each need extra input. The Stones can't keep going in a vacuum anymore. I guess that's fairly obvious. We found out the hard way by yelling at each other for five years, but we always do things the hard way.

The Stones got too big for me to really find how I can get the best out of them. When you're operating on that scale that is the juggernaut, it's like some sort of Frankenstein. You've created this thing and you're very grateful for it, but at the same time you wonder who's working for whom. Are the Stones working for me or am I working for the Stones? I think to keep that band together in the future, there's a definite possibility of some great Stones stuff to come. I'm not ruling out another golden period of the Stones if everything falls into place and the full moon's come in the right place [laughs]. I need to be well oiled, but it's not like I'm using this band for practice. To me, it's like, "Hey . . . I have somewhere else to go." There are five guys in this band, six guys . . . and twenty musicians, because they can all play different instruments and get different feels, different moods. And they all write. Everybody's multifaceted, so to me that's fascinating.

When that huge thing called the Stones unwinds, that's always my problem, really—not working with the Stones, or just not working. That's when I'd take up my darker pursuits. So just knowing that I have another team that is behind me is really comforting.

To me, music should never look like you're climbing Mount Everest to do what you do. The greats make it look as effortless as possible. You should be that much in front of what you're doing that you know what's coming next and you're rolling with it. You're prepared—you're not sort of straining every sinew just to keep moving. Things should float and have the power and the majesty. It has to fly. This is what music is all about, especially rock'n'roll music. It's like jazz. If jazz don't swing, it don't do nothing, and rock-

'n'roll comes straight out of jazz. It's a very simplified form of jazz, when it comes down to it. You can improvise over the thing as much as you want. It's the blues, basically, and without blues you wouldn't have jazz either. I can take this way back. I've got back as far as Corelli, 1698. I'm just trying to find the groove masters. I've been through Beethoven, Mozart, Vivaldi, and I've got to Corelli so far. That's what I'm really after—the stuff that moves, the stuff that shifts and is not agonizing or screeching to listen to. The idea of scrambling to get to the heights . . . it drives me mad watching guys trying to do that. It should drip like honey [laughs]. I don't know quite how to explain it, because you can't explain music . . .

January 6, 1993. Bill Wyman announces he is leaving the band.

KEITH RICHARDS: That's a good question [i.e., Is Wyman leaving?]. It should be aimed at Bill, but my thing is that he ain't out yet! He's in until he says he's out. It's really up to Bill. I don't want to change him, but I gotta go see him. After all, working with a guy for thirty years, I gotta at least look him in the eye and say, "Hey, where do we stand, Bill?" I'm not sure yet, and I have to find out, because if he really means it, and he really doesn't feel like doing it anymore, or can't get it together . . . I mean, I can't coerce him or put a gun to his head. I don't want a reluctant bass player, either. If it is true, we'll still go ahead, but I'll have to find somebody to fill a very large pair of shoes, and so will Charlie Watts, because that counts. I think if it was Charlie Watts, then we'd say, "We've had it," but I think given some care and some thought, that we can carry on. The Stones won't sound that much different. Charlie Watts came up with the best idea for keeping Bill in the band, which is to replace him with a girl bass player. That really might be too much for Bill [laughs] . . . He's such a chauvinist, Bill.

February 9, 1993. Mick Jagger releases *Wandering Spirit*.

MICK JAGGER: The thrust of this album is . . . Actually, it's not really a rock album per se. I don't want to put anyone off, but if you look at it, there are only maybe three rock songs on it in the traditional form. The rest is R&B, or country or gospel influenced, or rockabilly, or whatever, whereas with most Stones albums—though they contain other things—the thrust has really been harder rock.

I guess a solo album is my chance to express some other musical things, because the Stones is such a big project, especially if you're thinking about touring behind it. The album becomes a bit of an adjunct to a tour, so you're thinking, "Can I do this on stage? Will this work?" and all that, and it becomes part of something else. The next thing, someone's coming down from Canada saying, "Okay, we've got seventy shows lined up, what's the stage gonna be like?" So it all becomes part of a very big project. With a solo album you can do a folk song with just a fiddle if you want, because no one's going to say anything. With the Stones you can do all these things, but recently hard rock has become the focus, so maybe this is my response to that. For example, on a song like "Sweet Thing" I used the falsetto voice because I think it suited the groove. I like singing in falsetto, but just to be clear, "I'm not really a fairy!"

"Mother of a Man" was a reaction to the L.A. riots by someone whose response was to go and buy a gun, which a lot of friends of mine seemed to be doing. They'd go and buy a gun and join the Hollywood Gun Club and get their marksmanship up to scratch. I saw all these people doing gun practice when I did this picture [Freejack] down there. I hadn't used guns in a long while and I needed to look the part for the movie. I'd sort of gone off the idea of using firearms, so I went down to the shooting range thinking, "I hate this. I hate guns and I hate all this shit in America with all these guns. Everyone's got a gun—it's ridiculous!" I really didn't want any part of it, but I had to do it for the movie, so, "Okay, give me the gun." This guy from the FBI is there to help me and says, "There's the target," and I go . . . [shooting sounds] . . . firing a clip. I looked at it and thought, "Pretty good results. Okay, give me another gun" [laughs]. Then I got the top score and I said, "Give me something big, give me a semiautomatic!" I was just doing it for the movie, but I was quite enjoying it. If you're going to do something, you might as well be proud of the fact that you get good at it, and the better you are and the more conversant you are, the less likely you are to make mistakes if you ever have to use one. But guns are not something I want in my life.

To me this is like a '92, '93 record. I'm not trying to go into any new form of music, because there's nothing out there that I want to push or get involved with that I'm not already involved in. You know, rockabilly goes into gospel because those styles are very close, and then country music goes into blues and goes into rock and so on and so on. It's all part of one kind of popular music style that has existed for about fifty years.

April 20, 1993. Mick and Keith begin writing material in Barbados for what would become *Voodoo Lounge*. Charlie joins them ten days later.

MICK JAGGER: Yeah, I did go from work on my solo album straight into work on the Stones album. So yes, I was already in the groove, as it were. But the other side of that is that I just wrote a bunch of songs and now I have to write another whole bunch [laughs]. I did have a few things left over that I hadn't finished, like "Brand New Car," but I didn't have an awful lot else. So I went to Barbados and sat there at first thinking, "What am I going to do?"

We talked about the record, and we wanted to be focused and direct and to keep it simple. That's all well and good, but we still had to write the songs! We took a long time to write them—which is good, because I hate to rush that part—and we got a lot of good things, so we didn't waste a lot óf time in the studio.

I think this record has some of the good elements of the old Rolling Stones records without being too imitative of them. I was a bit worried initially about [engineer] Don Smith, who loves all that old equipment, tube amplifiers, and the like. Without realizing it they can start trying to re-create albums that they heard when they were young. It's a real danger, because once you've done it, I really don't want to do it again. I'd hear them whispering, "It sounds like *Exile on Main Street*," and I really didn't want to do that because I don't think *Exile* was a very good-sounding record. The performing was really good but the mix was awful. So I didn't want that, but then they said, "Oh, then you want it to sound very clinical," which I didn't either.

KEITH RICHARDS: I went straight off that tour [X-Pensive Winos] and went into writing songs with Mick and Charlie down in Barbados, with maybe a week off. I really had no time to discern the difference between the Winos and the Stones. I was just doing what I was doing. I knew that I didn't have to do any practising; I was already on a roll. It was funny, you've got the Winos and the Stones and one I love as much as other. We're all friends, anyway—everybody knows everybody. I first met Darryl through Charlie Drayton and Steve Jordan.

I think two days after I finished the last show with the Winos, Mick came to New York and we had a chat about what we were going to do about the record—how we saw it. Basically, after just sitting around a table in the afternoon, the only word that I remember that really stuck with me was "focus." We both said, "If we can be looking down the same telescope, we can pull the Stones really back in and get that 'feel' thing going." And that's what happened. Some things don't happen the way you want 'em exactly, but I've got to say I'm very, very happy with everything the Stones are doing.

One of the things is that I've got Mick to play harp more. I wanted him to get out of thinking about just being the lead singer—to start thinking that he had more to offer the band. I wanted to draw him into the band, and I think it worked. Mick has always knocked me out as a harp player. He's one of the best around, and I've always felt that his phrasing on harp was incredible. When it came to singing, sometimes he would put singing into another compartment and want to be more restricted in a way. I felt that playing the harp a lot more would automatically free up the way he phrases vocally, and it did. He's kind of like Louis Armstrong. He sang the way he played the trumpet. It's a unique style, but I think playing an instrument gives you more insight into a song.

MICK JAGGER: It's great fun, actually, playing harmonica not on a twelve-bar blues. I mean, twelve-bar is great but you've heard it so many times before. That's why it's so good on "Miss You"—which I didn't play—it was Sugar Blue, who's a fantastic player. It's good playing through those sequences because you don't get caught up in playing repetitious riffs. It's your own new riff, is what I'm trying to say. It's your new riff, which is the melody line screwed with in a blues way.

I mean, I love to just sit around and play the old blues stuff, but there's not that many new songs and even then a lot of them are just rehashes of the same old thing, so, like traditional jazz, it can become a moribund form. I think rock-'n'roll is not a moribund form because the more you get the very young people doing it, the more it will keep it alive. They'll always break the rules because they're not interested in rules, so it constantly regenerates. The virtue of rock'n'roll is that you're not stuck in a form like the blues. In rock'n'roll, if you want to change something, you just *do* it.

CHARLIE WATTS: The two albums [*Steel Wheels* and *Voodoo Lounge*] were different from most Stones albums because both times on both albums, we went to an island called Barbados. It could have been anywhere, but it happened to be Eddy Grant's place in Barbados on both counts. We spent three months there. Mick and Keith were there first and then I joined them and we just played. So by the time we got into the recording studio, we could play something and you'd go, "Oh, I remember that . . . I did this and that on it." You're already a third of a way to getting it together by doing that.

This time we also stayed at Ronnie Wood's house in Ireland and went over them all again for another few months. Then we went into the studio. By the time we started recording we really did have quite a few things down—thirty, in fact.

KEITH RICHARDS: Charlie has a whole new energy this time out. I think it has a lot to do with doing his own stuff. He was working all the time the Stones were off, and he made a very good record with Bernard Fowler. I think he realized that if you're going to do your own stuff, the buck does stop with you. He did say to me when we started this project last year [mumbles apologetically], "I sort of realized what you've been doing for thirty years" [laughs]. So everybody has come back with new insights, new ideas and experiences.

And we have a great new bass player, which to me was the one grey cloud on the horizon. I knew the rest of us were together, I knew there were some good songs around and that we were all ready for it, but if one of your engines has fallen off, what can you do? It turned out to be the least of our problems, and actually it went very smoothly. Darryl is fully integrating with Charlie and it's given an interesting new feel. It's fresh blood, after all. Darryl is incredibly accomplished, and he can also get down there in a funk. He's more precise than Bill and there's more power under there now.

That's one of the reasons Bill left. As I look on the upside of it, I think Bill realized that to do this gig you need to want to do it 110 percent at least. My way of looking at it now is that the minute you have some reluctance or doubt about it, you're already not on full power. In a way, I can now look on it as Bill stepping aside gracefully and letting the rest of us go.

I think one of my best ideas of last year was saying to Charlie, "Mick and I will say what we think about bass players, but you've got to decide." Charlie gave me a look and he said, "You're going to put me in the hot seat?" I said, "Once in thirty years, Charlie" [laughs].

CHARLIE WATTS: I know, it's awful, isn't it? I've never auditioned anybody before. It's not horrible, it's bloody hard work. We had four guys a day for a week! Seven days of it— you were just bassed out, I suppose they'd call it. I couldn't hear another bass at the end of the week. Darryl was the best of them. There were four guys on a really short list, and any one of them could have done the gig. They were all of the same musical calibre. In other words, they could play anything you put in front of them. It then got into a question of "feel" and do you think you could work with this guy for two years, or for however long it is? Luckily, Darryl was a very nice guy. He was a very pleasant man and a wonderful musician as well. This band doesn't call for that incredible sort of virtuoso bass playing, but he does have it, and if there was any room for it, he does have it, he could do it.

DON WAS: I knew Mick a bit but I'd never met Keith before. I went to an audition studio in New York, where they were trying out bass players. My interview for the job was listening to Keith tell me why he doesn't need a producer. So I left and didn't think I got the job, but I got a call and they asked me to do it. And I'm glad I did. They are masters of the rock'n'roll idiom. I learned a tremendous amount about music by working with these guys. *Steel Wheels*, which I really liked, was the appetizer to the main course, which [*Voodoo Lounge*] is. It was like a warm-up to this one.

I didn't know Keith before this record, and it was shocking to me to contrast the *Saturday Night Live* parody image—the "Mr. Change your blood every week" typical drug casualty of the seventies—with this vibrant, really intelligent, lucid, mind-racing character. He's the exact opposite of what you picture. The man is as creative as anyone I've encountered in my whole life. Whether he's doing a handwritten fax or playing guitar riffs, he's always inspired. It's a remarkable thing. I'd say he's at the peak of his powers. He's always grown as an artist and he's at a point where he's got a lifetime of experience on which to draw for inspiration.

Mick's contribution to this album has also been incredible. He's come up with some great lyrics and he's singing his ass off! There's an enthusiasm in the vocals that you'll hear right away. It's like, "Whoa, what got into him?" The other thing about Mick is that he's known as the guy who can put a tour together and go out on stage and then go back and check on the merchandise. But what people forget is just how deep his roots go in the blues. There were a couple of times where he'd pick up a National steel guitar and sing and play. He's just the natural inheritor of that tradition. They're both deep inside of what they're doing now.

May 3, 1994. The Stones take a cruise into New York to announce the Voodoo Lounge world tour of 1994–95.

MICHAEL COHL: Are the Stones still relevant in 1994? That's a tough one to narrow down, because there's a hundred different ways to define relevant. Is Bill Clinton relevant? Some days, people think he is, some days people think he isn't. I think he's always relevant because he's the president of the United States. If six million people are coming out to see the Rolling Stones in 1994–95, how can they not be relevant? Relevant, to me, means "Are they connecting with fans and are the fans interested in what's going on?" What's going on is a record and a tour. They will sell millions of records— they're going to sell millions of tickets. To me that means there are a lot of people interested in what they are doing, so how can they be anything but the *most* relevant, in that definition?

The difference from the last tour is that Steel Wheels was a new thing. It was like a couple that had been separated. They'd been married for a long time, separated for a long time, and were just getting back together and finding their sea legs. So nobody was sure what to do or how it was going to go, and they were working their way through it. It's much better this time. I think everybody's more relaxed. It's mostly the same faces, and there's much more of a camaraderie and a family feel to it.

CHUCK LEAVELL: The Steel Wheels/Urban Jungle tour began, in my mind, a completely new era in the Rolling Stones, especially in touring. It set a new standard, and not just for the band—maybe for others that came through as far as the stage is concerned, as far as the presentation, the music, and the flow from beginning to end. The challenge this time is how do you get close or maybe top what you did last time?

We went through the same process as with Steel Wheels. We had an eight-week rehearsal and did the same bit—played songs that the band hadn't done before. I think this time around the difference is that it's less of a greatest hits tour. Not all the songs will be as well known as some on Steel Wheels were, but they're equally if not more interesting. Like "Monkey Man," "Rocks Off," "All Down the Line," "Memory Motel," and "Wild Horses." The band hasn't done those songs in ages, and I think it's a wise decision because you can't go out and repeat yourself. If we go out and do 75 percent of what Steel Wheels was, it just won't work.

KEITH RICHARDS: What I'm hoping they're going to see is a show that isn't just locked into one set list. Obviously, a lot of the beginnings and the endings are pretty much going to be locked in, but we've rehearsed more songs than we've ever rehearsed before for a tour. In other words, we can keep it fresh—"Let's do this tonight," and change four or five songs. On the last tour it seemed to become a major thing to change one song, and two was out of the question. I have a feeling this time that we have more experience. And we'll be working with the same guys, so we can change four or five a night and alternate songs. It keeps it fresher for us, it keeps the crew more creative, and its also better for the audience in the long run.

The juggernaut thing can take over really quickly. It's so easy to do the same set list every night, and it's a very slick show but not necessarily the best you can give. So I'm really looking to change songs around a little more. There's some songs we've haven't done before, like "Monkey Man" is rocking in there this time. It's funny how certain songs at certain times suddenly pop up and suddenly everyone's into playing them and it suddenly sounds great, and it's a song that's never made it live-wise for you before. Suddenly "Ventilator Blues" is a possibility, and "Parachute Woman" and some other stuff [laughs]. Sometimes it's not so important that the audience knows every song. It's like an old friend—you've got to introduce him to the new friends, and the only way to do that is to play them.

MICK JAGGER: Yeah, the Steel Wheels stage was really good, but I think this one is interesting as well. I'm usually nervous on the first night, but after that I'm usually okay. The first night I'll be in . . . tatters. Wait, there's a song in here [laughs]. It's just that there's so much build-up with a big audience in a huge place and then there's all the press and it's never rehearsed enough. I mean, the songs are but then everyone forgets everything. I'll be blanking on the lyrics and Ronnie will blank on the solo but you get through it and hopefully the audience is with you. After that I just say "fuck it" and have fun with it, but it really is tough to have fun the first night, it really is [laughs].

1994. In early July, the Stones release "Love Is Strong." A week later, on July 12, they release *Voodoo Lounge*. On July 19, they do a tour warm-up performance at the RPM club in Toronto.

CHUCK LEAVELL: The RPM show was the best club gig I've ever done with a band, and I've done a few! Gosh, those are fun. If I had my way we'd do that about every three months, or every couple of months. It's a difficult thing to do, and I know why we don't, because of the logistics in putting it together, and you're "off time" is precious, especially to Mick, because he expends so much energy in one show. But they are so much fun, and RPM was great. I guess the thing that made it a stand-out was that it was Darryl Jones's first gig. Something else that I'll mention about that particular gig is that this particular line-up really is a leaner, meaner, tougher Rolling Stones. Steel Wheels was great, but this has a few less people, there's a little more room for everything to breathe, and it's tighter because of that.

DARRYL JONES: I have a feeling it's going to be pretty interesting. You know, it's the Stones. What can I say? I'm almost speechless. I love all these guys, I love the twang, I love the vibe, and I'm looking forward to a great, great time.

RON WOOD: You know what took years off my life? Seeing all the bras coming onstage. "Bill [Wyman], you're missing the scenery!"

August 1, 1994. The Voodoo Lounge tour opens in Washington, D.C. The tour will eventually gross US$121.2 million, making it the biggest-selling tour of all time.

MICK JAGGER: Coming offstage is difficult because you get so into the character you're playing on the stage, and then you have to come off and be just a regular person, plus there's all the adrenaline. So it can be difficult, but you just change out of your stage clothes and dry off and try and relax.

CHUCK LEAVELL: After a show? I tell you, the first thing that happens is that we all are herded into vans and quickly scurry away as the fireworks are going on outside. That's a big distraction for the band to make their great getaway, so the first thing that goes on is that everybody's in the van and we're talking. When I say everybody, there are several vans, and in my particular van there's Darryl, me, Bernard, and Lisa, and usually Arnold Dunn and maybe one of the security guys, Bob Bender. Sometimes there's one of the band members' kids if there's a lot of people out, or maybe there's one of the staff members in the van, so there's banter going on as to how the show went, what particular thing might have happened. The other day Darryl took a spill on the stage, so we were talking about that—"Man, are you okay? That was some fancy footwork!" This is the kind of thing that goes on in the van. When you get back to the hotel, and everybody goes up to their rooms, you change, you take your clothes down to the wardrobe, and kind of settle down, and maybe have a glass of wine or whatever. Then it depends.

Some nights you go to the bar and see some of the guys. Some nights Mick may call and say would you like to come up and have a bite to eat? Or Keith may call and say, "Hey, we got it going on up here, come check it out." Here's a perfect example: We played the last show in New York at Giants Stadium, we were hustled into the vans, out to the airplane to fly directly across the border to Toronto. Get there, go through customs, all of that, get your envelope with your key in it. Check into the room, it's now three-thirty a.m. Your bags have not arrived yet, they have to unload all that, so you wait for the bags, now it's four-thirty. The bags finally arrive. Okay, I'm ready for bed. Call the operator—"Please hold all my calls, unless there's an emergency, until noon the next day. Thank you very much." Get into bed. Ring, ring, ring. "Hello, Mr. Leavell? We have an emergency call from Ronnie Wood" [laughs]. "Woody, what's going on, man?" "C'mon up to Keith's room, c'mon!"

So it depends. There's those wacky nights that you do those things, and they're fun and you pay for it a little bit the next day. But hey, life wouldn't be the same without them.

1995. On October 30, the Stones release "Like a Rolling Stone." On November 10, they release *Stripped*. On October 15, 1996, they release on CD and video the fabled *The Rolling Stones Rock and Roll Circus*.

RON WOOD: The great thing about *Stripped* was that it was such an honest album. We didn't do any overdubs so it's just us playing live.

August 18, 1997. At the foot of the Brooklyn Bridge, the Stones announce their upcoming Bridges to Babylon tour.

MICK JAGGER: [Jumping down and addressing his question from the press area] I want to ask the Rolling Stones a very original question: Is this going to be your last tour?

KEITH RICHARDS: Yeah, this and the next five.

September 4, 1997. The Stones play a surprise kick-off show at the tiny (three hundred capacity) Horseshoe Tavern in Toronto.

MICK JAGGER: I think the Horseshoe gig was one of the better club shows we've done. There's always a lot of excitement around those types of shows, but sometimes they don't really come off too well. That one seemed to work and the material was coming together well. It's easy to play to yourselves in a rehearsal hall, but then when you actually play in front of people it's quite different. Then the big stadium shows are much more different because you've got all the lights and staging and you have to leap about and get the audience into it. It's much simpler in a small club because the audience is right there with you from the start.

In September, the Stones release "Anybody Seen My Baby," produced by Dust Brothers. Two weeks later, on September 29, they release *Bridges to Babylon*.

MICK JAGGER: I think it's a pretty good record. It's a notch up from some of the others we've done. The critics seem to like it, but I don't know how the punters will like it. I hope they do.

I started writing songs for this album last autumn, really, though they weren't intended to be on a Rolling Stones record. I thought I was writing songs for another solo album and was happily writing away when we decided to do another record with the band. So I took the ones I was working on that seemed to fit the band and brought them to Keith, and we worked on some of them together, and we also wrote some new ones.

On this album I wanted to try some new grooves, and so I talked to Charlie and we thought of some ways we could do this. I thought that some of the songs suited another kind of feel. So we eventually did some work on them outside, with the Dust Brothers, and then we brought those tracks back so that we could work on them with the rest of the band. So the album is a mixture of some new things as well as songs done in the sort of traditional way of recording with the Stones.

CHARLIE WATTS: It was a different way of working from the way we were used to but I had a lot of fun doing it. We were in L.A., which is great because it's full of musicians and producers. People like Wayne Shorter would drop by because he lives nearby the studio, or Jim Keltner would come by and offer to add some things. And I saw a lot of great jazz while we were there, just playing in the clubs. We worked with a couple of guys—John and Michael in particular, who are known as the Dust Brothers. As I say, it was a different way of working but very enjoyable.

KEITH RICHARDS: It was a different way of working but we kind of thought, well, "*vive la difference.*" So Mick would go a little more in the direction he wanted to go and I went a little further in my direction. We didn't waste a lot of time trying to reach a compromise on everything—just blending two things together.

We worked mostly with Don [Was] again because Don is such an easy guy to get along with. Now and again you find a guy that you feel like you've known him for years. The other great thing for the Stones is to have a producer who is also a musician. I think that shows up in the fact that our other best extended work with a producer was with Jimmy Miller, who is a drummer. He could get in the studio with us. The Stones respond to that more than to a guy that just happens to be a whiz with the faders behind the glass. Don Was's way of working really interests me, because he sits in the studio with the band while we're playing. He's almost part of it. You could look to him for a cue—it was very interesting. It cuts down that barrier between us. The control room sometimes can be like the Berlin Wall.

RON WOOD: I think this one's is a real peak for the Stones. I'd even say it goes back and compares well with classic albums like *Let It Bleed* and *Beggars Banquet*.

September 23, 1997. The Bridges to Babylon tour opens in front of 53,593 fans at Soldiers' Field in Chicago. The tour will gross US$89.3 million.

RON WOOD: This stage is another huge one and it looks great and everything, but my favourite part is when we walk across the bridge to the small stage and get to play the set in the middle of the people. Suddenly the seats you thought weren't that great are right up front. And for us it's great, because we can really vary what we play, because it's not all timed to light cues and all that. It's all about the music.

August 11, 1998. The Stones play Russia for the first time, at Luzhniki Stadium in Moscow.

CHARLIE WATTS: Mick was trying to make us go there for years, saying, "Oh, wouldn't it be great to play there" and all that, but as I grew up in the Cold War, I must admit I had these preconceptions. I thought it would be grey and dismal and snowing all the time. Everyone would look like Khrushchev and all that silly stuff. Of course, when we finally went there, I looked out my window and I could see Red Square and the Basilica and it was absolutely fantastic. It was magical—like we were in Disneyland, but the real thing.

November 2, 1998. The Stones release *No Security*, comprised of live material from shows in America, Buenos Aires, and Europe.

RON WOOD: For *No Security* we spent a lot of time figuring out what songs had been done for other live albums, because we didn't want to do anything that had been recorded before. On other live albums you have to go in and do some work on the tracks, but with this one we didn't. I didn't go to a studio once for overdubs. All the tracks are taken directly from the shows, so it shows we were pretty hot on that tour.

November 19, 2001. Mick Jagger releases his fourth solo album, *Goddess in the Doorway*. The first single, "God Gave Me Everything," features Lenny Kravitz.

MICK JAGGER: I don't need a band for my solo albums. It's pointless. I've got a very good band in the other world.

May 7, 2002. The Stones announce their upcoming tour in Van Courtland Park, New York, after a ride in a blimp emblazoned with the band's logo.

MICK JAGGER: At one time we had an idea that throughout the tour, competition winners would get a ride in the airship as a great prize, but I'm not so sure it's a prize as much as a forfeit. But we had a really good time in it.

We're going to do three kinds of shows on this tour—a

stadium show, an arena show, and a theatre or club show. In a place like New York, we'll do all three. So that's going to be fun for us. It's also a challenge for us to do these three kinds of shows where you have to jump from one to another. You get sort of used to playing a big place, so to change to a club will be difficult. The hard part for me is that one night I'll be doing the grand gestures and then in another venue it's just down to eyebrow movements. Sometimes I find it difficult moving from one to another, but we'll take a shot at it. Anyway, it will be a challenge and I think it will be fun.

As far as opening acts go, we're still signing some of them, but so far we've got Sheryl Crow, No Doubt, Buddy Guy, and Pretenders.

Regarding a new record, we just last night concluded negotiations between all the parties to release a "best of" Rolling Stones with two CDs going from 1963 to the present day. There will be all the hits and all the well-known songs and there will also be some new songs. That will be coming out in the early fall.

KEITH RICHARDS: A set list for the shows is still a bit down the road. It depends on whether we can remember them, but we're open to suggestions on that one.

MICK JAGGER: We like to do ones that we do know, but it's nice to find ones we've never done before. We're always looking for those. We'll try and do a different set list for each of the venues. Obviously in the stadium shows you have to do certain songs because people will be disappointed if they don't hear their favourites. You can't do all of them but you do have to do some of the well-known ones. With a club show you can do more or less what you want.

KEITH RICHARDS: One of the reasons we're doing this is that it's fun to play clubs and not to just play the same size venues all the time. It gives you a chance to do other stuff, things that don't necessarily work in a stadium.

Yeah, I guess we've got a gig to do. I mean, you know you're going to do it because you've been in on all the planning, but it's not until now that it actually hits you. It's like you've been drafted. On this day until the tour finishes, you're back on the road. That blimp ride marks the starting line. You sort of cut the anchor and off you go into the clouds, up in the sky, maybe even to Shanghai [laughs].

You know, I haven't been together with all four of these guys since we finished the last tour, which is almost three years ago. I've seen them all individually but suddenly you find yourself hovering above Manhattan together for the first time since you last walked offstage. What a place to meet!

With these guys it takes about two years to get antsy and then it takes about another year to put it together. The basic fact is that these guys want to do it and if people out there want to see it, you put those two things together and you get that magic.

CHARLIE WATTS: Whenever we play a club, it's like bedlam—it's mad! Fortunately, the club owners are good to work with—otherwise we'd never do them.

This won't be the last tour, but if it is that's fine. It won't be the last time we play. When we started the last tour, it was only to last a year and then something happened in the middle so it lasted two. If things on this tour are really great, the temptation will be to carry on. Keith's version is never to stop so that you don't have to face that start-up feeling again. It's a good idea, but there are other things to do in life, I think.

RON WOOD: It's getting to be like a habit. We've done the train, the boat, and the bridge. We'll probably do a submarine next time. I've always loved a challenge, so this tour will be great. We'll have to do our homework and pick some songs we've never played before, or at least haven't played for years.

August 16, 2002. After rehearsing in town for four weeks, the Stones play a surprise club gig at Toronto's Palais Royale ballroom, with Sharon Stone, Liv Tyler, Kate Hudson, and Dennis Quaid in attendance.

MICK JAGGER: It's great to get out here and play—I can tell you that. We've been here four weeks, but it sounds like four days [laughs]. It was great fun. We had a laugh. Thanks, everybody.

2002. On September 3, the Licks tour kicks off in front of 14,600 Bostonians at the Fleet Center. The North American leg continues until February 8, 2003 in Las Vegas. The tour is expected to gross US$90 million. On October 1, the greatest hits package, *40 Licks*, with songs from the band's entire career, makes #2 in its first week on the charts. On December 2, the Stones announce tour plans for Europe beginning June 4, 2003, in Munich. It will follow two weeks in Australia and three dates in Japan.

CHAPTER 9
Finale

MICK JAGGER: I don't really mind what anybody says about our story, because I don't think that accuracy is very important. What's important is that it's interesting . . . as long as it's fun.

I don't really like talking about myself. I think it's really boring. It's not easy being the centre of attention all the time. It's awful . . . and it's dangerous. People are always asking you about this and that. I just want to experience my life rather than having it examined all the time . . .

People always ask how long can we continue, and I just don't know. It's not a serious question. I just do what we do and it keeps going until, I guess, the fans don't want us anymore. You know, it's not like a typical career job where you work every day for many years and then you stop. In this band we work very intensely for periods and then we take time off. Some of the time it's quite a bit of work and it can be quite tiring, but it's also very exhilarating and has a lot of perks.

KEITH RICHARDS: I think I keep doing it because I'd go nuts if I stopped. I still believe there are even better days ahead for the band. We haven't stopped yet. We're not a nostalgia band like the Beach Boys—we're doing new things all the time. We make our own nostalgia every time we go out on the road [laughs].

My favourite Stones songs? Oh, I guess "Jumpin' Jack Flash," "Street Fighting Man," and "Tumbling Dice," if I have to have three . . . but then I've got to leave all my other babies out [laughs].

"Street Fighting Man" had always intrigued me, just for the sound. I'm just very proud of it. There's not an electric instrument on it except for bass, and it's one of the hardest sounds I've ever made, and I loved the sequence. "Jumpin' Jack Flash" because it's just such a great riff to play. You could play it all night . . . perhaps I do. I just keep turning it around [laughs] doing variations on that. If I say "Jumpin' Jack Flash," really, to me, I'm talking about fifteen, twenty other songs as well. To me it's a generic term. "Tumbling Dice," because it's a great groove. I remember how I felt when I wrote it and the way I felt when it came out. It's one of the closest to the way I heard it up here before it got made. They change—sometimes for the better—but this one I had mapped out and it came out just like I wanted it.

Favourite Stones albums? Probably *Exile on Main Street*, *Sticky Fingers*, *Beggars Banquet*, *Let It Bleed*, and *Some Girls*. I like quite a bit of that.

CHARLIE WATTS: The one thing this band has always had is a large following. People have always wanted to come and see Keith play guitar or to see Mick jump about and sing and entertain. There's as many people as buy the records and more. That's mainly why we work on the road—because people love to see us. I don't mean that egotistically. It's just a fact.

I suppose when we were in our late twenties we must have sounded one way. I don't know if we sound better than that now. I kind of think we do, but I don't know whether I'm right there or not. I can't see that—I can't see myself in those terms. When people say, "It's wonderful . . . it's the greatest this, that, and the other," I never see that. It's very nice to hear, it's very good for your ego, but I don't know whether to believe it or take it in. I just don't pay any notice of it apart from the thank you.

RON WOOD: We do have a lot of fun, and what we do is spread pleasure to an audience. I do believe that the music we put out gives people hope. It takes them into a surreal world for a while and takes all their troubles away. In light of all the bad things that go down, we just want to spread some smiles and get some serious grooves going with the audience.

ALEXIS KORNER: There are two reasons people get involved in music. Some guys just *have* to play. If they get paid for it that's great, but it's not essential. Others just want to get famous and make a lot of money. Mick has a real passion and a natural feel for music but he's motivated by the need for success, while Keith is just one of those people that *has* to play.

IAN STEWART: The band just keeps getting bigger and bigger. It's strange, really, but I must say I can understand it, because the band is still interested in music. It still plays like a band—it's not a put-on. It's not a hype the way so many of these rock'n'roll bands are. It's not all flash, the way The Who are—there's actually music to it. The band swings, and they're obviously all keen on what they're doing, so they've taken a generation with them. I think they could go on a lot longer if they wanted to.

KEITH ALTHAM: The basic characteristics of the individual people within the band—I mean, saving poor old Brian— are pretty much the same as they always were. I mean, I think Keith went through a very bad period where you didn't really feel you were on the same planet as he was, and probably weren't . . . but I think he's come through that. Once again, if you look at the Rolling Stones, what I said earlier on is still true today. Mick remains the superstar figure that he is—probably the most famous name in rock-'n'roll. Keith is still the man's man, he's still the one that actually holds the . . . the street level credibility awards, he's still kind of the outlaw figure who's never really ever quite given in to the establishment in any way, shape, or form. You couldn't imagine Keith Richards at Wimbledon watching a test match, could you, really?

PETER JONES: I've never seen a temperamental outburst from Mick Jagger. Mick Jagger, you know, is a cricket-loving, keep-fit guy at heart, really. There have been all the problems and so on, but the fact is, his interests are far, far removed from his image.

ALEXIS KORNER: I was certainly one of their first and one of their most fervent fans, and I still am. I think they are the greatest R&B band that ever came out of Britain. I don't see any reason to change that opinion, I really don't, and I'll tell you why—because they didn't *call* themselves that, they just *played* it. They played blues the way I hear blues—solidly, right the way through. Blues is not a form, it's the sound that some people make when they play. So yes, they are to me still the greatest R&B band ever!

I know that some of them are rather hung up about being what they would refer to as rock'n'roll idols at the age of forty, but I really don't see what they have to worry about as long as they still turn people on. That's the final criterion—do you turn people on? If you turn people on, you're entitled to whatever you get from it. You're entitled to the money, you're entitled to the titles, you're entitled to any of those things that you want, as long as you're doing it. Your age is totally immaterial. It's your ability to do it that is material, and absolutely nothing else. So they remain for me, the finest R&B band that's ever come out of Britain.

NORMAN JOPLING: Obviously, at the time one didn't realize they would be so successful. I knew they'd be big, but I didn't think they'd still be big in 1981. They didn't think they'd be big in 1981.

DICK TAYLOR: I think it's great. I'm really very pleased for them. Listening to them over the years, what they're doing now is inevitable. It all follows a line that is very logical. You can't get away from the fact that what they're doing follows on from everything they've done. Always—apart from *Satanic Majesties*, which went a little bit off course. But they obviously had to do that to get back to all the other things.

SID BERNSTEIN: To hang together for that long in today's society, it's difficult, with the pressures and the tensions, and the conflicts and the chaos that go on. But they've withstood all the problems, personal problems, other problems, and are still together. That's the miracle of it all, that they've lasted so long. I think it's because they don't play that often. Maybe that's what does it.

ERIC CLAPTON: I met the Stones before I even started playing as a professional musician, back in the days with Alexis Korner. Most of those guys were older than us so the Stones were the first guys I knew that shared a love of the blues that were the same age as me. They're probably the oldest friends I have, and we've been good mates since the beginning.

BOB BONIS: I think what keeps them relevant is that new kids still like their sound. They must—they aren't going just to see pop history. I've had friends asking me for tickets to the Madison Square Gardens show here in New York, people I haven't heard from in years. Their kids want to see it. Sixteen-, seventeen-year-old kids want to see the show.

PETER JONES: I think they deserve this prolonged reputation. I think that if you take them individually . . . For example, the quiet one—if you take Bill Wyman as being the quiet one. The guy is very creative. He's always been in the background onstage, but I talked to him at Midem [the annual French music festival] this last year and he was introducing some film music that he'd written, and really the guy is a talented, amiable, nice, and [I think now] respected musician. Charlie Watts could have been a great jazz man, had he wanted to be, had he wanted to go into the modern jazz field. I think [their success] is thoroughly deserved, if I have to say anything. The Stones have worked. I don't think anyone has given more to a public than Mick Jagger over the years.

I know about the pressures in the early days . . . the kinds of problems they went through early on in order to get any kind of recognition. I mean, they were living on the poverty line for a long while, in the hope that their music would win through in the end for them. I honestly think that their longevity in pop music is thoroughly deserved.

WILLIE DIXON: Yeah, there's no way you could dislike 'em because of their personalities. Personality is what makes people like you. Either you have a good personality or a bad one, and I think they have beautiful personalities. That could have a lot to do with their success over all these years, because when a lot of people like you they don't forget you too fast. The type of music they have, the youngsters like because the youngsters have a lot of energy to burn, and when [they] can find music to burn energy with that's what [they] want. When you get older, then naturally you don't care to burn energy—you wanna save it, if you got any.

DICK ROWE: When I look back on it all, I suppose it was quite exciting. When we first met, they didn't have any money at all, and of course they were up to all these tricks—a politer word than perhaps the right one. And there were incidents at petrol stations. Then later there were the jackets for the records, which gave us such a headache. In the end, I think it was a profitable relationship for both of us.

GLYN JOHNS: Very clever. I think they're both [Mick and Keith] very clever. But they're like spoiled brats. They just get away with whatever they want to and more power to them if they can, I suppose. It's their life, it's their music. I mean, maybe I haven't got the right to say it, but that's my opinion. It frustrates me because in the early days, watching them play, I knew there had never been anything like it. I'd never seen rock'n'roll played like that in my life and I never will [again]. We'll never see it [again] from them. I know bloody well I wouldn't cross the road to see them play now—I wouldn't care how big the club was. I wouldn't bother with it because I know it would be a disappointment. It wouldn't be as good as they used to be. They just don't have the same approach any more.

MICK TAYLOR: I think Mick and Keith are the Rolling Stones—they're the Rolling Stones identity. They write the music. Mick's the most organized one, yeah, definitely. He's the person who makes things happen, who makes decisions. Keith is the soul and the sound.

CHRIS KIMSEY: Since the "bad" old days they've changed quite a lot. There's definitely been an incredible improvement in the amount of energy and enthusiasm, especially from Keith. It's been remarkable. The band's taken on a new energy since then. It's really kicked everyone up the backside. Keith's energy now is so high, and he'll stay in the studio for hours, and he'll come with new riffs and things, which inspires Mick.

Working with the Stones, there's so much energy on the tape and on the record. When I work with other bands and they say, "Oh, make me sound like the Rolling Stones," I just laugh because there's an energy they have that no one else can really capture. There's a rawness. Other bands haven't got it, but the Stones have certainly!

CHUCK LEAVELL: Charlie Watts is the cornerstone. Absolutely, without a doubt, and everybody in this band knows that. There's an undying love and undying respect that we all have for Charlie. He's such a shy sort of individual that it's funny. If you'd say that to him he'd blush and he'd look down and probably deny it. "All I do is play a little drums . . ."

People say, "What are the Rolling Stones really like?" Well, they're four very individual human beings. They're all different from each other. Completely different, really. Maybe Ronnie and Keith are more alike than any other two, but even at that they're all very, very individual, and you take them apart and they're all interesting in their own ways. You can tell that by the solo projects, but you put them together, and there's just something there that comes along once in a millennium. It's just a certain combination, a formula like Pasteur running across his discovery or Thomas Edison. There's a moment, a combination of things that happen, which is magic and that applies to this band . . . to those four guys . . . no question about it.

KEITH RICHARDS: Apart from my family and my friends, I would have to say music is the most important thing in my life. I love music, I love playing it, I love my guitar. I even sleep with it [laughs].

Acknowledgements

This project has been part of my life for more than 20 years. During that time all of the people I've spoken with were, to a person, generous and respectful, sharing both their stories and their hospitality. Their contributions have been invaluable. Many very helpful people, for various political reasons, would rather go un-named. You know who you are and you have my thanks.

The original documentary was researched and written by myself and David Pritchard who later handed me his share of the headaches and the glories. It was started at the behest of Neil Sargent of TM Special Projects after the success of our documentary on The Beatles. Since then many people and companies have broadcast updated versions. Most helpful were Keith MacGregor, Ron Hartenbaum of Media America, Doug Adamson (formerly) at MCM in London and Glen McClain at ABC Radio International.

When we started the project it was Art Collins, then president of Rolling Stones Records, who lobbied for the band's involvement and through whom I met the amazing Jane Rose who has been incredibly supportive and helpful over the years.

There are several colleagues with whom I have traded interviews over the years: James Karnbach in America, Doug Adamson in Australia and Doug Thompson in Canada. They are responsible for some of the few interviews I did not conduct.

I would also like to thank Allen Klein and Andrew Oldham. Although neither would go on the record for the documentary or the book, I gained valuable insights into both them and the band through stories and letters they shared in our meetings.

Finally I have to express my sincere thanks to the band members themselves who have been unfailingly supportive and who regularly renew my faith in music.

Timelines: Many people have asked about the timeframes of the interviews. Early attempts at including the date of each interview became unwieldy and confusing so instead here is a guideline: The bulk of the interviews dealing with the history of the band and its members were conducted between the summer of 1981 and late spring 1982. (Obviously the interviews with Brian Jones were conducted in the 1960s by colleagues.) After 1982, interviews were conducted at the time of the event in question. So, if someone is speaking about the first British tour or the album *Let It Bleed*, their perspective is from 1982. If, for example, they are speaking about the Voodoo Lounge tour, the interview was conducted in 1994 and so on.

The chronology: Every effort has been taken to confirm the dates used. It is an amalgam of original newspaper reports cross referenced with the excellent information contained in James Karnbach's book *It's Only Rock'n'Roll* Bill Wyman's *Stone Alone* and a timeline written by Bill German.